To Gordon with love
from Isobel & Richard
20 February 1988.

# GARDEN BIRDS

*How to attract birds to your garden*

# GARDEN BIRDS

*How to attract birds to your garden*

## MIKE EVERETT

Consultant editors
Cyril Walker
Tim Parmenter

the
apple
press

A QUARTO BOOK

First published in 1985
Copyright © 1985 Quarto Publishing Limited
ISBN 1-85076-046-2

Published by The Apple Press
293 Gray's Inn Road, London WC1

This book was designed and produced by
Quarto Publishing Limited
The Old Brewery
6 Blundell Street
London N7

Senior Editor: Stephen Paul
Editorial : Liz Davies

Designers: Michelle Stamp & Alun Jones
Art Editor: Moira Clinch

Illustrators: Robert Morton, Tim Hayward, David Hurrell
courtesy of Linden Artists
Vana Haggerty, Norman Bancroft-Hunt
Chart Composition: Elly King

Art Director: Alastair Campbell
Editorial Director: Jim Miles

Typeset by Facsimile, Coggeshall
Colour origination by Hong Kong Graphic Arts, Hong Kong
Printed by Lee Fung Asco Printers Ltd, Hong Kong

# CONTENTS

# INTRODUCTION

THERE MUST BE HUNDREDS of books about gardens and gardening. Inevitably, most of these deal with the layout of gardens from the aesthetic or purely practical point of view and, of course, contain a lot of information on garden plants of every shape and size. Since gardening is an important and valuable leisure pastime for millions of people, none of this is particularly surprising—but the average naturalist might be forgiven for gaining the impression that many gardening authors pay rather little attention to the abundant wildlife which shares the gardens. All too often, perhaps, the emphasis is on the artificial or contrived, to the neglect of the natural—it begins, possibly, with the simple division of plants into flowers and weeds, or with the classification of insects, animals and birds as pests or nuisances if they should dare to interfere with the tidy, controlled and regimented garden in any way.

Before all the gardeners who have read this far snarl in disagreement and throw the book into the dustbin, let it be said at once that the intention is not to decry formal or well cared-for gardens, nor to advocate wild, untidy and basically unmanaged plots—far from it. The suggestion is that it is perfectly possible to manage a garden for all the traditional reasons (and in most of the traditional ways) and at the same time make it good for birds. Space will not permit very much comment about other creatures, such as insects, mammals, reptiles and amphibians, nor will it allow more than a brief mention of weeds and wild-flowers although you will find that these too often are compatible.

The motives behind maintaining a garden which you can share with birds could be debated almost endlessly, but the two main ones must involve the simple pleasure you derive from birds and a basic feeling that you are doing something to help them. The motives need be no more complicated than that.

The first part of the book is a guide to bird gardening. It considers the place of birds in the garden, the undoubted conservation value of gardens and habitat planning in the garden. This is followed by sections giving practical hints on the provision of water, what to plant and why, the safe use of garden chemicals, the problems of predators, bird feeding, and the provision of natural and artificial nest-sites.

Deciding what to include in this section, and indeed what to include in the rest of the book, has not been easy. It was first of all necessary to define what a garden means. The garden in the inner city is quite different from the garden in the countryside; some gardens adjoin the sea, or exist in mountain valleys, other are beside lakes and rivers and form clearings in forests and woods—an 'average garden' is therefore rather difficult to define!

Nevertheless, an attempt has been made to envisage such a thing—the sort of garden situation known to most people—but the boundaries have been kept fairly elastic, so as to include large gardens, gardens with lakes, rivers or streams alongside, those adjoining woodland and farmland, and so on. The definition has also been broadened to include the immediate grounds of schools, hospitals, factories and business premises, but large parks and 'estates' have been deliberately excluded. The list of 100 birds by no means includes all the species that visit gardens, for example, some people have birds like black grouse, turnstones and snow buntings in their gardens quite regularly, but it covers those which are regular in many gardens and a small selection of 'possibles' or more localized visitors.

*A beautifully laid out water garden (left) which is pleasing to the eye, but is less than adequate for attracting many bird species. It is unsuitable because there are no gaps between the plants to allow a safe access to the water's edge.*

*This rock garden (above) suffers from the same problems as the water garden: there is no clear area which slopes to the water's edge. The large lily pads, however, will provide smaller species with a place from which to drink.*

# THE BIRD GARDEN

A BIRD GARDEN can bring a great deal of pleasure, pleasure in the sight of birds and in the feeling that you are doing something to help them, and there is no need to seek any further justification.

## WHY A BIRD GARDEN?

PLEASURE BEGINS, perhaps, with the simple appreciation of colour and all the marvellous ways in which plumage details vary. Some birds are immediately striking, like a kingfisher or any of the woodpeckers, while others are more subtly attractive, like warblers and finches, or even (when you bother to look at them more closely) the more commonplace starlings and house sparrows. Then you begin to notice that birds move in many different ways: some hop, some run, others waddle. Some climb adroitly or, like tits, are accomplished acrobats. Some are very tame, even confident, while others are wary or unobtrusive. Once you have started to notice these things, you are already a birdwatcher. The next step is to learn which bird is which and to find out more about their lifestyles.

You can study this in detail in the second section of the book where you will find descriptions of 100 species, but there is no 'instant' way in which you can become an expert on bird identification. Learning your birds is a slow process of building up knowledge through experience, and a garden is one of the best possible places to start.

Note first the size—as big as a sparrow, smaller than a starling, and so on; then the general shape—slender like a wagtail, perhaps, or plump like a robin. Does the bird have a stout, seed-eater's bill, like a sparrow, or a fine, insect-eater's bill, like a warbler? How does it move? Does it run briskly and confidently, like a starling; hop in short spurts like a robin, or creep about rather furtively like a dunnock? Once you have gained a general idea of the sort

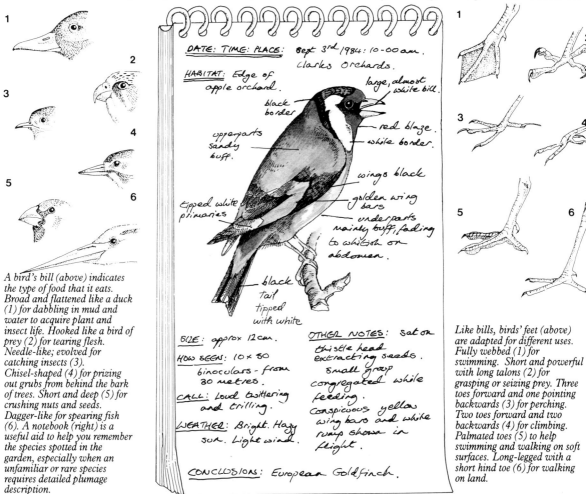

A bird's bill (above) indicates the type of food that it eats. Broad and flattened like a duck (1) for dabbling in mud and water to acquire plant and insect life. Hooked like a bird of prey (2) for tearing flesh. Needle-like; evolved for catching insects (3). Chisel-shaped (4) for prizing out grubs from behind the bark of trees. Short and deep (5) for crushing nuts and seeds. Dagger-like for spearing fish (6). A notebook (right) is a useful aid to help you remember the species spotted in the garden, especially when an unfamiliar or rare species requires detailed plumage description.

DATE: TIME: PLACE: Sept 3rd 1984: 10.00 am. Clarks Orchards.

HABITAT: Edge of apple orchard.

large, almost white bill.

black border

red blaze.

white border.

upperparts sandy buff.

wings black

golden wing bars

underparts mainly buff, fading to whitish on abdomen.

tipped white primaries

black tail tipped with white

SIZE: approx 12 cm.

HOW SEEN: 10 x 50 binoculars - from 30 metres.

CALL: Loud twittering and trilling.

WEATHER: Bright. Hazy sun. Light wind.

OTHER NOTES: Sat on thistle head extracting seeds. Small group congregated while feeding. Conspicuous yellow wing bars and white rump shows in flight.

CONCLUSIONS: European Goldfinch.

Like bills, birds' feet (above) are adapted for different uses. Fully webbed (1) for swimming. Short and powerful with long talons (2) for grasping or seizing prey. Three toes forward and one pointing backwards (3) for perching. Two toes forward and two backwards (4) for climbing. Palmated toes (5) to help swimming and walking on soft surfaces. Long-legged with a short hind toe (6) for walking on land.

of bird you are looking at, you can then move on to note the more obvious plumage features and the main areas of colour. Begin by looking at the whole upperparts, head and underparts; note particularly head and wing patterns, rump colours, whether or not the outer feathers in the tail are white—and so on. Once you have thoroughly mastered the most common visitors to the garden (and realized that even they might be tricky because of sexual differences, or seasonal plumages), finding that unusual or unexpected newcomer will be that much easier. You will also be much better equipped to start looking at birds away from the garden if, as often happens, bird gardening leads on to a wider interest in birds.

There is no doubt that feeding birds, providing them with water and, perhaps, nest-sites enhances your general enjoyment, especially since these often allow you to watch them at close quarters. But is there any substance in the feeling that you are also being useful to them?

Most bird gardeners can do little to offset the loss of some habitats which affects so many of the more specialized species, such as those of wetlands and heathlands. However, a positive contribution can be made towards the welfare of many woodland and woodland edge birds—birds of habitats which are fast disappearing in many areas. A carefully managed garden which caters for wildlife, especially if it can be designed to include plenty of trees and shrubs, is a positive asset. If you think of tens of thousands of sympathetically organized gardens as a great network of miniature nature reserves, your efforts begin to have real meaning—not just to you, but to the birds as well.

Feeding undoubtedly helps many small birds in winter, especially in very hard weather. In severe conditions it may become a significant factor in helping some vulnerable species to survive in reasonable numbers until

*The mixed-foliage border of a well-designed garden (above) with an expanse of lawn in front. The large variety of plants provides numerous insects and cover for warblers and more skulking species; the trees and bushes behind offer a selection of breeding sites, and the lawn in front provides an open area on which other bird species can feed.*

the following spring. Even if it is not, it is, of course, totally justifiable purely as a humanitarian response—and there is nothing wrong with that!

## BIRD CONTROL AND THE LAW

GARDENS CAN MAKE an important contribution to wildlife conservation and it is perfectly possible to maintain a fairly normal, traditional garden and at the same time make it suitable for a variety of bird species. This is an important point in conservation—conserving wildlife is not merely a matter of putting a fence around something and not touching it at all. Habitats are dynamic and often change if left alone, so active management may be required just to preserve the status quo. As habitats change, so the bird, animal and insect communities within them change. Deciding to leave a garden entirely to nature could actually reduce its value to birds because you are reducing its diversity.

Managing your garden as a bird habitat is one thing—but should you take the management one step further and include the creatures living within the garden environment? There may be very sound gardening reasons for, say, the control of insect pests, carried out with no harmful side-effects to wildlife (see pages 28 to 31)—but control of garden pests is unlikely to benefit birds in any way at all. (Nor will it harm them if it is carried out properly.) What about the birds themselves? It is very tempting to think of some birds as 'nice' and others as 'nasty'—should some of these be controlled in any way? The answer is a firm NO (with the provision that you may, of course, wish to control some species because they are damaging fruit etc). Birds do not live as isolated entities, but as components in a mixed, interacting community, in effect, sharing the available resources and not, as a rule, competing directly with one another. Nature maintains the balance, and you can destroy it all too easily if you interfere; the birds can look after themselves within this balance of nature.

To some extent, you do produce an entirely artificial situation when you create feeding centres for birds. Perhaps the balance may seem to break down at this point, when it is clear that some birds hog the scene at the expense of others—feral pigeons, starlings and house sparrows especially. While in the strict sense that is natural and represents a normal and predictable shift in the balance, it is quite understandable that you should wish to step in and help . . . but the way to do this is by a system of gentle deterrents, and not by any attempt to control the species whose tactics you resent!

Any form of bird control—and this includes the control of pest species in the garden—is in any case subject to the

*The destruction of crops (right) is a common problem. Rooks, pigeons and sparrows are among the main culprits, and the law stipulates that they may be 'killed or taken by authorized persons at all times'.*

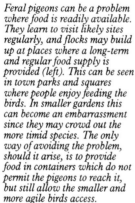

*Feral pigeons can be a problem where food is readily available. They learn to visit likely sites regularly, and flocks may build up at places where a long-term and regular food supply is provided (left). This can be seen in town parks and squares where people enjoy feeding the birds. In smaller gardens this can become an embarrassment since they may crowd out the more timid species. The only way of avoiding the problem, should it arise, is to provide food in containers which do not permit the pigeons to reach it, but still allow the smaller and more agile birds access.*

law, so it is as well to know what constraints the law applies. In the EEC, the Directive on the Conservation of Wild Birds provides the framework for the national laws adopted by member states, and works on the important basic principle that all birds are protected. It goes on to allow for certain exceptions—recognized pest species and certain birds which are accepted as quarry species for sporting purposes; but even then there are limitations on who can do what, and where, when and how. In Britain, the Wildlife and Countryside Act, 1981, gives full protection to all birds and special protection to the rarest species; this protection extends to nests, eggs and dependent young. Certain wildfowl and gamebirds are excluded at certain times of the year (so they can be shot legally)—but these need not concern us. There are also 13 species (the so-called 'pest list') which can be 'killed or taken by authorized persons at all times'. These are herring, great black-backed and lesser black-backed gulls (unlikely to concern most gardeners—unless you live at the coast and have herring gulls nesting on your roof . . .); woodpigeon, feral dove and collared dove; carrion and hooded crows, rook, jackdaw, jay and magpie; and starling and house sparrow. While these are listed because they are believed to cause damage to agriculture or gamebird populations, you could legally control any of them in your garden—although is is usually highly unlikely that any real need to do so would arise. an 'authorized person' means the landowner or someone acting with his or her permission—in other words, you can, for instance, shoot a starling in a garden you own, but not in your neighbour's garden unless you have his or her permission. Nor can you go out and kill the local magpies or crows without the consent of the owner of the land involved. The law also expressly forbids certain methods of killing, such as traps, snares, poisons and bird lime.

It is posssible to get a licence to control protected species if you can prove that they are causing serious damage, but in practice this is unlikely to be necessary and in any case you must try deterrent methods first. The law is quite complex; for more details, write to the RSPB (see page 156) for their free leaflet on the subject.

## THE ESSENTIALS: A BROAD OUTLINE

A BIRD GARDEN can exist in many forms, depending on its size and situation and, indeed, your own feelings on the subject. It could range from an almost wholly natural area to one which is intensively gardened in the traditional sense and yet is still good for wildlife. It is probably a mistake to think that a totally wild area is best for birds. Traditional gardening management is much more likely to produce a wider range of feeding opportunities than would normally occur in nature, especially through the planting of many varieties of plants and shrubs. A 50–50 compromise between 'wild' and 'tame' would be very suitable, but for most gardeners in most situations a mix of about 25/75 is perfectly adequate—in other words a normal, managed garden with provisions for wildlife.

The main factors to take into account are likely food plants; trees and shrubs for food, shelter, nest-sites and song-posts; the provision of water; where to put the winter feeding centre; whether to provide artificial nest-

*A patio garden situated in an urban area (above) can also be made suitable for birds. The only requirements are one or two bushy trees for nesting, a bird bath and a hanging feeder. Gardens located close to the coast will always produce a large number of species. In this instance (below) a freshwater pond and some low bushes would enhance the species' potential.*

*Small urban gardens, looked at individually, offer little for wildlife. However, a series of bushes in different plots (left) will provide a considerable amount of cover.*

*Access to water is often difficult for town birds. The provision of a simple bird bath (below) placed in an open area is a great help.*

sites; and the one which is so often forgotten—how to arrange things so that you can actually *see* the birds from your windows. At an early stage too, careful thought should be given to whether there are some parts of the garden from which you wish to exclude birds at certain times of the year, for example, parts of the kitchen garden or particularly vulnerable fruit crops. You may have to accept that the simplest and most foolproof way of protecting these is by caging them in entirely with netting.

Most of what follows in this book is aimed at people with at least a reasonably-sized garden, so perhaps this is the place to say a few words about tiny gardens, places with no garden at all and the grounds of factories, hospitals, schools and so forth. Any sort of widescale bird gardening may be out of the question, but there is still quite a lot that can be done.

In many cases, those with no gardens can still feed the birds in winter and enjoy watching them. Bird tables and feeding trays which can be fixed to windowsills are available, and tit feeders to hang in windows or attach to the glass with a rubber sucker can easily be found. Flat-topped roofs may be adjacent to your windows and these can make excellent, king-size bird tables. With a little thought and not too much expense, they might even be worth planting up with a few tubs of berry-bearing shrubs for the winter. Even in big cities and in the middle of big factory complexes you will be surprised at how effective

these relatively minor additions can be. There is no reason why nestboxes should not be put up on walls, as long as there are some gardens or areas with trees and shrubs not too far away where birds, like tits, can forage for the correct food for their young. Nestboxes for swifts and kestrels on larger buildings are worth considering.

Business premises may have lawns or grassy banks or even a few flowerbeds. They are much improved by the planting of ornamental, berry-bearing shrubs like berberis and cotoneaster, or with trees such as flowering cherries, rowan, the various whitebeams and crab apple—all very attractive to the eye and all of value to birds. Wherever there are trees such as oaks, scots pines, silver birch and so on—in other words native species—these should be left in situ. School grounds often provide exactly the right opportunities for planting trees and shrubs, and, of course, for erecting bird tables and feeders, and here bird gardening can have an educational function too. Hospital grounds sometimes provide equally good opportunities—for example, where it is possible for patients to look out of windows, feeding stations can be set up, or nestboxes erected. Birdwatching can, after all, be an excellent form of therapy.

Finally, some thought can be given as to whether such places might have an ornamental pond, or even a small lake—or, if not, a bird bath. Water is a sure attraction to many birds and is attractive on a formal lawn.

# GARDENING FOR BIRDS

IN PLANNING TERMS, gardens fall into two categories—wholly new, untouched sites and existing gardens. The first type obviously provides a lot of scope and can be planned from scratch, whereas in the case of an established garden it is a question of taking stock of what is already there and thinking about how it might be changed or added to.

## PLANNING THE GARDEN

BEFORE GOING ANY FURTHER, it is worth giving some thought to 'wild areas', which can be provided in either sort of garden. Remember that even an area designated 'wild' should not be an entirely neglected one—it will need a little management. It is usually best to maintain a wild area well away from your best flowerbeds and vegetable plots, simply to avoid the problem of weeds spreading to places where you do not want them. Choose a corner, or maintain a strip along a wall or fence where maintainance is easy and you can keep an eye on things. There is more about these areas later, but in passing note that plants like groundsel and shepherd's purse need little encouragement and should be retained to provide seeds for finches; thistles will attract goldfinches, as will teasels—which are also very attractive in their own right. Nettles may not be of much obvious use to birds, but they are invaluable to butterflies—if they can be left so that they grow close to or underneath buddleia, which attracts butterflies and a whole host of other insects, so much the better. Various grasses also provide seeds for small birds, but they also have a tendency to spread like wildfire and may need to be kept under control. Brambles too should be encouraged, perhaps in a corner of the garden or along a fence or wall. Birds enjoy blackberries just as much as humans and brambles can also provide nesting cover.

### Starting from scratch

A new garden plot requires a lot of thought before it is planted up. Look at the area around your garden and consider which birds are likely to come and what sort of conditions they would like. Think, too, whether there might be one or two local species which you might be able to attract by providing something special—a pond, perhaps, or a favourite food plant. Then draw up a plan, preferably on graph paper, taking into account the positions and likely eventual size of any existing trees and, of course, of other features such as clothes lines, garden sheds, greenhouses, fuel storage tanks and so on. Remember, too, to give early thought to any paths you may wish to lay out. Then plan where to put your flowerbeds, vegetable plots, shrubs and any trees you wish to plant, always bearing in mind lines of sight from

*Trees such as this* malus *(above) always provide excellent nesting sites for thrushes and finches. Fruits born by the tree, and insects attracted to it, are an important food source. Thistles (below) are attractive plants, which are pleasing to the eye. They will also coax more timid seed-eating birds into the garden.*

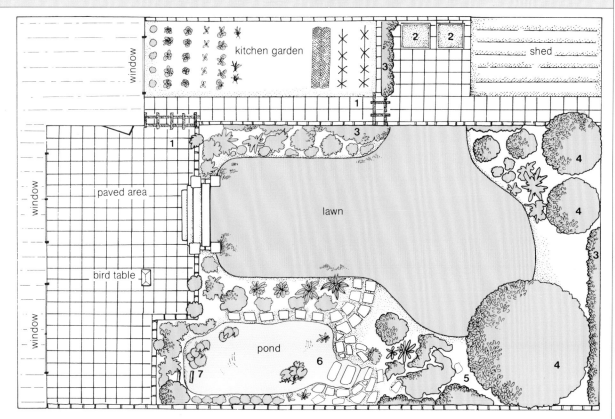

*A suggested plan for an average garden, incorporating all the features which will attract birds (above). It may, of course, be adapted to suit the individual situation. Pergolas (1) for climbing plants, which will provide nest-sites. Compost heaps (2) attract insects and, therefore, provide a natural food source. Hedges (3) which bear fruit, such as cotoneaster, have a dual purpose: they are useful as nesting sites, and their berries provide food in the winter. Taller trees (4), especially evergreens, allow roosting and are excellent nest-sites. A wild (5) area will provide food, in the form of berries, and cover for skulking species. A pond (6) with open shallows allows easy access for drinking. Perches (7) distributed around the garden will encourage flycatchers.*

*Although this landscaped garden (left) provides very little for birds in the immediate foreground, the mature trees in the distance give ample cover and nesting sites for large species.*

your windows so that you can actually see the birds which come. How much of the garden will be lawn? Don't be afraid to make your lawns a major feature and think in terms of planning the rest of the garden around them. Short grass maintained in the traditional way (but preferably with a little more tolerance than usual of clovers and buttercups) is used by a lot of birds.

Perhaps the most exciting possibility of all is to plan a garden pond. How big you make it, and what shape, will depend on the space available—but it will be a major attraction to birds and the insects on which many of them feed. If you are fairly close to larger water areas, streams, rivers or canals, think of the kingfisher as a likely visitor and provide both small fish and one or two suitable perches; remember too that ponds provide homes for frogs, toads and newts and also the chance to grow some interesting and very attractive plants.

**Adapting the old**
If you have a well-established garden (or are moving into a house which has one) and if, so far, little thought has been given to providing for birds, the first thing to do is to take stock of what is there and decide what should be retained, and where and how alterations might be made.

Large lakes with surrounding vegetation (right) will encourage many water birds such as ducks, swans, rails and herons. If the water level can be regulated so as to leave muddy margins, wader species may be tempted to rest and feed while on migration. Wet areas also harbour large numbers of insects which will attract swallows and other insect eaters.

The benefits of having a mature woodland (left) in a garden are enormous — many hole-nesting species, such as woodpeckers, treecreepers and tits, can find suitable cavities in which to breed and find food. It is important, however, that dead branches and trees (below) should be left, for they are important providers of nest-sites and food items.

On pages 20 to 27 you can see which plants, shrubs and trees to look for, or to add, but here is some general guidance about trees.

### Trees

Mature trees are an asset in any garden, providing as they do song-posts, a variety of sources of natural food and many nesting-places. All too often there seems to be a tendency to regard them as a nuisance or potential source of danger, and to lop off big branches or even to think of felling. Obviously, where there is a distinct danger to houses, or if overhanging branches are a nuisance to neighbours and passers-by, some action is desirable—but try to keep tree control to a minimum and always seek professional advice first.

The other great temptation is to remove dead trees because they are unsightly, or to take off dead branches. In fact, dead wood often harbours a lot of insect food which is sought by woodpeckers, nuthatches, treecreepers and tits; it often provides opportunities for hole-nesters, like tits, to breed and, above all perhaps, for woodpeckers to excavate nest-holes. Furthermore, dead limbs are used as drumming-posts by the spotted woodpeckers in late winter and spring. So you should think twice before taking down dead wood—try to retain some of it if at all possible. It is, after all, a vital component of any woodland habitat and one which to some extent you can replicate in the garden.

## ON THE WATERFRONT

IF YOU ARE LUCKY ENOUGH to move into a house with a river frontage, or a lake or decent-sized pond at the foot of the garden, spend some time watching what happens before planning any changes. Find out which waterside plants are growing there and which birds are using them for food or shelter. Large areas of reeds or so-called 'bulrushes' may extend right across your frontage, and it is perhaps tempting to clear them away to give a clear view across areas of open water—but it may be much better to create a couple of large gaps in the cover, retaining some of it at either end and in a clump or two in the middle. This broken edge effect is likely to prove more attractive to more bird species than either a clear shoreline or a continuous, unbroken line of vegetation. By producing little bays and inlets you will provide loafing spots for duck, feeding areas for snipe and open crossing points which might help you to spot more furtive birds like the water rail. You might also attract a fishing heron and, if you provide one or two strategically placed perches, regular visits from a kingfisher.

If you are fortunate enough to have a long frontage on to a lake, it could pay dividends to think in terms of creating a length of irregular shoreline, with miniature bays, promontories and shallows. This will probably involve you in many hours' manual labour, but the chance of attracting more waterfowl and perhaps migrant waders like green and common sandpipers will make it very worthwhile. A big post in the water will also be useful as a perching place for a number of birds.

In upland areas, some gardens back on to rocky or fast-moving streams, where common sandpipers, dippers and grey wagtails may all occur as breeding birds. Generally, it is not possible to manage the foot of your garden to attract these species, although a contrived bit of gravelly shore might help wagtails and sandpipers and a garden pond should certainly attract the former. If there is none in place already, it would be worth positioning a couple of large, round-topped stones in the water where you can see them. All three birds will find them and use them—dippers may pause to feed in the eddies around them.

One final point concerning water frontages: a relatively swift-moving lowland stream, particularly on chalk, may provide you with the opportunity of growing your own cress if you have the room to divert the water across a shallow area. This leads not only to good eating, but produces excellent conditions for a number of birds, including wagtails and pipits. If you live in a suitable area there will be cress farms locally where you can see how the system works and (if you are not likely to present a serious commercial threat) local cress-growers may advise you.

### Water for birds

Most people, of course do not have rivers, streams, lakes or ponds at the foot of their gardens, but for many bird gardeners the provision of water is often one of their first considerations. Birds need water to survive; you can provide it quite easily, either as a simple drinking or bathing supply, or in the form of a manmade pond.

Bird baths are available in a variety of forms, either on pedestals or as precast or moulded mini-pools for placing at ground level. All of these are perfectly acceptable to birds, but you can just as easily make your own, using an upturned dustbin lid or a small sheet of heavy gauge pond-liner. If you do make your own, remember to give the birds easy access from gently sloping sides, or via a brick or stone placed in the water. Remember that shallow water is all that is needed; keep it clean of leaves and debris and change the water regularly.

Water is important in winter and, even if you do not maintain a year-round supply for your birds, you should endeavour to provide it in hard weather. The problem is, of course, that water freezes easily—so what is to be done? *On no account* should you add any form of anti-freezing substance to the water: the chances are that it will do some harm to the birds. You can, of course, adopt the irksome course of going out and breaking the ice regularly, or adding warm water at intervals, but nowadays most people think instead of installing a simple heater to maintain the water temperature above freezing point. An aquarium heater, available at any good pet shop, does the job perfectly well but it will, of course, require external, weatherproof wiring—a local electrician should be able to advise you on this aspect. If you are putting water out in a shallow container, for example a dustbin lid, it is very effective to raise the whole affair on bricks and place a simple nightlight in the space underneath it.

### Making a pond

Making an artificial pond is an exciting prospect (at least, it is once you've dug the hole). This is in any case a popular and common practice among gardeners, and many of the better gardening books give excellent advice on what to do. A formal garden pool—even a fairly sophisticated water garden—will provide good conditions for birds, but in many ways a purpose-built pool is better. The only constraints are how much you want to spend and how much space you have available.

Broadly speaking, the aim is to produce a pond with a slightly irregular outline, shallow at the edges (or at least at one end) and not more that 1m ($3\frac{1}{4}$ ft) deep in any place. It should provide 'walk-in' access to birds and easily accessible drinking and bathing places. Through a mixture of native and more exotic plants, it can be both visually attractive and a good source of food for birds. A pool can be designed in conjunction with another garden

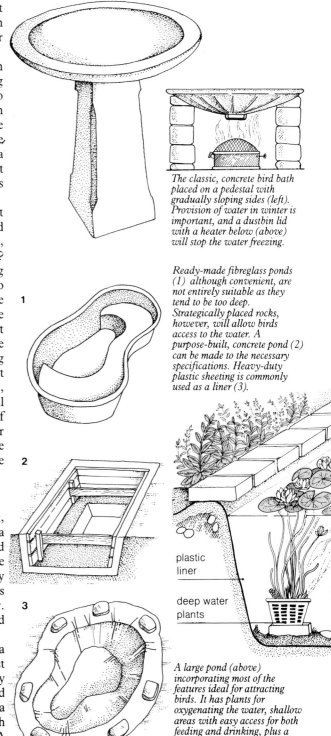

The classic, concrete bird bath placed on a pedestal with gradually sloping sides (left). Provision of water in winter is important, and a dustbin lid with a heater below (above) will stop the water freezing.

Ready-made fibreglass ponds (1) although convenient, are not entirely suitable as they tend to be too deep. Strategically placed rocks, however, will allow birds access to the water. A purpose-built, concrete pond (2) can be made to the necessary specifications. Heavy-duty plastic sheeting is commonly used as a liner (3).

plastic liner

deep water plants

A large pond (above) incorporating most of the features ideal for attracting birds. It has plants for oxygenating the water, shallow areas with easy access for both feeding and drinking, plus a fountain where birds may bathe.

feature—an adjacent rock garden perhaps. This could also provide a simple waterfall system whereby water is pumped up and returned to the pond by gravity, producing oxygenation which is essential for a successful and productive pond. The alternative is to stock the pool with plenty of oxygenating plants, hornwort, for example.

A heavy clay soil provides a ready-made pond-liner which will cost you nothing other than a lot of sweat and toil. But soils with good drainage require entirely artificial techniques for which there are three alternatives. It is possible nowadays to purchase quite large, moulded glass fibre ponds which are excellent for the small garden. Their major disadvantage is that the size and shape is predetermined by the manufacturers. Preparing a

concrete lining, and coating it with plastic paint, gives you much greater flexibility, but is laborious and, once completed, very difficult to alter in any significant way. A better alternative is to line your excavation with heavy-duty polythene sheeting, which is no more expensive than the other methods and is much more flexible in design terms.

At all stages of construction, extreme care must be taken not to damage or puncture the sheeting. It is important to provide a reasonably smooth base on which to lay the sheeting and then to lay it generously, to allow for its movement and settling when soil is placed upon it, and again when you add the weight of the water. Allow a wide overlap at the edges and do not trim off the surplus until the whole pond is completed and filled. Again, be

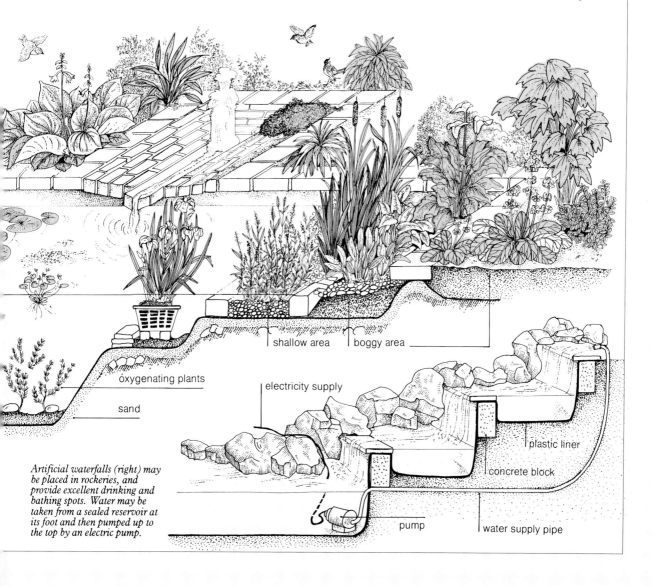

*Artificial waterfalls (right) may be placed in rockeries, and provide excellent drinking and bathing spots. Water may be taken from a sealed reservoir at its foot and then pumped up to the top by an electric pump.*

shallow area    boggy area

oxygenating plants

sand

electricity supply

plastic liner

concrete block

pump    water supply pipe

very careful not to damage the sheeting if any large stones, plant containers etc are to rest on it.

Rainwater would eventually fill your pool, but it is better and faster to do it from the tap, using a hosepipe. Add a few buckets of water from a local pond to help introduce the first micro-organisms to the new environment. Allow the water to settle for about two weeks (topping up the level if necessary) before any planting is undertaken. The layer of soil you have placed on the pond-liner will provide most of what you need for planting, but plants in containers can also be placed as required; use some of the soil from the excavation to build up a low surround to incorporate the overlap of the sheeting and to provide a good moisture-retaining base for waterside plants.

## Stocking the pond

Many of the plants available commercially for garden ponds will be suitable, but, for a more natural look, a much better strategy is to introduce a majority of native species—the sort of things that grow in real ponds in your district. However, the law places certain restraints on the uprooting of wild plants, even common ones. Be sure that you have the necessary permission before going to your local pond for supplies; take only a few plants of the kinds you need and cause as little damage as possible while doing so. Choose only places where these plants are abundant. In many ways, it is often better to scrounge what you want from neighbours or friends with established ponds. As already mentioned, hornwort is an excellent oxygenating plant. Some other useful species

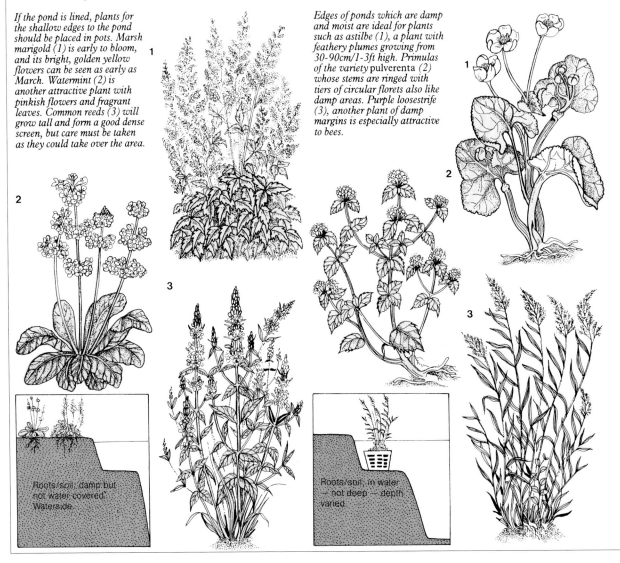

*If the pond is lined, plants for the shallow edges to the pond should be placed in pots. Marsh marigold (1) is early to bloom, and its bright, golden yellow flowers can be seen as early as March. Watermint (2) is another attractive plant with pinkish flowers and fragrant leaves. Common reeds (3) will grow tall and form a good dense screen, but care must be taken as they could take over the area.*

*Edges of ponds which are damp and moist are ideal for plants such as astilbe (1), a plant with feathery plumes growing from 30-90cm/1-3ft high. Primulas of the variety* pulverenta *(2) whose stems are ringed with tiers of circular florets also like damp areas. Purple loosestrife (3), another plant of damp margins is especially attractive to bees.*

Roots/soil; damp but not water covered. Waterside.

Roots/soil; in water — not deep — depth varied.

you can introduce include water mint, water forgetmenot, water plantin, marsh marigold, marestail, yellow flag iris, bogbean, purple loosestrife, frogbit (floating), amphibious bistort (floating) and (at the deepest parts) water lilies. Reed grass *(phalaris)* will grow well around the wet edges, as will bog arum, primulas and various ferns. Reedmace will form big, attractive stands and may need some control as your pond matures; unless you have a lot of room or are prepared to carry out continuous management it is probably not a good idea to introduce the highly invasive and fast-spreading common reed *(phragmites)*.

There is a good chance that the common toad (and perhaps newts) will colonize unaided—but here, too, you can ask a friend or neighbour for spawn or tadpoles from a

well-established pond. A supply of the spawn of the common frog could be even more valuable. This has become a scarce animal in many districts, and founding a new, protected colony could be an important local conservation project. Remember that both frogs and toads require easy access into and out of the pond—gently sloping banks or strategically placed stones will help them. They also like flat stones placed in the water, both at and just under the surface. During hot weather watch for falling water levels and adjust the exits accordingly.

Bird gardeners will welcome visits by kingfishers and grey herons, but the latter can be unpopular in gardens where ponds are stocked with goldfish and other ornamental species. Netting over the water is an effective way to stop predation, while erecting simple string or wire

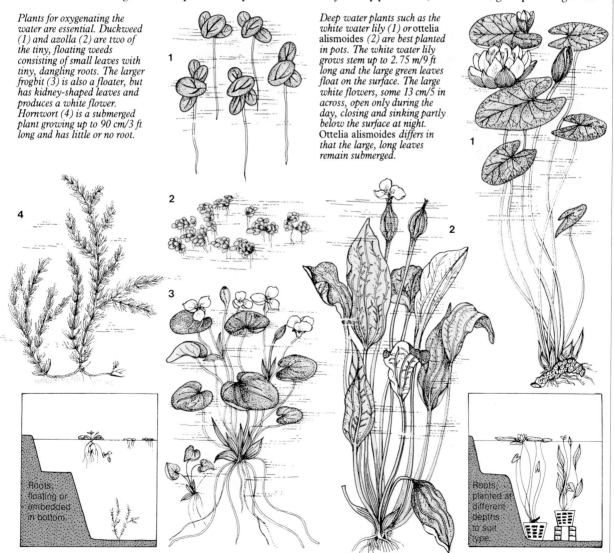

*Plants for oxygenating the water are essential. Duckweed (1) and azolla (2) are two of the tiny, floating weeds consisting of small leaves with tiny, dangling roots. The larger frogbit (3) is also a floater, but has kidney-shaped leaves and produces a white flower. Hornwort (4) is a submerged plant growing up to 90 cm/3 ft long and has little or no root.*

*Deep water plants such as the white water lily (1) or ottelia alismoides (2) are best planted in pots. The white water lily grows stem up to 2.75 m/9 ft long and the large green leaves float on the surface. The large white flowers, some 13 cm/5 in across, open only during the day, closing and sinking partly below the surface at night. Ottelia alismoides differs in that the large, long leaves remain submerged.*

Roots, floating or embedded in bottom.

Roots planted at different depths to suit type

lines around the edges of the pool can also be an effective deterrent. Model herons or heron-like birds often make bird gardeners groan with distaste, but they, too, can prove quite effective deterrents in the short term. Fortunately, grey heron predation tends to be rather seasonal, at least at garden ponds, usually involving mainly young birds in late summer and autumn.

## TREES AND SHRUBS

TREES PROVIDE BIRDS with song-posts, roost-sites, nesting-places and food, either directly through their seeds, nuts or fruits, or indirectly through the insects they attract. Anything with reasonably thick foliage might provide a roost-site; ornamental evergreens are best for this, but beyond planting a few of these there is not much you can do. The shrubs described later are often better. Similarly, you should not worry too much about providing song-posts; most birds will use whatever is available, including roofs, television aerials, wires, as well as trees and bushes.

### Trees

As far as possible, existing trees—especially native or long-established kinds—should be retained. Ideally, too, you should not be in too much of a hurry to remove dead

*The beech (left) with its seed, the 'mast', falling in autumn will attract many types of finch; it is also favoured by tits, nuthatches and woodpeckers.*

*The alder (right) is a favourite of the siskin, especially when planted in damp areas. Redpolls also feed on the seeds in the tiny cones and warblers thrive on the insects.*

*Mountain ash (left) with its crop of bright red berries is a colourful addition to any garden. Mistle thrushes are very partial to the fruit as well as other thrushes and blackbirds.*

*The oak (above) is probably host to more species of insect than any other tree, thus supplying food for many bird species; pigeons and jays feed on the acorns.*

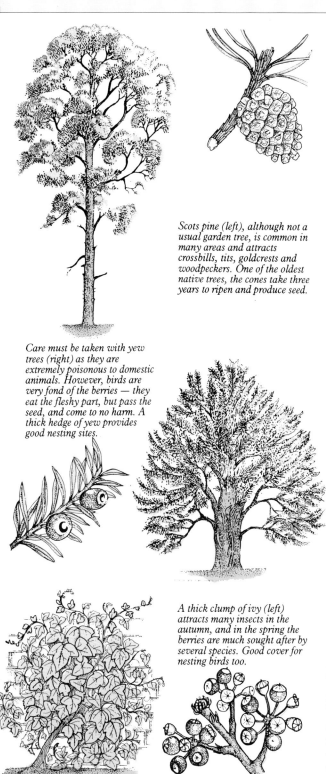

Scots pine (left), although not a usual garden tree, is common in many areas and attracts crossbills, tits, goldcrests and woodpeckers. One of the oldest native trees, the cones take three years to ripen and produce seed.

Care must be taken with yew trees (right) as they are extremely poisonous to domestic animals. However, birds are very fond of the berries — they eat the fleshy part, but pass the seed, and come to no harm. A thick hedge of yew provides good nesting sites.

A thick clump of ivy (left) attracts many insects in the autumn, and in the spring the berries are much sought after by several species. Good cover for nesting birds too.

wood as this can often provide useful insect food and potential nest-holes for several species. If you have enough room, elm is a thoroughly worthwhile tree and even one with Dutch elm disease, though unsightly, will be of benefit to birds for several years after its infection and death. If it is safe, think about retaining it for a time.

Trees to retain and trees to plant can be dealt with together. Important considerations in both cases are preferred soil type, eventual height and size and the likely spread of the tree—and whether it is safe to have it close to the house. Remember, too, that many trees are relatively slow-growing and will not reach maturity for a long time. Big trees really belong in big gardens. For most people, smaller species have to do instead—but many of these are of equal value to birds.

Small ornamental conifers and maples, while very popular, are of limited value to birds, except that they provide some cover and nest-sites. Most are of little value for food. Native or well-established species are far better. The oak *quercus robur* is used by some 300 species of insects, provides nest-sites and grows acorns which are much appreciated by woodpigeons and jays. Willows too are immensely rich, with some 250 insect species recorded and a useful supply of seeds in the autumn. As with oaks, some of the ornamental varieties are almost as good as the native kinds. Poplars may have up to 100 insect species on them; silver birch can have as many as 225 and its catkins provide good spring feeding for redpolls and other small birds. Beech trees provide nuts in autumn—the popular beechmast which is eagerly sought after by, among others, chaffinches, greenfinches and winter-visiting bramblings. More than any other tree, perhaps, the hornbeam is likely to attract the shy and elusive hawfinch, especially if there are several trees together and a drinking pool nearby. Ash is another useful tree: bullfinches are particularly fond of ash-keys. The rowan or mountain ash would be a beautiful garden tree even if its berries attracted no birds at all—but thrushes and blackbirds love them!

Cherry trees of various kinds, crab apples and several ornamental trees in the whitebeam group all produce fruits which are attractive to birds, especially thrushes, sometimes hawfinches and, in the occasional winters when they appear in large numbers, waxwings. Holly provides excellent cover, roosting and nesting places and berries. Gardeners (unless they are also avid wine-makers) tend to look askance at elder, but it is a good berry-bearing and insect-rich species, favoured by many small birds in autumn especially. Hazel, too, is a good tree for its cover and its nuts. There are, in fact, many more useful trees in the broadleaf group: spindle, the limes, wayfaring tree, bird cherry, and field maple, for instance.

Special mention should also be made of alder, which likes wet or very damp places and is a likely species alongside rivers or lakes. It is another very rich 'bird tree', popular with tits, warblers, treecreepers and, especially, redpolls and siskins.

Of the conifers, yew is one of the best, providing thick cover and berries which, while they are harmful to man and domestic animals, are eaten by many birds like thrushes and greenfinches. Coal tits and goldcrests feed on the insects in yews and also in the native Scots pine. This handsome tree (and several of its close relatives) produces cones which also attract coal tits (and crested tits) and, of course, crossbills. Both the European and the Japaneses larches are similarly excellent trees for birds— and so, in fact, are many of the larger exotic conifers widely planted in bigger gardens, such as cedars and redwoods.

Fruit trees must be mentioned. Apples in particular are a favourite of many birds, such as thrushes and waxwings. Bullfinches may damage the buds in spring, of course, making them unpopular with gardeners at that time. If you can, leave a few apples on the trees for the birds, and some windfalls on the ground.

At this point, some mention must be made of ivy, which grows both on trees and on houses. It actually does little harm to trees, despite popular opinion, and can be kept within reasonable bounds on walls. Few plants are as good for birds: ivy provides cover, nest-sites for many species (eg blackbirds, song thrushes, robins and spotted flycatchers), a rich variety of insect food and a late and welcome supply of berries from January to March.

### Shrubs

Many of the general observations made about trees apply also to shrubs. Again, soil requirements, size, spread and so forth have to be taken into account. Many of the larger, denser species provide potential nest-sites and some of the very large kinds, if planted in groups, may also provide cover for winter roots. At first sight, a mass of rhododendrons might seem useful, but, while birds roost and occasionally nest in them they generally provide little insect life or food and allow precious little to grow in their dense shade. Attractive though they are, while in flower, there are many better choices for the bird garden.

A wild, natural hedge, with hawthorns, perhaps blackthorn, wild roses, brambles, the odd small tree and all the many plants associated with such a habitat will be immensely rich in food for birds. Such things are well worth preserving, or even creating if at all possible. For many gardeners this is not a realistic proposition and they will have to think instead of a more formal hedge. If so, privet is very good; so is holly and, while it is slow-

growing, a yew hedge is probably even better still.

Rose bushes, especially climbers, are good for insects and their fruits. Honeysuckle, too, provides succulent berries and masses of insect food, as well as good nesting places; firethorn is attractive in a different way but every bit as good. There are many shrubs which you can plant for their berries, such as several kinds of berberis, snowberry, guelder rose and of course cotoneaster, especially *c simonsii* and *c x watereri. Cotoneaster horizontalis* grows over and along walls and is the waxwing shrub par excellence. Other attractive shrubs of

*Several garden varieties of hawthorn (above) are available and these can make an excellent hedge for birds to nest in. The red berries are much favoured by redwings, fieldfares and blackbirds.*

*Try to be sure to get a female holly tree (below) as only these produce the red berries which attract the mistle thrush, fieldfare and redwing. The holly also makes a good hedge.*

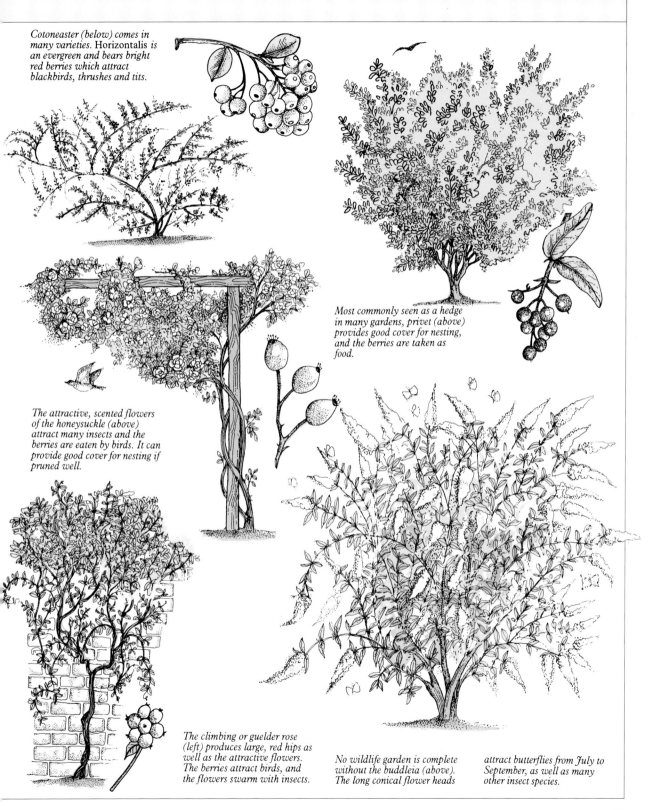

*Cotoneaster (below) comes in many varieties. Horizontalis is an evergreen and bears bright red berries which attract blackbirds, thrushes and tits.*

*Most commonly seen as a hedge in many gardens, privet (above) provides good cover for nesting, and the berries are taken as food.*

*The attractive, scented flowers of the honeysuckle (above) attract many insects and the berries are eaten by birds. It can provide good cover for nesting if pruned well.*

*The climbing or guelder rose (left) produces large, red hips as well as the attractive flowers. The berries attract birds, and the flowers swarm with insects.*

*No wildlife garden is complete without the buddleia (above). The long conical flower heads* *attract butterflies from July to September, as well as many other insect species.*

good value to wildlife include dogwood, Japanese quince and Russian olive.

Finally, there is buddleia, often called the 'butterfly bush'. Its principal attraction is indeed for butterflies, which may come in vast numbers, and for this reason alone it is a must in any wildlife garden—but it attracts masses of other insects too and so is used by many birds in late summer and autumn.

## FLOWERS AND WEEDS

A GARDEN WHICH IS RICH in flowering plants is generally also one which is rich in insects and, therefore, one which will attract a good many birds. To this extent, the more traditional idea of gardening is already valuable to wildlife. Flowerbeds which incorporate a good mixture of classic garden plants and shrubs form ideal mini-habitats, especially when the flowers chosen also provide seeds for birds. Well-vegetated banks covered with lesser periwinkle, or possibly large periwinkles, form excellent alternative borders, rich in insect life and also provide cover for voles (which are generally not regarded as

significant garden pests).

Good all-round plants for birds include forgetmenots, cornflowers, cosmos, asters, scabious, evening primrose and antirrhinums; many ornamental thistles and grasses are good for seeds, and may be easier to control than their wild counterparts. Sunflowers are a must in a good bird garden, not only for their seeds, but also for the many insects they attract. The list of worthwhile plants is actually a very long one—a shortened version would include michaelmas daisy, hebe, iceplant, petunia, sweet rocket, night-scented stock, valerian, pink, thyme, primrose, godetia, lobelia, candytuft, clarkia, mignonette, balsam, marjoram, honesty, aubretia, lavender, foxglove, larkspur and wallflower.

The sort of flowerbeds which are the best of all for birds and other wildlife are, unfortunately, the kind which are anathema to most gardeners—ones where weeds (or to be more fair to them, wildflowers) are allowed to co-exist with garden plants. A half-managed or 'lazy gardener's' flowerbed is ideal in many ways, but in the interests of commonsense it would be wrong to recommend letting the weeds run riot and take over altogether; this would in

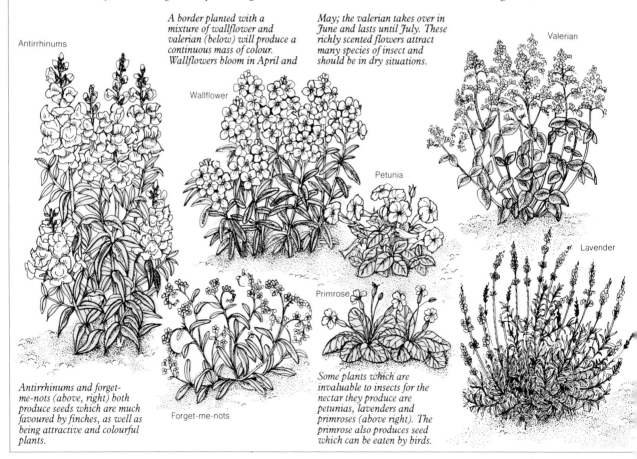

Antirrhinums

Wallflower

*A border planted with a mixture of wallflower and valerian (below) will produce a continuous mass of colour. Wallflowers bloom in April and*

*May; the valerian takes over in June and lasts until July. These richly scented flowers attract many species of insect and should be in dry situations.*

Valerian

Petunia

Lavender

Primrose

Forget-me-nots

*Antirrhinums and forget-me-nots (above, right) both produce seeds which are much favoured by finches, as well as being attractive and colourful plants.*

*Some plants which are invaluable to insects for the nectar they produce are petunias, lavenders and primroses (above right). The primrose also produces seed which can be eaten by birds.*

*Sunflowers (left) are not only attractive, but if left to seed they provide invaluable food for finches and tits. The seeds can also be collected for putting out on the bird table in the winter.*

any case ruin the habitat. Totally bare soil between garden plants is unnatural, but is an accepted ideal in the garden—a good compromise is a flowerbed with garden plants and some wildflowers and some bare soil between them; this seems to be the mixture birds like best of all.

Many bird gardeners try to set aside a strip or a corner which is, effectively, a weed garden in which wild plants are allowed to grow, with some control and, of course, some consideration of the views of the neighbours. Wild grasses are a problem because they are highly invasive and spread like wildfire. They can be contained if you have a reasonably large garden and if you expend a lot of energy on occasions, but are perhaps best avoided in small gardens. Nettles, too, need control, but a space should be set aside for a nettle-patch, if at all possible. Their main value is to several species which lay their eggs on nettles and whose caterpillars then feed on the leaves, but birds can of course benefit from the caterpillars. One of the most useful things to do for a good butterfly garden is to plant nettles in close proximity to buddleia. Thistles (which may need careful control) and teasels are attractive in their own right and also attract goldfinches

*Poppies (below) will brighten up any garden with their bright red flowers, and the seeds produced are attractive to finches.*

*Thistles (below), if left to seed, are a favourite of goldfinches and linnets, while the nettle is an invaluable food plant.*

Poppy

Nettle

Thistle

Dandelion

Buttercup

*Dandelions and buttercups (left, above) generally thought of as weeds, are nevertheless colourful plants and attract many species of insect.*

*Dandelion seeds are also eaten. Care must be taken that these do not spread too much and take over the garden.*

to their seeds. Poppies provide seed for birds (note that there are also several useful cultivated varieties which may be just as good). Other valuable weeds which produce seed for wild birds include some which are traditionally uprooted whenever they show up in most gardens—docks, sorrel, ragwort, groundsel and dandelions. Many umbellifers are also rich in insects, but beware the huge and spectacular giant hogweed which is now naturalized in many places. It is a menace to humans because it can cause a painful and very unpleasant skin rash and is best avoided altogether.

Finally, a traditional, mown lawn is very good for birds; it is even better if you allow clovers, buttercups and cranesbills to grow in it. Blackbirds, thrushes, robins, wagtails, starlings and many others find a rich supply of invertebrate food on lawns. Long, unmown grass is distinctly less useful to most birds, but could be maintained in small clumps or at the edges of a lawn in larger gardens.

## CONTROL METHODS

THERE ARE A GREAT MANY CHEMICALS available to the gardener for use in pest control; the bird gardener should see that they are not harmful to wildlife.

### Slugs
Frequent garden pests, they can be caught and destroyed by simple traps—a shallow, but steep-sided container sunk in the ground and filled with a sweet liquid works very well; so does a hollowed-out half orange placed open side downwards. Chemical slug killers contain *metaldehyde* and *nuthiocarb*, both of which can harm

 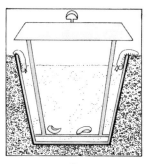

*Dangerous slug jugs or trays containing beer or the chemical* methaldehyde *(above) should be buried in the soil and covered to safeguard pets, birds and other wildlife. The snail trap (right) uses a powerful attractant to lure snails and slugs, and* methaldehyde *finishes them off.*

## CHEMICALS IN THE GARDEN
### Weedkillers
Most herbicides do not harm animals and birds, but care should be exercised in spraying. Remember, too, that some weeds (groundsel, thistles, docks etc) are beneficial to birds.

| SPECIFIC USES | RECOMMENDED TREATMENT |
|---|---|
| **Established lawns:** | |
| Clovers | Mecoprop with 2,4-D, dicamba or ioxynil. |
| Daisy | 2,4-D with mecoprop or dicamba. |
| Dandelion, creeping buttercup and plantains | MCPA, 2,4-D or 2,4-D mixtures. |
| Moss | Lawn sand based on ferrous compounds |
| Variety of weeds | MCPA with dicamba or 2,4-D with dicamba or mecoprop. |
| **Newly sown lawns:** | Ioxynil. |
| **Newly laid lawns:** | No herbicides for at least six months. |
| **Paths, drives and tennis courts:** | Simazine or paraquat granules. |
| **Vegetable gardens and flower beds:** | |
| Clearing weeds before planting | Glyphosate. |
| Removing annual weeds from ornamentals, strawberries and certain vegetables | Propachlor granules. |
| **Problem weeds:** | |
| Couch grass | Dalapon, used when grass is growing vigorously, but among fruit trees and bushes, apply in November when tree is dormant. Glyphosate can also be used. |
| Bindweed, coltsfoot, dock and horsetail | MCPA, 2,4-D or 2,4-D mixtures. |
| Dandelion | 2,4-D or 2,4-D mixtures. |
| Ground elder | Dichlobenil, when desirable plants cannot be damaged. |
| Nettles | MCPA, 2,4-D or mecoprop. |

## Insecticides

As far as possible, care should be taken to see that beneficial insects like bees and ladybirds are not affected when insecticides are applied.

| SPECIFIC USES | RECOMMENDED TREATMENT |
|---|---|
| **Ants** | Permethrin, pyrethrum. |
| **Aphids** | |
| — on fruits | Spray before blossoming with dimethoate, formothion, malathion or chlorpyrifos. |
| — on vegetables and ornamental plants | Fenitrothion, malathion or pirimicarb. (Some plants can be damaged by these — check before use). |
| **Blackcurrant gall mite** | Lime sulphur. |
| **Caterpillars on vegetables** | Chlorpyrifos, derris or permethrin. |
| **Cabbage fly** | Bromophos or chlorpyrifos. |
| **Carrot fly** | Bromophos or chlorpyrifos. |
| **Codling moth** | Chlorpyrifos, permethrin or fenitrothion. |
| **Cutworms** | Bromophos or chlorpyrifos. |
| **Onion fly** | Bromophos or chlorpyrifos. |
| **Raspberry beetle** | Derris dust, fenitrothion or malathion. |
| **Red spider mite** | Derris (roses), dimethoate, malathion or chlorpyrifos. |
| **Sawflies** | Chlorpyrifos, dimethoate or fenitrothion. |
| **Thrips** | Derris (roses), fenitrothion or malathion. |
| **Wasps** | Carbaryl. |
| **Winter moths on fruit trees** | Chlorpyrifos, fenitrothion or permethrin. |

## Fungicides

Most are unlikely to harm birds or animals, but may affect fish if used too close to garden ponds. Mercury-based compounds such as *calomel*(*mercurous sulphide*) should not be used!

| SPECIFIC USES | RECOMMENDED TREATMENT |
|---|---|
| **Blight on potato and tomato:** | Copper, maneb or zineb. |
| **Bulb and corm diseases:** | Treat before planting with quintozene dust; dip in benomyl or thiophanate-methyl. |
| **Dumping-off of seedlings:** | Copper or quintozene; thiram (as seed dressing). |
| **Leaf spots:** | Benomyl, copper, maneb (roses), thiophanate-methyl, thiram or zineb. |
| **Mildews:** | |
| Downy | Zineb |
| Powdery | Benomyl, copper, dinocap, sulphur, thiophanate-methyl. |
| **Moulds:** | |
| — on soft fruit | Benoyml, dichlofluanid, thiophanate-methyl or thiram. |
| —on vegetables and pot plants | As above. Under glass use tecnazine. |
| **Rusts:** | Maneb, thiram or zineb. |
| **Scabs on apples and pears:** | Benomyl, copper, sulphur (not sulphur-shy varieties), thiophanate-methyl or thiram. |
| **Turf diseases:** | Quintozene or thiophanate-methyl. |

wildlife and pets. Do not sprinkle such baits in the open, but be sure to place them under a board, brick or flowerpot where birds and hedgehogs cannot reach them—or the poisoned slugs.

It is also worth mentioning that the compounds used in the treatment of roof timbers will kill bats. If you have bats in your roof but need to treat your timbers, consult an expert through the organizations listed on page 156.

### Rodent control

The control of rodents may be necessary in some circumstances. Where mice are eating fruit or bulbs stored indoors, a standard breakback trap is ideal, but must not be used outdoors. Rodenticides can be used where voles or mice are eating garden plants, but they should always be placed in a covered situation where birds cannot get at them. The same applies to the rat poison, *warfarin*, which should be placed in a pipe or inside a pile of bricks and stones.

### Birds

Birds are often best kept off vulnerable fruits by netting, but this is not always predictable. Two safe bird repellents

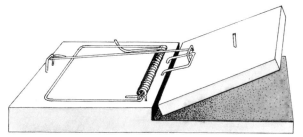

*Where mice are a pest to crops or stored vegetables, the simple backbreaking trap (below) is not to be recommended for outdoor use, as birds are just as likely to get caught.*

*To discourage birds from eating fruit crops, a plastic kestrel mounted on a flexible pole (left) which moves in the wind, or an enclosed fruit cage is the best solution. The cage (below) consists of small mesh netting supported on a frame of metal poles. Care must be taken that no gaps are left — birds will find their way in through them, but then may not be able to escape so that you may have to dismantle part of the cage to let them out.*

Although insect pests are not desirable, if you want to have a complete avifauna in your garden you have to accept that some insect damage is inevitable. If the damage to fruit-bearing plants becomes, or achieves, plague proportions you may wish to resort to chemical pesticides. It must be remembered, however, that all pesticides are poisonous and must be used sparingly, for they are not only toxic to birdlife but can also be dangerous to pets and even humans. It is best to spray (left) on days when there is no wind, so that you prevent the chemicals spreading over a wide area, and causing unnecessary mortalities (above).

are *Anthraquinone*, used to protect buds, and *ammonium aluminium sulphate* which can be applied to flowers and vegetables. Both are quite effective.

### Using chemicals

All garden pesticides are poisonous; you should use them only where you have positively identified the pest involved and you should bear the following points in mind.

Do not buy any pesticide which does not include details of its ingredients on the container and then buy only as much as you need. Obey the manufacturer's instructions, keep the chemicals out of the reach of children and pets and always be scrupulously careful to wash your hands (and any utensils) after use. Do not contaminate any

source of water, particularly ponds, streams and ditches; fish can be affected even by diluted chemicals.

Avoid spraying in windy conditions, which will spread chemicals to places where you do not want them—this is particularly important when using herbicides. Do not spray plants in flower, when there is a real risk of harming bees and many other nectar-feeding or pollinating insects; but if you must do so, spray in the evening.

Safe disposal is as important as safe storage. Solid remains should be sealed firmly in their containers and put in the dustbin; empty containers can go there too, but should be thoroughly rinsed out first. Surplus liquids must be effectively diluted before disposal and should then be emptied into a WC or an outside drain.

By following the guidelines given here it is possible to

use many standard garden pest control methods without causing any harm to wildlife. For further information contact the organizations listed on page 156.

## PREDATORS

THE MOST DIFFICULT CONCEPT for many bird gardeners to grasp is the relationship between garden birds and their predators—the other birds (or animals) which kill and eat them or rob their nests of eggs and young. To many people, wild creatures are 'nice' or 'nasty'; understandable though this may be, it is a fundamentally wrong way to look at nature. Predators and their prey exist in balance with one another, except

where man introduces unnatural or artificial factors into the equation, and the numbers of predators are a reflection of the amount of prey available to them. Predators do not actually 'control' the numbers of their prey species, as is often supposed. Nor is predation 'cruel'—there is really no difference between a blue tit catching and eating a caterpillar, and a sparrowhawk raiding a bird table.

If you live in an area where sparrowhawks occur, they will almost inevitably be attracted to a busy feeding station and a smash-and-grab raid on your bird table may well become a regular, even daily, event. This may distress you, but there is nothing you can do about it. You must accept it as perfectly normal and, indeed, realize

*A cat's natural instinct is to hunt prey, and this kitten attempting to catch a dove (right) shows the problem common to bird and pet lovers. The main problem is not necessarily one of predation, but there may be sufficient disturbance to keep many bird species away from otherwise suitable areas.*

that by providing food which concentrates many small birds in one area, you are in effect providing food for sparrowhawks. Their predation on small birds is only one of a series of natural factors, including starvation and disease, which results in high mortality, especially among inexperienced birds in their first winter.

## Cat control

Fortunately, though, natural predators are relatively scarce in the garden and it is also likely that we will see very little of their comings and goings. Cats, however, are another matter. They are not natural predators since they occur in unnaturally high numbers, at a much greater density than would be possible for a wild predator. Nor

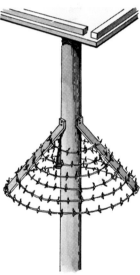

*A barbed-wire skirt (above), or inverted cone, prevents predators such as rats, cats and squirrels reaching the food table.*

*If cats are fitted with a collar and bell, this will warn birds of their approach and prevents predation. The collar (above) should be elasticated to prevent strangulation should the cat get caught on an obstruction.*

are they in any way limited by a natural food supply since they are domesticated and fed by us.

It is exceptionally difficult to keep cats out of gardens without resorting to the erection of close-mesh fencing or all sorts of anti-cat devices such as wires and broken glass along the tops of walls, which are not only unsightly but also tend to upset the neighbours! Commercial cat-repellents are often quite effective in the short term, but of course are expensive since they have to be used more or less continuously. All sorts of ingenious methods have been used to keep cats away from bird tables and feeders, including wire skirts below the table and projecting wires around about; feeders should certainly be situated as far away as possible from likely jumping-off points in trees, on walls and so on. Probably the best and simplest way to lessen the numbers of deaths caused by cats is to fit them with collars and bells.

## Bird control

Magpies, jays and crows are all expert nest finders and for part of the year take the eggs and young of small birds. Crows are likely to do so only in large, quiet gardens since they are very wary birds, but jays may do so in well-timbered areas and magpies almost anywhere. Since magpies cause more argument and more concern than almost any other garden predator—cats included—let us consider the case for and against them.

Magpies are partial and seasonal predators: for most of the year they feed mainly on invertebrates and a variety of other foods, and only rarely kill birds. Most probably never do so at all. Their nest-robbing activities occur over a relatively short period and even then probably provide only a very small part of their diet. It is true that they may clean out a lot of nests in a small area, but their victims can withstand even heavy predation of this sort and will almost always move elsewhere and nest again. Any apparent decline or disappearance is, therefore, likely to be only temporary and in the long term the total numbers will not be affected. The situation is continuously monitored by the wildlife trusts and there is no evidence of a decline attributable to the activities of predators, and certainly none which correlates to increasing numbers of magpies.

As with sparrowhawks, so with magpies: you should learn to accept their nest raids as natural and inevitable, however much that may distress you at the moment when it happens. It is quite proper, of course, to take action against magpies and indeed jays and crows, using legal methods (see page 10). However, magpie control is hardly justifiable in the majority of situations, although exceptional circumstances can sometimes make it necessary.

# FOOD AND FEEDERS

NOBODY KNOWS FOR CERTAIN when man consciously began to feed birds around his dwelling place, but it must have been going on for thousands of years—no doubt developing quite naturally through the habits of some species which scavenged around the homesteads. It may always have been done for purely altruistic reasons, but it has also been done to catch birds for keeping as pets—or for the pot. Nowadays, feeding birds is standard practice in many countries.

## FEEDING BIRDS

PROVIDING FOOD ATTRACTS BIRDS and gives many people a lot of pleasure (which is no bad reason for doing it), but does it really have any conservation value? This is a difficult question to answer, not least because it is very difficult to measure what effect feeding has on the numbers of small birds. However, it is quite reasonable to assume that it is very beneficial to some species, at least in periods of prolonged severe weather and, especially, prolonged snow cover. Birds will very quickly find regular and reliable sources of food and will return to them again and again; they may come to rely on them, so it is very important, in hard weather at least, to continue a feeding programme once you have started it.

It is not necessary to feed birds all through the year.

*Some features of the ideal bird garden (below). The old tree stump with food crammed in cracks and a central hole makes an ideal low level, natural bird table (but is open to predation or unwanted visitors). The table, which is on a long pole, has a plastic sleeve to prevent cats from climbing up, and the inverted tin higher up will deter squirrels. The suspended nut basket is a further attraction.*

nut basket

inverted tin

old tree stump

plastic sleeve

*In winter, fallen fruit left on the ground or stored and then put out later is welcomed by birds such as these starlings (left). It is also a favourite food of blackbirds, redwings, fieldfares and other thrushes.*

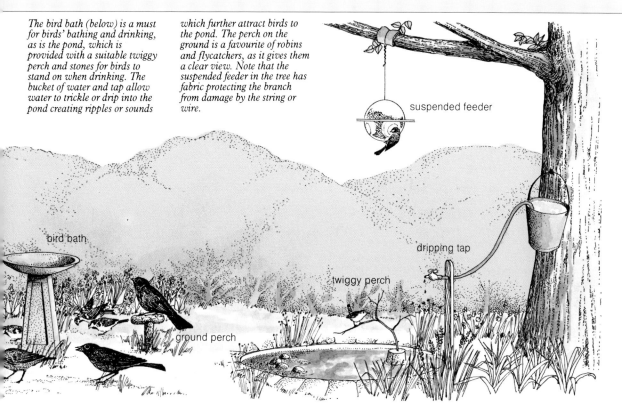

*The bird bath (below) is a must for birds' bathing and drinking, as is the pond, which is provided with a suitable twiggy perch and stones for birds to stand on when drinking. The bucket of water and tap allow water to trickle or drip into the pond creating ripples or sounds which further attract birds to the pond. The perch on the ground is a favourite of robins and flycatchers, as it gives them a clear view. Note that the suspended feeder in the tree has fabric protecting the branch from damage by the string or wire.*

suspended feeder

dripping tap

bird bath

twiggy perch

ground perch

Natural food supplies should be readily available from spring to autumn and, importantly, are the resources to which birds turn when feeding their young. Feeding in the garden is, therefore, unnecessary (and indeed not recommended) outside the winter months. Water on the other hand, can be made available all the year round, and is especially important during very cold weather.

Before discussing food and feeders in detail there are a few basic points to bear in mind. The first concerns 'competition' at feeders. Many people resent the bullying, over-confident attitudes of starlings or the abundance of house sparrows and feral pigeons. You cannot seriously hope to exclude any of these birds altogether, but you can manage them to some extent. Some feeders are accessible by holes only, or by spaces in mesh surrounds, which can exclude pigeons and starlings at least, and sometimes house sparrows. Unfortunately, though, a hole which is too small for a starling will also keep out blackbirds and thrushes. A rather better solution is probably to try to maintain two or three different feeding stations at once, well spaced out if possible, and to separate different kinds of food. This allows more individual birds to feed at the same time with some segregation—but it isn't foolproof!

Grey squirrels are fun to watch, but even a feeder well out of jumping range of a tree or wall may prove accessible to them. An inverted biscuit tin two-thirds of the way up the post of a bird table, with a plastic drainpipe placed like a sleeve over the post below it, is an effective and simple way of keeping grey squirrels at bay.

It is important to keep feeding stations reasonably clear of rotting food and to clean away old scraps so as to avoid the risk of disease and infection; do not allow uneaten food to lie around on the ground, where it is likely to attract rats and mice. The odd field mouse will probably be a welcome visitor, but lots of house mice and certainly lots of brown rats will not. Rats, incidentally, also carry a strong risk of introducing *salmonellosis*, which can cause heavy and distressing mortality among garden birds. Ideally, feeding sites should be moved once or twice during the winter and the feeders thoroughly cleaned in spring.

## WHAT TO FEED — AND WHERE

THE SIMPLEST WAY TO FEED BIRDS is to scatter bread and other scraps on the ground, on a windowsill or on a flat roof. This almost invariably attracts hordes of house sparrows, starlings and pigeons, but it is also very useful in attracting some species which hardly ever visit bird tables or other feeders. Its big disadvantage is that it may also attract rats and mice. It is generally better to concentrate feeding at two or three sites, using a bird table and other feeding devices. This makes general hygiene easier, enables you to provide food close to the cover which is important to some species, means better protection from marauding cats and, last but not least, provides you with a much better chance of actually watching your guests. Ground-feeders can be provided with a small amount of food below bird tables and will, of course, be useful for the frequent spillages.

### The basics

Many people believe that white bread is bad for birds— this is not so, but it can be hard and therefore very difficult for birds to break up and swallow, so it should be soaked in water first. The same general rule applies to other kinds of bread, all of which are very acceptable to many species. Biscuits, cake remnants, cooked pastry leftovers and all the crumbs which accumulate in breadbins, biscuit barrels etc are all worth putting out. Remember that most garden birds have very small mouths, so break it all up.

The list of kitchen scraps you can put out is almost endless. Small pieces of cheese are a favourite with many birds; so are bits of fat and, as a special treat, suet. Suet can be provided in small pieces, as a block which tits and nuthatches can chip away at (it is best to secure it by wire, or hang it from a convenient branch), or rammed into a hanging container. Many people push bits into cracks in trees for tits and woodpeckers, or even create special feeding stations for them on old tree stumps. Suet, lard or dripping also forms the basis of the popular 'bird cake': it is melted down and poured over a mixture of seeds, dried fruit, nuts, cake crumbs, cheese and virtually anything else you care to add. When hardened, this can be placed on a bird table, hung up in a container (in which it can be left to set beforehand,) or crammed into a hole in a stump or tree-trunk. The proportions of the bird cake are roughly 227g ($^1/_2$ lb) of fat to 453g (1 lb) of mixture.

Bones too attract tits, nuthatches and woodpeckers, as well as starlings, either for the fat and meat left clinging to them or for the marrow inside. They are best hung up, and care should be taken with broken bones (especially poultry bones) left on the ground if you have a dog or a cat. Odd pieces of meat are relished by many birds. At least some should be minced up for small insectivorous birds like wrens and dunnocks. Minced meat has also been recorded as being eaten by birds like snipe and water rail in hard weather. Robins and tits will enjoy it at any time. Incidentally, commercially available cat and dog foods can also be put out for many small birds. Bacon rind, cut into small pieces, cooked or uncooked, is another firm favourite. Many people ask whether the salt content

of bacon (and indeed other foods) is harmful to birds, but there is no evidence to suggest that the amounts present have any ill effects. Many of these meaty foods will help small insectivorous birds, which generally have the hardest time finding enough to eat in severe weather, as long as what you provide is broken down into very small fragments. The so-called 'ants' eggs (really pupae and larvae) which you can buy very cheaply in pet shops are also very helpful to these species. If you can obtain them, mealworms (flour beetle larvae) are also very useful. Robins are said to sell their souls for them—they will at least come rapidly and may take them from your hand.

### The titbits

Nuts of course, are very popular. Almost any kind will do, but peanuts are the best (not, however, the excessively salted variety available in pubs etc), either strung up in their shells, placed in a nut basket, suspended in the mesh bags in which they now come prepacked, or simply scattered on the bird table. Peanuts can be bought in bulk from many pet shops and commercial bird food suppliers; they sell like the proverbial hot cakes, so lay in a good supply. Tits, nuthatches and even great spotted woodpeckers will delight you with their antics where nuts are hung up for them. They will even come right up against windows. Greenfinches, too, will soon find them and, if you are in an area where they occur in winter, so will siskins. Unfortunately, house sparrows are also very fond of nuts and will very quickly learn how to get at them. One way to prevent them from taking more than their fair share is to hang the nut basket inside a glass jar, leaving only the base of the basket accessible. Tits and siskins can cope with this, but sparrows find it rather difficult. Half a coconut can be suspended for tits and nuthatches, and once emptied, the shell makes a useful bird cake container. Dessicated coconut should *not* be put out as it may swell up inside the bird.

Many kinds of mixed, small vegetables and dried peas, lentils etc are useful additions to the menu; dried fruits, especially currants and sultanas, are also firm favourites with many species. Whole or half apples are much appreciated by blackbirds and all the other thrushes, including winter-visiting fieldfares and redwings. Leave a few windfalls and any damaged apples for the birds, and if you can, set aside a small proportion of your crop against the possibility of hard weather later on. Oats, oatmeal, maize flakes, puppy meal and all kinds of 'bird seed' can also be put out—a seed hopper is recommended to avoid too much spillage. Most commercial wild bird foods contain a high proportion of seeds among their many ingredients, and can be recommended; they sometimes lead to strange things growing in the garden in spring too!

# FEEDING REQUIREMENTS

**Grey heron:** Fish, eels, frogs, small mammals and large insects

**White stork:** Frogs, reptiles, large insects and small mammals

**Mallard:** Mainly plant matter; also insects, molluscs and seeds

**Mute swan:** Aquatic plants, grass or cereals

**Sparrowhawk:** Birds up to the size of the woodpigeon; large insects

**Kestrel:** Small birds and mammals, insects and worms

**Red-legged partridge:** Seeds, vegetable matter, buds, flowers and insects

**Partridge:** Seeds and vegetable matter

**Pheasant:** Seeds, insects, plant shoots and grain

**Water rail:** Insects, molluscs, worms, grain and plant material

**Moorhen:** Aquatic plants, grasses, seeds, insects and molluscs

**Coot:** Aquatic plants, grass, insects, small fish, seeds and molluscs

**Snipe:** Worms, insects, grass and seeds

**Woodcock:** Worms, insects, seeds and grass

**Herring gull:** Carrion, fish, worms, molluscs, crustacea, insects, seaweed, garbage

**Common gull:** Fish, molluscs, insects, worms, scraps

**Black-headed gull:** Fish, molluscs, insects, worms; seeds, grass and refuse

**Feral pigeon:** Grain and seeds

**Stock dove:** Seeds, grain, fruit, roots and green shoots

**Woodpigeon:** Grain, seeds, vegetables, plants, acorns and berries

**Turtle dove:** Seeds

**Collared dove:** Grain, seeds, fruit

**Barn owl:** Small mammals including mice and voles; small birds and insects

**Tawny owl:** Rats, mice, voles, small birds, frogs and worms

**Little owl:** Insects, worms, small mammals and birds

**Scops owl:** Crickets, grasshoppers, moths, beetles, mice and small birds

**Ring-necked parakeet:** Fruit, berries, seeds and nuts, especially peanuts

**Cuckoo:** Insects, especially caterpillars

**Swift:** Insects caught on the wing

**Kingfisher:** Small insects, but mainly small fish

**Hoopoe:** Chiefly insects and their larvae; worms, lizards and small mammals

**Wryneck:** Insects, especially ants

**Green woodpecker:** Larvae of wood-boring beetles and ants

**Great-spotted woodpecker:** Larvae of wood-boring beetles, spiders, nuts and berries

**Lesser-spotted woodpecker:** Larvae of wood-boring insects, spiders and berries

**House martin:** Entirely insects

**Swallow:** Solely insects

**Meadow pipit:** Insects, worms and spiders

**Pied/white wagtail:** Flies, mosquitoes, beetles and seeds

**Yellow wagtail:** Small insects

**Grey wagail:** Insects, larvae, small fry

**Starling:** Worms, spiders, insects, seeds, fruit and berries

**Golden oriole:** Large insects, caterpillars, fruit and berries

**Jay:** Acorns, beetles, fruit, nuts, eggs and nestlings, small mammals

**Magpie:** Large insects, small mammals, carrion, fruit, eggs and grain

**Jackdaw:** Large insects, fruit, nuts, spiders and eggs

**Rook:** Worms, caterpillars, acorns and grain

**Carrion/Hooded crow:** Worms, small mammals, eggs and nestlings; insects and carrion

**Waxwing:** Chiefly insects, berries, buds and fruit

**Wren:** Flies, small beetles, spiders, ants and earwigs

**Dipper:** Small aquatic insects and their larvae; molluscs and small fish

**Dunnock:** Small insects, spiders and seeds

**Sedge warbler:** Flies and other small insects, spiders and berries

**Icterine warbler:** Insects and caterpillars, fruit and berries

**Melodious warbler:** Small fruits such as berries; insects and their larvae

**Garden warbler:** Insects such as flies, caterpillars, small beetles and spiders; berries in autumn

**Blackcap:** Insects, fruit and berries, especially elderberries and snowberries

**Whitethroat:** Insects and berries

**Lesser whitethroat:** Small insects and berries

**Sardinian warbler:** Small insects, fruit, seeds and berries

**Willow warbler:** Aphids, beetles, spiders, worms and small berries

**Chiffchaff:** Flies, small caterpillars, aphids and small beetles

**Goldcrest:** Small insects and spiders

**Firecrest:** Small insects and spiders

**Pied flycatcher:** Insects of all kinds, usually taken in the air

**Spotted flycatcher:** Insects of all kinds, usually taken in aerial pursuit

**Black redstart:** Insects; also spiders and millipedes; occasionally berries

**Redstart:** Insects and berries

**Nightingale:** Various insects, earthworms, spiders and berries

**Robin:** Insects, spiders, worms and berries

**Fieldfare:** Insects, worms and grubs, fruits and berries

**Redwing:** Earthworms, snails, insects and their larvae; also fruits

**Blackbird:** Insects, worms, kitchen scraps, fruits and berries

**Song thrush:** Snails, earthworms, insects and their larvae; fruits and seeds

**Mistle thrush:** Fruits, especially of mistletoe; slugs, worms and insects

**Long-tailed tit:** Small insects, spiders, seeds and buds

**Marsh tit:** Insects, seeds and berries

**Willow tit:** Small insects, berries and seeds

**Crested tit:** Insects, caterpillars, conifer seeds and juniper berries

**Coal tit:** Beetles, flies, spiders, seeds and nuts

**Blue tit:** Aphids, spiders, caterpillars, fruit, grain and seeds

**Great tit:** Mainly insects; also seeds, fruit and buds

**Nuthatch:** Large insects and their larvae; spiders, earwigs, seeds and nuts

**Treecreeper:** Insects and their larvae; spiders

**Short-toed treecreeper:** Invertebrates, woodlice, weevels, beetles, earwigs; also seeds

**House sparrow:** Virtually anything, but especially seeds

**Tree sparrow:** Mainly seeds; also insects

**Chaffinch:** Seeds, fruit and insects

**Brambling:** Insects, caterpillars; seeds in winter

**Serin:** Seeds, insects and elm buds

**Greenfinch:** Seeds, tree and flower buds, berries and insects

**Goldfinch:** Seeds of dandelion, thistles, insects and their larvae

**Linnet:** Small insects, caterpillars and weed seeds

**Redpoll:** Insects and seeds

**Crossbill:** Seeds of pine cones, insects and berries

**Bullfinch:** Insects, berries, seeds and buds of fruiting trees and flowers

**Hawfinch:** Seeds, especially of hornbeam; insects, berries, beechmast

**Yellowhammer:** Plant shoots, seeds, insects and worms

**Reed bunting:** Insects, snails, caterpillars and seeds

**Siskin:** Seeds of alder, birch, spruce and pine

37

Sunflower seeds are perhaps the most popular seeds of all, much loved by greenfinches in particular—they are usually included in wild bird mixtures, but can be bought separately. You can, of course, grow your own and enjoy the sunflowers themselves before they become bird food.

One of the great pleasures of feeding birds is that there is almost no limit to the menu: follow the guidelines given here, but experiment with your own ideas too.

## ALL KINDS OF FEEDERS

THE CLASSIC BIRD TABLE is a simple, flat board mounted on a post. It is actually available in a wide variety of forms, from very simple to rustic (and sometimes quite awful)— but the birds have no eye for what may please *you* and their requirements are very simple. Whether you buy a ready-made table or make one yourself, following the basic instructions given here, is really up to you. Incidentally, there is no reason why a plastic table should not do just as well as a more traditional wooden one.

Ideally, a bird table should sit securely on a firm post approximately 1.5 m (5 ft) above the ground, not too far from cover, but out of the jumping range (from walls and trees) of cats and grey squirrels. It should have a roof to keep the food fairly dry (the roof can also incorporate a food hopper) and should have a low surrounding rim to avoid too much spillage of food on to the ground below. Gaps in the rim or holes bored in the table itself will assist in draining off rainwater. It is also possible to place bird tables on walls or window-ledges by using metal or wooden brackets, or to hang them up by cords or chains.

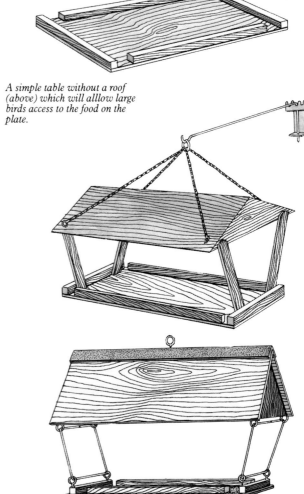

*A simple table without a roof (above) which will alllow large birds access to the food on the plate.*

*Two types of hanging tables (above). The latter with a removeable tray which is suspended from the roof.*

*An exploded diagram of a typical bird table (below). Remember that the roof segments should overlap to cut* *down leaks onto the base plate, and that the coaming is incomplete to allow easy drainage and cleaning.*

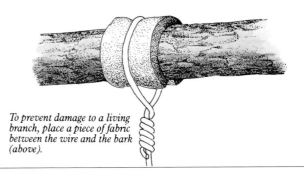

*To prevent damage to a living branch, place a piece of fabric between the wire and the bark (above).*

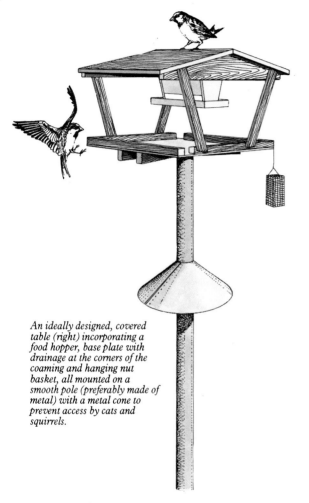

An ideally designed, covered table (right) incorporating a food hopper, base plate with drainage at the corners of the coaming and hanging nut basket, all mounted on a smooth pole (preferably made of metal) with a metal cone to prevent access by cats and squirrels.

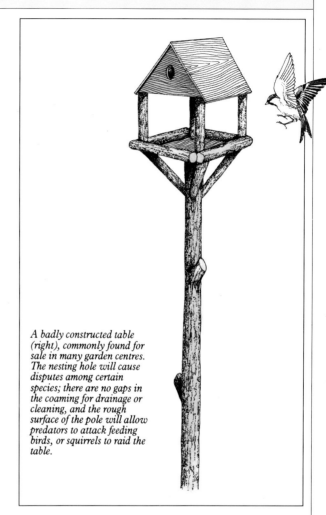

A badly constructed table (right), commonly found for sale in many garden centres. The nesting hole will cause disputes among certain species; there are no gaps in the coaming for drainage or cleaning, and the rough surface of the pole will allow predators to attack feeding birds, or squirrels to raid the table.

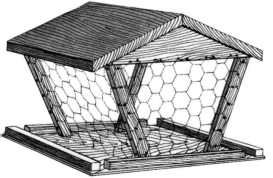

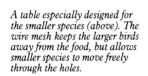

A table especially designed for the smaller species (above). The wire mesh keeps the larger birds away from the food, but allows smaller species to move freely through the holes.

Many species like to perch on a good vantage point before venturing onto tables, or down to water. A strategically placed perch (above) will help them to make up their minds.

Nuts can be strung from the sides and nut baskets and other feeding devices can be suspended from them.

Purpose-built metal or plastic nut and scrap baskets come in a variety of shapes and sizes and are available quite cheaply from many sources. Many shops now sell nuts prepacked in inexpensive sausage-shaped bags and these have proved highly popular and very successful. They have the advantage that they can be hung almost anywhere. There is now an enormous range of garden bird equipment available, including food hoppers, tit bells, windowsill trays and so on, some of them incorporating several features at once and others with covered feeding areas accessible only to tits.

You can, of course, make your own feeding devices. A tit bell—which is basically some sort of inverted container for fat-based bird cake and the like—can be made from half a coconut shell, an empty yoghurt container or even an old jam-jar. Other jars of various sizes can be mounted or suspended horizontally and will provide excellent feeders which keep the food dry and all in one place. You can also create sheltered ground feeding stations by using simple screens which will not only protect the food you put down, but also give some protection from predators.

One further tip: some garden birds, like wrens, do not come very readily to feeders and although they may come to food on the ground they really prefer to feed under cover and in thick vegetation. Heavy snow cover greatly reduces their options, so be prepared to clear snow away for them and open up areas of undergrowth and hedge bottoms for them. Small supplies of minced meat scraps, fat, cheese and 'ants' eggs' can also be useful.

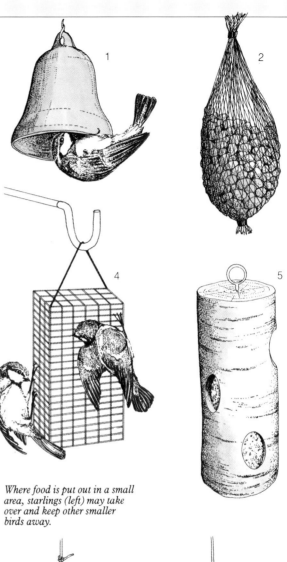

*Where food is put out in a small area, starlings (left) may take over and keep other smaller birds away.*

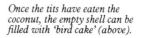

*Once the tits have eaten the coconut, the empty shell can be filled with 'bird cake' (above).*

*Similarly, this empty plastic yoghurt carton (above) can be filled with fat, nuts and seed, and then suspended.*

40

The tit bell is very popular with blue, great and coal tits when filled with 'bird cake'. The nut bag (2) is suitable for finches and tits. The seed hopper (3) means you can put out a lot of nuts and seed at once, rather than constantly renewing supplies. Nut baskets (4) are very popular, but make sure there are no sharp edges or points, as these can damage birds' legs. A simple device for 'bird cake' is the birch log (5) drilled with holes and then filled with fat, a favourite of woodpeckers and nuthatches. Another type of hopper (6) is the globe — this also keeps the food dry and can only be used by small birds. A nut feeder (7) and drinking cup on a long plastic pole.

A hole bored in the middle of a tree stump (above) and filled with suet, fat and seeds makes an ideal feeding station.

A suspended glass jar (above) filled with seeds and nuts will entice tits and finches, and also keeps the food dry.

An alternative method is to secure the jar in the fork of a tree (above). Clear glass allows the birds to see the food.

Peanuts still in their kernels and threaded on to a piece of string (above) makes the tits work harder and is fun to watch.

41

# HOMES FOR ALL

HOWEVER YOU MANAGE THE TREES in your garden, natural hole nest-sites are always at a premium. In many gardens there will be none at all. Nestboxes provide an ideal substitute and while their basic design caters for hole-nesters, boxes can also be adapted to suit other species, particularly those which like ledges and sheltered cavities. Here are some of the main factors to bear in mind when considering nestboxes.

## BASIC CONSIDERATIONS

NESTBOXES CAN BE FITTED to walls or trees, according to what is available. There is no hard and fast rule about how high they should be placed, but 'out of reach' (of humans and cats) is a good rule of thumb. Around 3 m (10 ft) up is fine, but probably no lower than 2 m (6½ ft). The sheltered side of a wall or tree is best, but many boxes are also in exposed situations. It is always best to place the box so that it faces away from the prevailing wind or rain direction and also away from the greatest heat of the sun,

in other words not facing due south. A sheltered and reasonably well hidden situation is necessary for open-fronted boxes used by robins, pied or white wagtails and spotted flycatchers.

Once a box is in use, it should be disturbed as little as possible: it is best not to examine the contents at all, but if for any reason you must do so, exercise great care and make your visits as brief and infrequent as possible. You may also realize at some point that something has gone wrong, and a quick inspection may reveal deserted eggs or even dead young birds. You may have caused desertion yourself by disturbing the box too much, but there is also a chance that cold weather may have caused the adults to desert eggs, or a failure in the food supply has led to the starvation of the young.

Direct predation from cats, weasels, squirrels or even great spotted woodpeckers is also possible. Strategically placed wires or obstacles may deter cats, but squirrels are notoriously hard to keep away from nestboxes. Metal cones at the entrance holes of boxes have stopped weasel

*To reduce the size of a nestbox entrance, and thereby make the box more suitable for a smaller species, a length of wood (which doubles as a perch) can be nailed across it (left).*

*If the hole in a nestbox is slightly too large, house sparrows (right) will take it over. While not always unwelcome guests, they can deprive birds such as blue tits for which these nestboxes are intended.*

*When suitably placed in the fork of a tree, or low down in vegetation, and where water cannot get in, old kettles or jugs (above) make ideal nesting sites for robins.*

*When attaching a nestbox to a tree, be sure to place it away from side branches so that predators, such as cats (right) cannot get near them.*

predation (the animals cannot climb around them to get at the holes) and metal plates fitted around the entrance frustrate most squirrels, who have to enlarge the hole by gnawing before they can get inside. Woodpeckers may be deterred by this method too, but can, of course, break into a wooden box from any direction. It is best to accept that a certain amount of predation is inevitable. Wasps, bees and earwigs may colonize a nestbox. Earwigs cause the birds no problem and can be left alone; wasps and bees are probably best left alone too (although a professional bee keeper can remove a swarm for you) and rather than meddle with them, it would be better to put up another box nearby.

Once a box has been used, there remains the question of whether or not to clear it out. The nest débris, plus perhaps old food remains or even a rotting dead chick, will attract insects and bird parasites, some of which may be harmful to next year's young, so it is best to clean out used boxes, but not until early spring. Things should be left as they are during the winter as nestboxes may be used by tits and sometimes wrens for roosting—or even may be occupied by dormice, which are well worth protecting because they are quite uncommon in many areas. Remove the box completely, clear out all the contents and pour boiling water over the interior to kill off any remaining parasites. Check for repairs to the lid or sides and make these good. A wood preservative (but *not* creosote) can be applied and will lengthen the life of a wooden box. Given proper care and attention it should last for many years and give excellent service.

As with bird tables and feeding devices, so with

nestboxes: there are many different kinds on the market in the basic design range, some perfectly acceptable, but others hopelessly inadequate. Bear in mind the size and hole position mentioned previously and look carefully at fixing methods. Wooden boxes are generally better than plastic ones, although some of the latter have proved very successful. Remember that birds are not influenced by style—only by certain simple requirements, which are usually not too difficult to provide.

## NESTBOXES IN DETAIL

THE BASIC NESTBOX is about 250 mm high and 150 mm deep (10 in × 6 in), with a sloping, hinged roof (or a removable front panel) and an entrance hole, near the top, on either the front or the side. It exists in various styles, or can be made very easily from a plank about 1450 mm long, 150 mm wide and 15 mm thick (4³/₄ ft × 6 in × ¹/₂ in). The internal floor size should be at least 100 mm × 100 mm (4 in × 4 in) and the entrance hole about 125 mm (5 in) from the floor. The box is best secured by battens, or via an elongated rear panel, preferably using screws. Nails will do, but should be galvanized rather than the wire kind. Among the birds likely to use such a box are blue, great, marsh and coal tits, redstarts, pied flycatchers, nuthatches and tree sparrows. By confining the entrance hole to a diameter of 27 mm (1 in) for coal, blue and marsh tits, 30 mm (1¹/₅ in) for great tits and 32 mm (1¹/₃ in) for redstarts, pied flycatchers and nuthatches, house sparrows and starlings can be kept out.

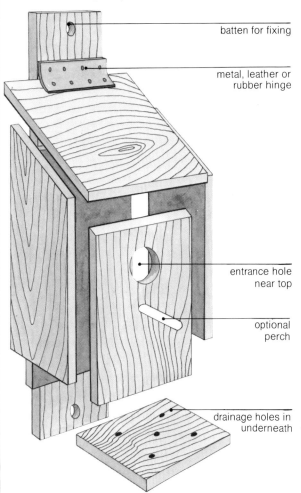

batten for fixing

metal, leather or rubber hinge

entrance hole near top

optional perch

drainage holes in underneath

*An exploded view of a typical nestbox (above) showing the ease of construction. The hinged lid allows viewing of the contents. The perch will give good views of the adults before entry.*

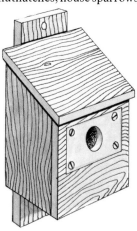

*The metal plate (above) stops birds like the house sparrow enlarging the hole.*

*This open-fronted box (above) is ideal for species like the spotted flycatcher and robin.*

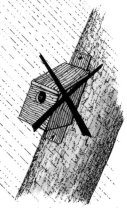

*Always try to position the box facing away from the prevailing wind and, if possible, tilted slightly downwards (above) to*

*prevent rain from entering and soaking or even drowning the nestlings.*

By increasing the dimensions of this basic box, larger hole-nesting birds can be encouraged to breed. A box with internal floor dimensions of 200 mm × 160 mm (8 in × 6⅓ in), with a hole 250 mm (10 in) above the floor and about 70 mm (3 in) wide can be used by jackdaws and stock doves, and of course starlings. By doing away with an entrance hole on the normal size box and removing half the front panel, an open-fronted nestbox can be provided, suitable for robins and pied wagtails. Spotted flycatchers prefer a shallower front, which means the removal of about two-thirds of the panel.

Boxes have been developed for a wide range of other birds, not all of which occur in gardens. There is now a standard design for tawny owls which has proved very successful. It should be at least 3 m (10 ft) up, preferably more, and placed at an angle of about 45 degrees to the horizontal, either on a main trunk, in a substantial fork or on the underside of a large limb. Tawny owls are likely to nest in large, well-timbered gardens, but it is important to remember that boxes must be situated well away from paths or regularly used areas (which includes paths and roads outside your property). Tawny owls can be bold and aggressive in the defence of their young and will attack people coming too close, sometimes with extremely painful results, so exercise great care in putting up tawny owl boxes—think first whether you really have enough room for them.

Barn owls are not garden birds in the normal sense, but may well occur around large properties, farm building complexes, factory sites and the like. They have declined

*To avoid damage to trees use a leather strap (above) to fix nestboxes to them.*

*If a suitable angled branch is not available, an owl box can be fixed at an angle (above).*

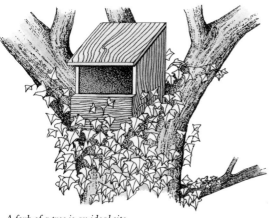
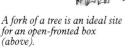

*A fork of a tree is an ideal site for an open-fronted box (above).*

*A tawny owl box strapped to the underside of a branch (above). It may also be used by stock doves and jackdaws.*

45

in many areas and one reason for this is the loss of nest-sites through the removal of old trees or the demolition or modernization of old buildings. A box could be erected for them in a dark corner of a suitably quiet outbuilding, or in the upper part of a modern barn. Barn owls need freedom from disturbance, but unlike tawny owls will not attack people. Feeding primarily on small rodents, especially rats and mice, they are worth having around. Kestrel boxes are really only suitable for people with large, rather open areas adjacent to their houses or places of work. Kestrel boxes can be placed on trees or even on poles in open fields.

Swifts, swallows and house martins are all often associated with human habitations and can all be attracted by the provision of the right kinds of nesting places. Swifts generally choose holes (usually under the eaves) in large, old buildings (often long-standing traditional sites), but may also use specially constructed nestboxes placed at eave or gutter level on high walls. Swallows simply require a suitable ledge or shelf in a porch, outhouse, garage or garden shed, which can be designed and fitted for them quite easily; but remember to allow them some means of coming and going.

House martins build a deep cup-shaped nest of mud which is affixed to walls, almost always just below a gutter or the eaves, but sometimes in the angle at the end of a gable. They are highly colonial and often nest in large numbers at traditional sites, but new colonists can be attracted by using the custom-built artificial nests advertised in several ornithological magazines. One of the main problems with house martins is the mess they make on walls and windows, prompting many people to set about removing their nests. A better solution is to place a 150 mm (6 in) board below the nest to catch most

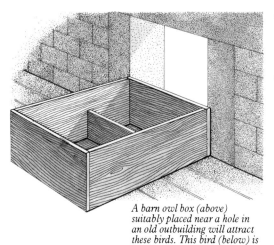

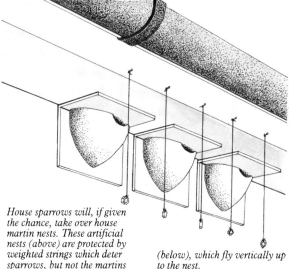

A barn owl box (above) suitably placed near a hole in an old outbuilding will attract these birds. This bird (below) is leaving the nest behind the bricks.

House sparrows will, if given the chance, take over house martin nests. These artificial nests (above) are protected by weighted strings which deter sparrows, but not the martins

(below), which fly vertically up to the nest.

of the droppings. Another thing which worries people is the way in which house sparrows try to take over house martin nests; it is difficult to do much to help, but some success has been achieved by hanging lengths of wool vertically downwards to upset the sparrows without affecting the martins, as the latter, unlike the sparrows, swoop up to the nest from underneath.

Treecreepers nest in crevices in big trees or behind pieces of loose bark and are always possible breeders in large, well-timbered gardens.

Space does not permit mention of all the other species which might possibly be attracted, but further details are available in the publications listed on pages 156 and 157. Birds are not the only creatures to use boxes, and at a time when bats are finding it difficult to find undisturbed roosting places there are good reasons for putting up one or two bat boxes in the garden.

*A kestrel box (above) should be placed 6-9m (20-30 ft) up on a pole, or tree. The roof should be waterproofed.*

*Bats also need roosting sites. Place the box (above) 3.5-4.5m (12-15ft) up in a tree.*

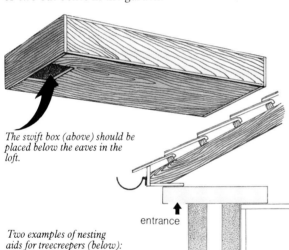

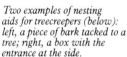

*The swift box (above) should be placed below the eaves in the loft.*

entrance

*Two examples of nesting aids for treecreepers (below): left, a piece of bark tacked to a tree; right, a box with the entrance at the side.*

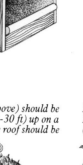

*Wrens will nest in a variety of objects such as flowerpots, coconuts and pipes (above, right). They also use conventional nests (below).*

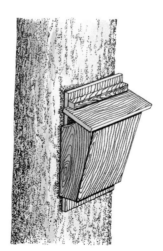

# DIRECTORY
## *of 100 garden birds*

# HOW TO USE THE DIRECTORY

ATTRACTING BIRDS to your garden requires not only a fair degree of gardening skill but also a working knowledge of the particular demands and characteristics of individual birds. The following directory contains detailed information on distribution, plumage, size, preferred habitats, nesting habits, food requirements and sources and much more for 100 species.

The directory provides both comprehensive ornithological information *and* readily accessible details for easy and quick reference. Four of the 100 species—swallow, robin, blackbird and house sparrow—have been selected for special features, while the remaining 96 species are dealt with in a single page format as shown.

① Outline maps of Europe give detailed distribution information. Taking into account migratory patterns, the maps show summer distribution (in green), winter distribution (in diagonal hatching) and all year distribution (in green with diagonal hatching).

☐ Summer distribution

▨ Winter distribution

▨ All year distribution

---

WARBLERS : *SYLVIIDAE*

# WHITETHROAT *Sylvia communis*

COMMON, AS A BREEDING BIRD, throughout the whole of Europe, the whitethroat, a summer visitor, is declining in numbers due to the drought in the Sahel, its principal wintering quarters. Once the commonest sylvia warbler in Britain, the population crashed in 1969, when only a quarter of the population returned—it has never recovered its former status. However, numbers have marginally improved.

The male upperparts are brownish grey, the wings are chestnut-brown, the head and nape are grey, and the throat is white. The underparts are white, and the breast is suffused with pink in the spring. The outer feathers of the dark tail are white. The female upperparts are similar to the male's but the head is browner and less grey. The breast and flanks are buffer and less pink. Juveniles are browner above than adults, and the white throat is less defined. The underparts are buffish, and the outer tail feathers are dirty white. Adults have a bright, clear, pale brown eye with a clear-cut iris, and a whitish eye ring. In juveniles the eye is a muddy brown. The call is a sharp, hard *tak-tak* with a scolding *churr*. The song, often emitted in a fluttering, dancing flight, is a short, scratchy warble consisting of rapid notes ending in a shrill chatter. It will also sing from a prominent perch on top of a bush or from deep cover.

A skulking, restless bird, constantly on the move, it dives in and out of cover, looping up in display flight, and appearing out of bushes and hedges with its crown feathers raised, its tail fanned and with a scolding voice.

The whitethroat is a bird of varied habitat ranging from low, thorny bushes, brambles, open areas of scrub, hedgerows and commons, to willow beds, banks of ditches and young conifer plantations, near any form of cultivation.

The diet consists of small insects foliage and, in the autumn especially most other sylvia warblers, it eats be

The nest, usually sited low down, built cup of grass and roots made by th lined by the female with fine roots, w

It is not often seen in gardens in th However, on autumn passage, it may searching for berries.

## FACTS AND FEATU

☑ **Plumage** upperp Male: c female sexes underp with pe white. **Habita** and b young **Food Nest** in the tall pl

14 cm/5½ in

♀

♂

*The whitethroat is a summer visitor which is more likely to be seen between late April and September. It is a skulking species and likes brambles in which to breed (above).*

110

50

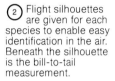

(2) Flight silhouettes are given for each species to enable easy identification in the air. Beneath the silhouette is the bill-to-tail measurement.

**21 cm (8 in)**

(3) The nest symbol (when ticked) indicates that the species will nest in a garden if the right environment is provided.

(4) The nestbox symbol (when ticked) indicates that the species will come to a feeding area if the appropriate food is put out.

(5) The bird table symbol (when ticked) indicates that the species will come to a feeding area if the appropriate food is put out.

(6) The plant symbol (when ticked) indicates that certain plants will be a positive attractant for some species. Details of these plants can be found in the main entry for each relevant species.

(7) Family name, English and scientific.

(8) Species name, English and scientific.

(9) Main entry, containing comprehensive details of distribution, plumage, behaviour, breeding, nesting habits, calls and songs, migratory patterns and much more.

(10) 'Facts and features' box for easy reference. Containing distribution map, flight silhouette with bill to tail measurement, symbol panel and abbreviated information on plumage, habitat, food and nest.

(11) Specially commissioned artwork showing detailed plumage breakdown and, where necessary, showing the difference between male and female plumages.

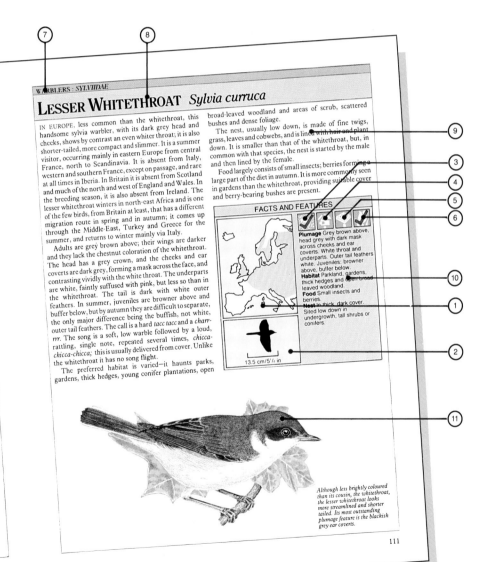

WARBLERS : *SYLVIIDAE*

# LESSER WHITETHROAT *Sylvia curruca*

IN EUROPE, less common than the whitethroat, this handsome sylvia warbler, with its dark grey head and cheeks, shows by contrast an even whiter throat; it is also shorter-tailed, more compact and slimmer. It is a summer visitor, occurring mainly in eastern Europe from central France, north to Scandinavia. It is absent from Italy, western and southern France, except on passage, and rare at all times in Iberia. In Britain it is absent from Scotland and much of the north and west of England and Wales. In the breeding season, it is also absent from Ireland. The lesser whitethroat winters in north-east Africa and is one of the few birds, from Britain at least, that has a different migration route in spring and in autumn; it comes up through the Middle-East, Turkey and Greece for the summer, and returns to winter mainly via Italy.

Adults are grey brown above; their wings are darker and they lack the chestnut coloration of the whitethroat. The head has a grey crown, and the cheeks and ear coverts are dark grey, forming a mask across the face, and contrasting vividly with the white throat. The underparts are white, faintly suffused with pink, but less so than in the whitethroat. The tail is dark with white outer feathers. In summer, juveniles are browner above and buffer below, but by autumn they are difficult to separate, the only major difference being the buffish, not white, outer tail feathers. The call is a hard *tacc tacc* and a *charr-rrr*. The song is a soft, low warble followed by a loud, rattling, single note, repeated several times, *chicca-chicca-chicca*; this is usually delivered from cover. Unlike the whitethroat it has no song flight.

The preferred habitat is varied—it haunts parks, gardens, thick hedges, young conifer plantations, open broad-leaved woodland and areas of scrub, scattered bushes and dense foliage.

The nest, usually low down, is made of fine twigs, grass, leaves and cobwebs, and is lined with hair and plant down. It is smaller than that of the whitethroat, but, in common with that species, the nest is started by the male and then lined by the female.

Food largely consists of small insects; berries forming a large part of the diet in autumn. It is more commonly seen in gardens than the whitethroat, providing suitable cover and berry-bearing bushes are present.

**FACTS AND FEATURES**

**Plumage** Grey brown above, head grey with dark mask across cheeks and ear coverts. White throat and underparts. Outer tail feathers white. Juveniles: browner above, buffer below.
**Habitat** Parkland, gardens, thick hedges and open broad-leaved woodland.
**Food** Small insects and berries.
**Nest** In thick, dark cover. Sited low down in undergrowth, tall shrubs or conifers.

**13.5 cm/5¼ in**

*Although less brightly coloured than its cousin, the whitethroat, the lesser whitethroat looks more streamlined and shorter tailed. Its most outstanding plumage feature is the blackish grey ear coverts.*

111

# GREY HERON *Ardea cinerea*

GREY HERONS are large, long-necked, long-legged birds with huge, blue-ended wings and powerful, dagger-shaped bills. The predominant colours are grey, black and white. Adults are grey above and on the offwing, with blackish flight feathers; they are whitish below with some black on the flanks, and white on the head and neck. There is a distinctive black band running back from the eye and ending in long, narrow black plumes; the foreneck is streaked blackish. Immature birds are much drabber and greyer on the head and neck and also lack the black head and neck markings.

Grey herons are common over much of Europe, where they are characteristically birds of lowland lakes, riversides, marshes and other freshwater habitats, but in many areas they are equally well-known as a coastal species. They normally nest colonially, building large stick nests in high trees, but in some regions they also nest on low bushes or in reedbeds or even on low cliffs, both coastal and inland.

In flight, herons retract their necks and proceed with slow, deep, steady flaps—but they can also soar well, often at great heights. While they sometimes swim in search of fish, or even plunge awkwardly into water from the air, grey herons normally hunt with stealth and great patience from the bank or by wading or standing motionless in shallow water. The prey is seized with a lightning thrust of the bill; it may be fish, frogs, small mammals or even small waterbirds or their young.

Grey herons will visit gardens with extensive water frontages and also those with garden pools, returning repeatedly, if not deterred, to those stocked with fish. Being wary and easily disturbed, they often come in the very early morning or in the evening. In many cases marauding herons are young birds which visit chiefly in late summer and autumn. Damage can be prevented by netting small pools completely, or by stringing wires around their perimeter or across the water area; a dummy bird—perhaps a garden ornament suitably painted—often proves a good short-term deterrent.

## FACTS AND FEATURES

**Plumage** Back and wings grey; neck, head and belly white. Black crown, blackish streaks on foreneck and flanks. Juveniles: greyer; no black markings.
**Habitat** Lakes, ponds, rivers, marshes and estuaries.
**Food** Fish, eels, frogs, small mammals and large insects.
**Nest** Communal, large platform of sticks and twigs built in trees or on ground in reedbeds.

91.5 cm/36 in

*Unlike storks and cranes, herons fly with their necks tucked into the body. Although common in parts of its range, shooting has decreased its numbers dramatically in central Europe. Extreme cold weather conditions also take their toll on young birds, when frozen lakes and streams prevent them from feeding.*

# WHITE STORK *Ciconia ciconia*

THE WHITE STORK IS UNMISTAKABLE—a huge, slightly off-white bird with black flight feathers, a long neck, a long, pointed red bill and long, pinkish red legs. Young birds are browner on the wing feather and have much duller bills and legs.

Unlike herons, storks fly with their necks outstretched and the legs extending behind, slightly drooping below the horizontal. They glide often and are masterful soaring birds; in direct flight, the huge wings have a rather slow, steady and powerful action.

In some countries, white storks nest in trees. However, it is far more common for them to nest in close association with man, frequently on buildings, including private houses. They feed in low-lying wetlands, damp fields, etc and not necessarily beside water, eating a wide range of prey including frogs, reptiles and large insects. On the ground, they move with a slow, deliberate gait, holding the body rather horizontally, picking and jabbing with their bills while feeding.

The white stork's long and close association with man, and its status as a popular and harmless bird has ensured a long history of freedom from any kind of persecution. Indeed, it is widely regarded with affection, and features strongly in the folklore and traditions of many countries. It is often considered lucky to have a stork's nest on the house-top or chimney and there is a long history of providing artificial nest-platforms or iron 'nest-baskets' for the big birds.

Sadly, habitat disappearance due to drainage and changing patterns of land use, plus pollution and, probably, the disappearance of prey species through the use of agricultural chemicals, have made the white stork a rare and declining species in its former haunts in north-west Europe—although it remains tolerably common in Spain and Portugal and in parts of eastern Europe. In some countries—France, Germany and Switzerland, for example—there have been extensive captive breeding programmes which have been quite successful in restocking the wild population.

*Although this stork has had a long association with man — and it is thought to bring good luck if a pair nests on your property — its numbers are decreasing. The major reason for this is the lack of suitable food: the numbers of frogs and toads (the major food items) have been greatly reduced by the practice of draining marshes.*

## FACTS AND FEATURES

**Plumage** Body, including head and neck, white. Wings white with black flight feathers. Long red legs and bill. Juveniles have browner legs and bill.
**Habitat** Damp fields, marshes.
**Food** Frogs, reptiles, large insects and small mammals.
**Nest** Usually near human habitation, in trees, on ruins or buildings.

1 m/40 in

# MALLARD *Anas platyrhynchos*

♀          ♂

*The mallard is probably the most familiar duck in the region — it may be found frequenting even the smallest of ponds and lakes. Nests may be located under bushes or even on buildings, often far from water. Males loose their bright plumage during the summer and resemble females.*

THE MALLARD IS BY FAR THE COMMONEST and most familiar wild duck over much of Europe—a well-known, and in some places, almost semi-domesticated species, it is also the ancestor of most forms of domestic duck. The wild drake has a yellow bill, a bottle-green head and neck, with a narrow white neck-ring, a dark, purplish brown breast and a largely greyish body, with a black stern; the tail is whitish with characteristically stiff, black, upward-curving central feathers. The duck is beautifully mottled in brown and buff and has a creamy tail. Both sexes show a wing-patch (speculum) which is purple, edged with black and white.

Mallard are surface-feeding ducks, found on virtually all kinds of freshwater (and on coastal marshes etc in winter) and very commonly in cities, towns and villages. They respond quickly to feeding with bread and grain, and many town birds are very tame. In the wild, mallard are mainly vegetarian, feeding by dabbling or up-ending in shallow water or while wading; a few insects, molluscs, crustaceans and other invertebrates make up the remainder of the diet.

Gardens adjoining any reasonably sized area of freshwater, or a river or canal, may be frequented by mallard, where they may come ashore to loaf in groups— or to be fed. Bread, cake, biscuit fragments, grain and waste vegetables, including potatoes, are all acceptable.

Occasionally mallard will nest in holes in big trees and they may also be tempted to use special duck baskets if provided, but most nest in deep cover where the duck constructs a beautiful, deep nest lined with a thick layer

## FACTS AND FEATURES

**Plumage** Male: green head and neck separated from body by white ring. Breast brownish; body grey; rear black; tail white with black curled, central feathers; yellow bill. Female: brown and buff mottling.
**Habitat** Freshwater lakes, ponds and rivers; coastal waters, estuaries.
**Food** Mainly plant matter, also insects, molluscs and seed.
**Nest** Holes in trees, but mainly on the ground in dense vegetation.

58.5 cm/23 in

of down and feathers. The normal clutch size is 10 to 12 eggs. Nests not infrequently occur in large gardens, or those with suitably dense cover, usually, but not invariably, fairly close to water. The female leads the ducklings to the water soon after they have hatched— often a fairly hazardous journey, but one which we can sometimes make a little easier by opening gates, removing obstacles, keeping cats at bay and, if necessary, even providing a little gentle shepherding!

# MUTE SWAN *Cygnus olor*

IN MANY COUNTRIES IN EUROPE, except in Britain and Ireland, the mute swan is not at all numerous or well-known; its main area of distribution is from the Baltic and Poland across eastern Europe.

Swans are at once identified by their great size and all-white adult plumage, the mute swan being distinguished from the other two European species by its gracefully curved neck and an orange bill with a black base and a prominent black knob (larger in the male). Juveniles are a pale greyish brown colour, with greyish bills, becoming patchily brown and white as they grow older. Another feature not shared by the other swans is the characteristic, rhythmic and surprisingly loud sound made by the wings in flight. While not actually mute (it makes assorted snorting, wheezing and hissing sounds), this species is not highly vocal like the other two.

A small amount of animal food is taken, but the mute swan is essentially vegetarian, eating aquatic plants (which its long neck enables it to reach at some depth), but also grazing on fields of grass or, sometimes, cereals. It is semi-domesticated in many places, responds well to feeding (similar foods to those given for mallard) and is not infrequently installed on lakes and ponds as an ornamental bird. It has declined markedly in parts of Britain, mainly through lead poisoning, of which the major source is the discarded angler's weights, which the swans pick up while feeding.

Mute swans may frequent large, open gardens adjoining lakes and rivers; should they nest, they are best left well alone—while stories about them breaking legs are probably folklore rather than fact, they are very aggressive while breeding and could seriously hurt small children. This same aggression and their frequent intolerance of their smaller waterbird neighbours makes their presence on small waters a doubtful blessing.

## FACTS AND FEATURES

**Plumage** Adult: all white; orange bill with black knob at base. Juveniles: greyish brown, bill grey.
**Habitat** Grassy fields, marshes, open freshwater lakes, ponds, rivers, estuaries or coastal waters
**Food** Aquatic plants, grass or cereals.
**Nest** Usually near the water's edge or in shallow water, a large platform of plant material lined with down.

1.5 m/60 in

The large nests of this species may be placed on small islands, lake edges, or river banks (above). They are particularly aggressive when breeding, and will drive away any intruder.

# SPARROWHAWK *Accipiter nisus*

THE MALE SPARROWHAWK is little bigger than a blackbird—a small, rather compact hawk with dark blue-grey upperparts and crown, a white chin, orange cheeks and the underparts closely barred with orange-brown. The tail is broadly banded with grey and black. Females are considerably larger, with much browner upperparts, a whitish eye stripe and whitish underparts closely barred with dark brown. Both sexes show a bright yellow eye and have relatively long, thin yellow legs.

*The sparrowhawk is a bird of hedgerows and woodland where it hunts its main prey of small birds. The male is much smaller than the female and has bluish grey upperparts. The characteristic flight is a series of wingflaps followed by a glide and it can often be seen soaring on flat wings above woodland.*

♂  ♀

Sparrowhawks usually nest in mature trees in copses or woods, and often in conifer plantations, but may breed in large gardens with sufficient good sized trees and little disturbance. For the most part, though, their presence in gardens will be as hunters.

The typical hunting method is a smash-and-grab approach: flying low and fast, twisting through cover and around obstacles, slipping from one side of a hedge to the other, the sparrowhawk relies on a surprise attack to secure its prey. All that may be seen is a fast-moving, low-flying bird, either dark grey-blue or brown, with rather short, blunt-ended wings and a longish tail. The prey consists of small birds, snatched in one or both feet and carried off to a plucking place—some way off, if the birds are nesting locally, or close by at other seasons.

Sparrowhawks are quite common over much of Europe, wherever there is good tree cover, but are rare or even absent in some areas, such as most of East Anglia. They are by no means uncommon in towns and villages and are frequent garden visitors. Hunting birds might appear at any time, but they can be particularly regular at bird tables and established feeding stations where they know there is a guaranteed source of prey. Many people actively dislike them because they kill and carry off small birds. They find it particularly distressing when this happens at bird tables, but sparrowhawks belong just as much as blue tits or robins and have just as much right to take advantage of a readily available source of food. It is wrong to regard them as cruel, or to believe that they have any long-term effect on the numbers of small birds.

## FACTS AND FEATURES

**Plumage** Male: upperparts, including crown, dark, bluish grey; underparts whitish barred with brownish orange. Female: upperparts, including crown, brown; underparts barred with brownish black.
**Habitat** Mixed and coniferous woodland, farmland, hedges with tall trees.
**Food** Birds up to the size of wood pigeon; large insects.
**Nest** Platform of twigs lined with leaves, placed in a tree.

28-38 cm/11-15 in

# KESTREL *Falco tinnunculus*

BY FAR THE MOST COMMON BIRD OF PREY throughout most of Europe, the kestrel is also the one with the most catholic choice of habitats. It occurs almost anywhere, including the heart of the largest towns and cities.

Adult males are handsome birds, with pale blue-grey heads and tails (the latter with a broad, black band near the tip), chestnut upperparts finely spotted with black, and streaked buffish underparts. Females are much duller, being mainly reddish-brown above with dark barring. Kestrels have fairly long, painted wings and ample tails. Direct flight is with rapid, rather clipped wingbeats interspersed with glides. On the wing, the most distinctive feature of this bird is its persistent habit of hovering while it hunts for the small mammals which are usually its main prey.

Kestrels nest in holes in trees, cliffs and buildings, on ledges and sometimes in the old nests of other birds, crows and magpies, for example. Many large, older buildings—office blocks, factories, warehouses, churches—provide possible natural sites for this very adaptable species; nests have even been recorded on large, broad windowledges. Trays or open boxes can be provided for them in urban settings, and purpose-built boxes (see page 44) can be erected in farm buildings, or trees, or (as has been done successfully in the Netherlands, for example) even on poles in open fields.

The main prey is usually small mammals: mice, voles and shrews. They are typically caught in a short pounce from a vantage point, or from the characteristic hovering position. Many large insects, earthworms and other invertebrates are also eaten, and urban kestrels catch and eat large numbers of small birds.

People are often tempted to take young kestrels from the nest for falconry. In Britain, this is an offence unless a licence to do so has been granted. Furthermore, it is an offence to keep a kestrel in captivity if it is not registered by the Department of the Environment. For further information on the subject of conservation, see Bird Control and the Law pages 10 to 12.

*The grey head and black-tipped grey tail separate the male kestrel from the female. It is frequently seen perched on trees, telegraph poles or overhead power lines searching the ground below for prey.*

## FACTS AND FEATURES

**Plumage** Male: upperparts chestnut spotted with black; head and tail blue-grey, tail has broad black band. Underparts buffish streaked black. Female: upperparts brown barred dark brown or black. Brown tail barred.
**Habitat** Farmland, villages, towns, moorland, cliffs— almost anywhere.
**Food** Small birds and mammals, insects and worms.
**Nest** On buildings, cliff ledges, holes in trees, or old nests in trees.

33—35.5 cm/13—14 in

# RED-LEGGED PARTRIDGE *Alectoris rufa*

THE RED-LEGGED OR 'FRENCH' PARTRIDGE is an introduced species in Britain, confined mainly to the southern half of England and parts of Wales. In Europe, where it is native, it is confined to France (except the north and north-east), north-west Italy, Portugal, Spain, the Balcans and Corsica.

At reasonable range, it is easily distinguished from the grey partridge by its striking plumage. It has a long white stripe above the eye, a dark stripe through the eye joining the broad, broken-edged black band around the whitish throat, a pale grey breast, and flanks strongly barred with lavender, black and chestnut. The bill and the legs are red. As the bird flies away, it shows a bright chestnut tail. Its voice is also distinctive—a loud, rhythmic *chuck, chuck-er* or a slower, rather harsher single note.

Red-legs are birds of open countryside, especially arable farmland, but you will also find them in any areas of waste ground, open hillsides, scrub, plantation edges, vineyards and the edges of marshes; while clearly very adaptable, they prefer dry, open areas. They are likely to occur on open ground around factories and works. Sometimes they wander into large gardens, especially where these adjoin open fields, and occasionally they nest there; you may even find them right up against the walls of occupied houses. Red-legs require a reasonable amount of thick ground cover for nesting, but they are also hard-weather visitors to most suitably situated gardens, where they may come to grain and scraps.

They are largely vegetarian, but also eat a small quantity of insect food. Chicks depend heavily on insects—until they are 10 days old, about 30 per cent of their diet consists of insects. In many parts of England, red-legs do not seem to have suffered from changing agricultural practices in the way that grey partridges have done and they are often very common on open farmland. Their numbers are artificially maintained for shooting, in some areas, by releases of captive-bred birds. The population also becomes mixed by the release of the closely related chukar or various hybrid forms.

## FACTS AND FEATURES

**Plumage** Upperparts brown; long, striking, white supercilium; dark stripe through eye joining streaky black on neck. Chin white, breast bluish grey, flanks broadly striped with black and chestnut. Red bill.
**Habitat** Farmland, waste ground, vineyards and dry heathland.
**Food** Seeds, vegetable matter, buds, flowers and insects.
**Nest** Under bushes, in hedgerows or among vegetation.

34 cm/13½ in

*The red-legged partridge is a bird of open farmland and vineyards (above) where hedges and bushes provide cover for the nest. The female may occasionally lay two clutches in different nests, the male incubating one, she the other.*

# GREY PARTRIDGE *Perdix perdix*

THE GREY PARTRIDGE is found over most of Europe, except most of Scandinavia, most of Spain and parts of Mediterranean Europe, and eastwards into Asia. It is native in the British Isles, but has declined markedly in most areas (as indeed it has throughout Europe) following the introduction of modern, highly mechanized (and usually chemical-based) farming. Insecticides are implicated in many areas, as these can particularly affect the diet and the survival of young chicks, half of whose food may come from insects.

This is a slightly smaller and relatively less rounded bird than the red-legged partridge, but the two are similar in many ways. They are ground-dwelling, mainly vegetarian birds, with rather short but very strong legs—fast and capable fliers, but when possible preferring to escape on foot. Both run very rapidly, the red-leg probably rather faster than the grey, however. Both are also gregarious and form small flocks outside the breeding season. The red-leg not infrequently perches on posts, walls and even roofs—the grey only rarely does so.

At any distance, the grey partridge looks fairly nondescript—a rotund, predominantly brown (not grey) bird with almost no neck and a small head. Close to, however, it is actually a handsome bird, with a chestnut-orange face, a grey neck and breast, and pale flanks boldly barred with chestnut; the back is light brown with buff streaks. The tail, which only becomes obvious in flight, is chestnut, like that of the red-legged partridge.

The sexes are almost alike, although females are duller and browner than males. The male shows a conspicuous, large, dark horseshoe mark on the lower breast (most obvious when he stands upright)—females either lack this mark altogether or show only a trace of it.

Grey partridges occupy very similar habitats to red-legs and indeed, on arable land at least, both species may occur together. Like the red-leg, the grey partridge occurs on all sorts of open areas adjacent to works and factories, as long as these are relatively undisturbed. They will come for food into large gardens adjoining farmland, especially in hard weather. Big, quiet gardens near open land and with suitable cover may hold breeding pairs.

*The dark chestnut horseshoe mark on the male's breast is much reduced or absent in the female. The cackling 'kirrick kirrick' call advertises the birds' presence.*

## FACTS AND FEATURES

**Plumage** Upperparts brown, finely mottled with buff; chestnut orange face; grey neck and breast. Flanks pale barred with chestnut. Large, dark horseshoe on lower breast of male, less obvious or non-existent on female.
**Habitat** Farmland, moorlands, heathland with cover.
**Food** Seeds and vegetable matter.
**Nest** On ground, in vegetation for cover; a hollow lined with dead leaves.

30.5 cm/12 in

# PHEASANT *Phasianus colchicus*

A COCK PHEASANT IS UNMISTAKABLE — a large, handsomely proportioned and very colourful gamebird with a long, pointed tail. The origins of pheasants are complex and involve many introductions or releases of different forms, so that they are now highly variable in appearance. However, the majority have a predominantly copper-coloured body—beautifully spotted, barred and scalloped with black, browns and buffs—paler wings and rumps and light tawny or chestnut tails with narrow, dark, transverse bars. All have a slight crust at the rear crown, large scarlet face-wattles and bottle-green heads; the majority also have a narrow, but conspicuous white collar. A fairly common form is more or less blackish-green all over. Females are markedly smaller and are typically rather pale brown above, mottled in buff and black, and paler still below, with a much shorter tail than the male.

Originally an Asian species, reaching the easternmost limits of Europe as a truly wild bird, the pheasant has been introduced throughout much of middle Europe for a very long time. Its arrival in Italy, for example, was in Roman times and it has been present in Britain since Norman times at least. It is now widespread and common, generally associated with farming country with at least some woods, copses or shelterbelts. In many areas numbers are artificially maintained at high levels for shooting by extensive rearing programmes. While the rearing of pheasants for sport has undoubtedly helped to preserve some woods and other valuable cover in many parts of Britain, it has also led to the extensive and wholly unjustified persecution of birds of prey and owls.

Like partridges, pheasants are mainly vegetarian and so will come to feeding stations and do very well on the food put out for most other birds. An extra supply of grain for them is advisable if they come regularly. Where they are common they will come frequently to large gardens, especially if these adjoin woodland. Poultry food is also taken readily. A roosting female or two is a possibility in a large garden—so is a small roost in trees.

## FACTS AND FEATURES

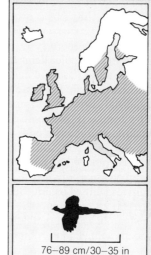

**Plumage** Male: copper coloured with buff, brown and black. Bottle-green head and neck, red face wattles and usually a white neck ring. Long, brownish tail with dark transverse bars. Female: pale, buffish brown, mottled with black.
**Habitat** Farmland, scrub, woodland and marshes.
**Food** Seeds, insects, plant shoots and grain.
**Nest** On the ground among cover.

76–89 cm/30–35 in

*The male pheasant is sometimes polygamous, mating with several females which can lay their olive-brown eggs in a single nest. The nest is normally placed on the ground well hidden in dense undergrowth, and the hen alone undertakes the incubation of the eggs and the rearing of the young.*

# WATER RAIL *Rallus aquaticus*

*A secretive and rarely seen bird of the reedbeds (above), the water rail is often only indicated by its blood-curdling cries. Fleeting glimpses as it moves quickly through cover, or when it takes a short flight above the reeds are all you can expect.*

ONE OF THE PROBLEMS with writing a book about garden birds is that there are many species which might just possibly occur, or actually do so in very limited circumstances. The water rail is one of these. Most bird gardeners will never see one—but it is always a possibility if you live beside a lake, river or ditch; more than just a possibility perhaps, if there is a large freshwater wetland nearby. It is very unlikely to occur in the breeding season, but is much more likely in winter, especially in severe weather. Water rails will forage near or below bird tables and other feeders and in extreme conditions even on open lawns. A fair-sized garden pool is also likely to be an attraction, if it includes a lot of cover—so is a cress-bed, even a small one.

The water rail resembles a small, slim moorhen with a long, slightly decurved reddish bill; it has a similar but dingier and much less obvious white 'horseshoe' under the tail. The upperparts are dark olive-brown, streaked blackish, while the sides of the head, the throat and breast are slate grey; the flanks are barred black and white. It is a furtive, rather shy bird, as a rule, soon bolting into cover if alarmed, or fluttering away into hiding with dangling legs. The normal gait is deliberate and suspicious, with frequent halts and a nervous flicking up of the short tail, but at times it allows itself to be observed very easily. The way in which it insinuates its narrow body through the thickest vegetation is quite remarkable.

Water rails are omnivorous, but with a strong leaning towards animal foods—mainly insects, worms, crustaceans, molluscs and small fish. Vegetable matter taken includes grain, seeds, berries, grass and small roots. These visitors to gardens are likely to be able to eat much of the normal fare provided for other birds, but they can be attracted and sustained by minced meat morsels, fat and bacon rind.

## FACTS AND FEATURES

**Plumage** Adult: upperparts brown, streaked darker; sides of head, throat and breast slate grey; flanks barred black and white; undertail whitish; bill red. Juvenile: no grey; flanks brown and buff; bill less red.
**Habitat** Reed and willow beds, ditches and cress beds.
**Food** Insects, molluscs, worms, grain and plant material.
**Nest** Hidden low down in dense vegetation.

28 cm/11 in

# MOORHEN *Gallinula chloropus*

THE MOORHEN IS A WIDESPREAD and common bird, inhabiting almost every kind of freshwater habitat from marshes and the edges of lakes and rivers to streams, ditches and tiny ponds. All it requires is water and some degree of cover, so it may well take up residence at larger garden ponds or be a frequent visitor to them. It may also come readily to food put out for other birds, at times, even travelling some distance from water.

Although rather shy in many Continental countries, it is often reasonably tame in Britain and is thus a familiar bird to many people, and a regular visitor to many gardens. Given enough room and freedom from disturbance, it is also quite likely to nest on ponds in large gardens. It builds a fairly substantial nest near the water's edge or low in branches above the water and may be encouraged to do so by the provision of a simple platform in a bush or by the construction of a small, well-vegetated island.

Adult moorhens are glossy blue-black on the head, neck and underparts and very dark brown on the back and wings, with a distinctive white line along their sides, and a conspicuous white 'horseshoe' under the tail—frequently visible as the tail is cocked and flicked upwards. The bill and frontal shield are bright red, with the tip of the bill yellow; the legs and very long toes are green, with a red 'garter' just below the feathering on the upper leg. Juveniles are browner overall, with pale throats and dull greenish bills; downy chicks are black with red bills. The moorhen has a variety of calls but the commonest call is a loud and very distinctive *purruk*.

The natural food of the moorhen is similar to that of the water rail, but with a predominance of vegetable food—seeds, fruits, grasses, aquatic plants etc. A well-stocked, well-vegetated garden pond will provide plenty to eat, and, in winter, moorhens seem very happy with the usual food put out for other garden birds; some individuals will even fly up on to bird tables to feed.

## FACTS AND FEATURES

**Plumage** Adult: dark, slate-grey with dark brown back and wings; white stripe on flanks. Bill and frontal shield bright red; bill tip yellow. Juveniles: brown; no red on bill and frontal shield; white chin and throat.
**Habitat** Fresh water with vegetation or cover.
**Food** Aquatic plants, grasses, seeds, insects and molluscs.
**Nest** In reeds at edge of water or low in branches over water.

33 cm/13 in

*When swimming, the moorhen often flicks its tail up, showing the conspicuous white undertail sides. In the breeding season, moorhens are very aggressive — they can be seen balancing on their tails in the water and striking at each other with their long toes.*

# COOT *Fulica atra*

*The coot's nest is usually on the ground in vegetation (above) and often near water. Both sexes incubate the eggs, and, when hatched, the young are brooded by the female and fed by the male for the first few days. Note the wide lobes on the long toes which help propel it through the water.*

THE COOT PREFERS LARGE AREAS of water, only rarely coming to garden ponds, small streams or ditches. However, it is always a likely visitor to gardens, especially ones with large lawns, which adjoin lakes and rivers. It is markedly gregarious outside the breeding season and may occur in quite large numbers.

Coots come out of the water to graze on short grass (and often arable crops). In the water they feed mainly on the soft stems and leaves of aquatic plants, but to some extent also on various aquatic invertebrates and even small fish. Unlike the moorhen, the coot dives well, frequently bobbing back up at the surface of the water with a beakful of broken-off vegetation. Its more aquatic way of life is reflected in its heavily-lobed toes, designed more for swimming than wading.

Adult coots are easily identified, being simply slate-black all over (but quite glossy on the head and neck), with a brilliant white bill and frontal shield. Seen at close quarters, they have red eyes, which add to what seems to be a slightly disagreeable facial expression—indeed they are quarrelsome neighbours and fight frequently. Chicks are black, with amazingly bright-red, naked heads; juveniles are greyish brown with whitish throats and forenecks. Like moorhens, coots are often reluctant fliers, but both actually fly very well and are capable long-distance travellers.

Coots will sometimes come to food put out for other

## FACTS AND FEATURES

**Plumage** Adult; overall slate-black, glossed on head and neck. Bill and large frontal shield white. Juveniles: brownish with whitish face, neck and breast. Bill greyish, frontal shield very small, also grey.
**Habitat** Lakes, large ponds, marshes and rivers.
**Food** Aquatic plants, grass, insects, small fish, seeds and molluscs.
**Nest** On branches or in reeds at water level.

38 cm/15 in

birds and they are certainly fond of bread. They may well breed where gardens adjoin lakes or large, slow-flowing rivers, building a bulky nest in vegetation in or beside the water, or among branches which reach down into it. They, too, can be encouraged by the construction of small platforms or floating or static islands.

# SNIPE *Gallinago gallinago*

GARDENS WITH FAIR-SIZED PONDS, or those which adjoin lakes and rivers may attract a number of wading birds, of which the snipe is probably the most frequent in most areas. Snipe prefer areas with plenty of waterside vegetation and open, muddy ground or small shallow pools to feed from. Apart from creating such areas—usually only feasible in large gardens—or keeping open large ditches alongside the garden, it is difficult to do much to attract snipe. Visits are most likely in hard weather, when snipe will come out on to open areas and even on to lawns and grass borders in search of food. Because they are highly specialized feeders, probing deep into mud in search of invertebrates, it is difficult to feed them, but there is a very good chance that they will take minced meat or dogfood and catfood. Since they appear to require a lot of gait to aid digestion, mix some (or alternatively any small, hard seeds) in with the meat.

Although they appear in the open often enough, snipe are usually first seen only when flushed—zigzagging wildly away with a loud, hoarse *schaaap* call. The very long straight bill, golden buff stripes down the back and obvious white corners to the tail are usually easily seen. On the ground, the bill appears disproportionately long; the back stripes are conspicuous, too, and there are longitudinal dark stripes on the head.

The much smaller Jack snipe *lymnocryptes minimus* also visits garden pools and wet places. It is only about as big as a song thrush and has a much shorter bill than the snipe. Jack snipe sit tight until the last possible second, rise almost at your feet—nearly always without calling—and fly a short distance, without much zigzagging, before dropping back into cover again. The stripes on the back are brighter than those on snipe and there is no white on the tail. They are exceptionally dificult to see on the ground, but they have a very distinctive up-and-down movement while feeding, as if they were on springs instead of legs.

## FACTS AND FEATURES

27 cm/10½ in

**Plumage** Upperparts dark brown with buff stripes on mantle; head pale buff with dark stripes on crown. Neck and breast buff with dark streaks and spots. Underparts white, flanks barred dark brown.
**Habitat** Muddy edges to ponds, wet meadow, marshes and boggy moorland.
**Food** Worms, insects, grass and seeds.
**Nest** Well concealed on the ground, in grass tussocks or in vegetation.

*When flushed, this snipe rises and zigzags away with hoarse calls. The drumming sound heard during the breeding season is made by the outer tail feathers which vibrate as the bird dives through the air.*

# WOODCOCK *Scolopax rusticola*

THE WOODCOCK IS A LARGER and altogether bulkier bird than the snipe, although basically rather similar in appearance. Its wings are more rounded, and, even when flushed, it lacks the wild, panic-stricken flight of the smaller bird. Woodcock are a rich, almost chestnut brown colour, beautifully marked with black, dark brown and buff, and with dark bars *across* the crown, not lengthways as in snipe. The bill is long and straight, carried pointing downwards, and, on the ground, the legs appear very short.

Woodcock usually spend the day sleeping on the ground, in woods or thick cover. They fly out at dusk to feed in damp areas or around the margins of lakes and marshes, returning to their roosts around dawn. A large garden, especially one with plenty of shrubs or other suitable cover may attract the woodcock for food or, in hard weather, for shelter. The feeding considerations are similar to those which apply to snipe. You could also, supply freshly turned leaf litter or soil (and, if possible, chopped up earthworms) as additional sources of food.

Woodcock sometimes nest in very large gardens with lots of trees forming copses or miniature woods; if there is woodland close by and access is easy, they may also bring their chicks into the gardens to feed.

For most people living in well-wooded areas, however, the woodcock is always much more likely to be seen from the garden than actually in it; this is because males have a curious 'roding' flight around their home areas. The purpose of the flight is to attract females rather than to advertise territorial rights. From early spring onwards, the males emerge at dusk and fly round and round quite large areas, often following a more or less regular route and reappearing over the same spot every few minutes. While roding, they have a curious, slow, flicking wing action and repeatedly call, in sequence, a loud and far-carrying *tsiwick* and a quiet, deep, double or treble grunting noise—the latter only audible at close range.

## FACTS AND FEATURES

**Plumage** Upperparts rich chestnut brown, barred and scalloped with buff and black, crown and nape dark brown with pale buffish bars. Underparts pale buff, finely barred darker. Tail rufous. Long, straight bill; flesh at base darker towards tip.
**Habitat** Open woodland, copses, young plantations.
**Food** Worms, insects, seeds and grass.
**Nest** Well concealed in bracken or dead leaves.

34 cm/13½ in

*Very much a bird of the woodlands, during the breeding season, the woodcock can be seen flying over the trees proclaiming its territory. In the daytime, however, it is reluctant to take to the air, only leaving its place of concealment at the last possible moment.*

# HERRING GULL *Larus argentatus*

HERRING GULLS ARE WIDESPREAD around the coasts of Europe, but much more numerous around northern and Atlantic coasts than in the Mediterranean. They spread inland in large numbers in winter, but are hardly likely to be garden birds other than in coastal areas and seaside towns; even then they will be mainly winter birds, coming to food scraps put out for other birds. Where they do so, they are bold enough to need no encouragement at all.

Identification of gulls is difficult until you get to know them. The adult plumage is distinguished by white head, neck and underparts, light grey back and upperwing, the latter with a black tip with prominent white marks, and a white tail. The heavy bill is yellow, with a red spot near the tip, and the legs are pinkish (or yellow in the Mediterranean and in eastern Scandinavia). Juveniles are streaked brown, with darker primaries and tail, and a blackish bill. There are several immature stages in which the birds become progressively paler and greyer on the back and wings. The small, yellow-rimmed eye, in combination with the angle of the heavy bill, gives the herring gull a distinctly mean expression.

Herring gulls are very vocal, especially when in groups, and while breeding. Young birds produce a variety of thin, mewing or squealing noises and adults a range of barking and laughing calls—plus the loud *yodelling* so often heard around harbours and fishing ports.

In a growing number of seaside towns, herring gulls are becoming a nuisance through their habit of nesting on buildings, including private houses. This has led to increasing complaints from householders, and local authorities are faced with the extremely difficult problem of removing them effectively and humanely. Established colonies are hard to remove, and, even if individual birds are legally killed or trapped, others soon move in to take their place . . . the answer to this vexed problem is far from clear, but in places not yet taken over by gulls, individual householders or the owners of buildings should deter first colonists as soon as they appear and nip the problem in the bud.

## FACTS AND FEATURES

**Plumage** Adult: head, neck, breast and belly white. Mantle and wings pale grey; tail white. Wings have black tips with white marks. Juveniles: pale buff streaked with brown, dark band at tip of tail.
**Habitat** Sea coasts, rubbish tips; reservoirs and farmland in winter.
**Food** Carrion, fish, worms, molluscs, crustacea, insects, seaweed, garbage.
**Nest** On roofs of buildings, on the ground or cliff ledges.

56 cm/22 in

*The natural breeding habitat of the herring gull includes cliffs, beaches and low-lying grassland on islands. Both parents incubate the eggs, of which there are usually three or four. The larger size and heavy yellow bill with a red spot distinguish it from the similar common gull.*

# COMMON GULL *Larus canus*

*Out of the breeding season, this species may be seen in urban areas, and during the winter months it will venture into gardens to take food from the bird table. It is smaller than the herring gull and has a yellowish green bill and green legs.*

THE POPULAR NAME 'Seagull' is something of a misnomer. Most European species commonly occur, and even breed, inland, and the common gull is a prime example. Actually, 'common gull' is also rather misleading: although this is indeed a widespread and fairly numerous bird, it is normally outnumbered in many areas by both herring and black-headed gulls. Its main breeding grounds are in northern Europe, where many colonies are on moorland and lakes well away from the sea. In parts of Scandinavia it is encouraged to nest in the gardens of lakeside houses by the provision of special nesting-trays, the aim being to farm the eggs for human consumption!

Superficially, adult common gulls resemble herring gulls, but are much smaller, only a little larger than the much more familiar black-headed gull. The back and upperwings are slightly darker than in the herring gull, the much slighter bill is plain greenish-yellow and the legs are a dirty greenish colour. A larger eye set in a much more rounded head presents a very different and much gentler facial expression. Immatures are at first streaked and dark on the upperwings, with a prominent black tip to the white tail; they become lighter and greyer as they grow older. They have pale bills with dark tips and brownish legs.

The following comments apply both to this species and to the black-headed gull (see page 68). It is not at all difficult to establish feeding stations for the smaller gulls in places where they are common. They will in any case soon find feeding stations set up for the other birds, and

## FACTS AND FEATURES

**Plumage** Adult: body, head and neck white; mantle and wings grey; rump and tail white. Bill yellow-green, legs greenish-yellow. Juveniles: streaked with buff with dark brown wings. Black band at tip of tail. Bill pale with dark tip.
**Habitat** Moorland, lakes and reservoirs, farmland.
**Food** Fish, molluscs, insects, worms, scraps.
**Nest** A hollow formed on the ground, lined with plant material.

40.5 cm/16 in

will readily pluck up the courage to drop in, coming quite regularly to bird tables, especially in hard weather. They often forage on football pitches and school fields (seeking worms and other invertebrates), often in large numbers. They will quickly come to bread and all manner of other scraps thrown out for them, even coming very close to buildings and into quite small gardens. Flat roofs provide excellent feeding stations for gulls and can be utilized as such even in built-up areas.

# BLACK-HEADED GULL *Larus ridibundus*

GARDENS BESIDE OR NEAR THE SEA, or alongside the larger lakes and rivers, are the most likely ones to attract hungry gulls—but with this species, particularly, the term 'seagull' is most inappropriate. Many black-headed gulls breed inland, forage around inland waters or over farmland and fields, descend in droves on city parks and town centres and come readily to feeding stations—including those in gardens. It is a fair bet that a great many black-headed gulls never see the sea at any time.

General feeding is covered under common gull (see page 67), so this is the place to say a bit more about gull identification, which is complicated at first but can be a fascinating pastime. Most field guides give full details—see the specialist book on gulls in the list on page 156. Successful identification begins with the realization that gulls, depending on their size, take a varying number of years to progress from juvenile to adult plumage, with several immature stages in between. Having established the size of the bird and whether it is an immature or an adult, it is then necessary to pay attention to bill and leg colour, general body colour and, particularly, the pattern and distribution of colour on the wings and tail.

Fortunately, the black-headed gull is a relatively easy one to identify. Adults conform to the usual gull pattern—white with grey backs and upperwings—and in breeding plumage have chocolate-brown hood. The bill and legs are crimson. In autumn and winter, the dark hoods is lost and is replaced by small, blackish marks before and behind the eye. Juveniles are patchily brown above, and immatures are grey and black on the wings, with dark-tipped, yellowish bills and yellowish or orange legs. Immatures, too, have head-markings like winter adults. At all ages, there is one striking feature which immediately distinguishes the black-headed gull—a very obvious white leading edge to the outer part of the wing, contrasting with the dark (almost black in adults) underside of the outermost flight feathers. Confusion is likely only with a few other rare or uncommon species which are unlikely to appear in most gardens in any case.

## FACTS AND FEATURES

**Plumage** Adult in summer: body white, back and wings pale grey, chocolate brown hood; red bill and legs. Adult in winter: dark marks in front of, and behind, the eye.
**Habitat** Marshes and saltings, lakes and pools on moorland, estuaries and farmland, parks in villages and towns.
**Food** Fish, molluscs, insects, worms; seeds, grass and refuse.
**Nest** In grassy tussocks, or on ground.

35.5-38 cm/14-15 in

*The bright red bill and legs, together with the chocolate brown hood, depict the adult black-headed gull. It is a very shy bird, in most gardens, and rarely alights on the ground, preferring to hover and snatch food in its bill and then fly off to devour it.*

# FERAL PIGEON *Columba livia*

THE WIDESPREAD AND VERY FAMILIAR domestic or feral pigeon is mainly associated with human habitation and is most often a bird of towns and cities—and their gardens—although you will find that it is by no means uncommon in many rural areas. It is descended from the wild rock dove, which still exists in its pure form around the extreme northern and north-western coasts of Scotland, around the coasts of Ireland and both coastally and around inland cliffs in parts of southern Europe. Wild and feral forms frequently intermingle and breed together.

The species is widely kept in captivity and has, indeed, been domesticated in Europe for at least 2,000 years. It was widely kept in specially-built dovecotes, some of which housed hundreds of birds, and it was treated as an extremely important source of food. It was this large, free-flying domesticated population which gave rise to a large feral population, which very quickly adapted to breeding in the wild and living in close association with man.

The feral population is entirely self-supporting, but is continually augmented by lost or escaped birds, including many homing pigeons. Where large populations occur in rural areas, they are classed as agricultural pests which may be killed or taken at any time by authorized persons (for further information see page 10); control measures are often taken, not always very effectively, against large urban populations.

While ornamental pigeons are often provided with dovecotes, few people provide (or see any need to provide) artificial sites for feral birds. Many people feel that their population is far too big and, rather illogically, most ornithologists tend to ignore the feral pigeon or pretend that it does not really exist. Many townspeople get a lot of pleasure from feeding pigeons—not always with the approval of their neighbours. However, most bird gardeners would prefer not to play host to these invasive and numerous birds, largely, one suspects, because they appear to have such prodigious appetites. In many ways, then, the feral pigeon is a rather controversial bird.

*Many colour varieties, from pure white through brown to black, have been bred. Feral pigeons are descended from the rock dove which inhabits the mountainous regions in Europe. The feral birds, after escaping, often take up residence in urban areas where they have become something of a nuisance.*

## FACTS AND FEATURES

**Plumage** Very variable—from blue grey with glossy green patch on neck, two black bars in inner wing and black tip to tail, to black and white, brown, brown and white plumages, with or without wing- and tail-bars. Many show a white rump.
**Habitat** Widespread: cities, towns, gardens, parks and farmland.
**Food** Grain and seeds.
**Nest** On a ledge, or in a hole on buildings.

33 cm/13 in

# STOCK DOVE *Columba oenas*

THE STOCK DOVE is reasonably well-distributed in Europe, but does not occur in the extreme north or in parts of the Mediterranean. It is an easily overlooked species, and while it occurs in smallish flocks, it is not usually particularly numerous. There seems little justification in treating it as an agricultural pest and, indeed, it now enjoys the status of a protected species in the United Kingdom.

Stock doves are rather smaller than woodpigeons and about the same size as rock doves or feral pigeons. They are a darker, more uniformly blue-grey than either of these. They show no white anywhere in their plumage; there is a glossy green patch on the sides of the neck, and the throat and breast show a distinct virous tinge. In flight, two short, broken, black wingbars are visible, but a more obvious and very useful identification feature is the way in which the blue-grey wings seem to have a dark border. The grey tail has an obvious dark band at the tip. Stock doves have a very distinctive circling display flight in spring. The song in a deep *oo-woo*, with the second syllable clipped and abrupt.

Favoured habitats include coastal and inland cliffs, quarries, sand-dunes, sometimes ruins and old buildings, as well as woodland, parkland and large gardens with old trees which will provide suitable nest-holes. Mature trees with holes will certainly provide breeding opportunities in large gardens. Stock doves also respond quite well to the provision of nestboxes of the large, standard design (see page 44) can may also nest in various other boxes, crates, barrels and so forth provided for them. I have seen stock doves nesting in plastic cider barrels with an opening in one end—and also ornamental pigeon-houses.

For the most part, stock doves feed in the fields and in open country, often in company with woodpigeons, feeding on grain and seeds, the roots, shoots and leaves of many plants (including crops) and various fruits and berries. As a general rule, they tend not to come to feeding stations in gardens, at any rate not as readily as woodpigeons or feral pigeons.

## FACTS AND FEATURES

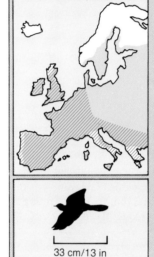

**Plumage** Overall blue grey, slightly paler on underparts. Glossy green patch on sides of neck. Breast tinged red. Two short, black bars on inner wing. Black end to tail. Juveniles duller, browner, lacking green gloss on neck.
**Habitat** Parks, forest edges, farmland, large gardens, cliffs and ruins.
**Food** Seeds, grain, fruit, roots and green shoots.
**Nest** In holes in trees and buildings.

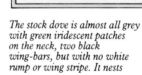

33 cm/13 in

*The stock dove is almost all grey with green iridescent patches on the neck, two black wing-bars, but with no white rump or wing stripe. It nests commonly in disused farm buildings, churches, holes in trees, and it will also use nestboxes.*

# Woodpigeon *Columba palumbus*

THIS FAMILIAR BIRD is the largest and bulkiest of the European pigeons and doves. It is basically grey-blue-grey on the head, a darker, duller grey on the back and wings, with the flight feathers noticeably darker, and paler below with a purplish-pink wash on the breast. There is a glossy green and purple patch on the sides of the neck, above a conspicuous white patch (which gave the bird its old name of ring dove). In flight, the blackish tail shows a broad white band on the underside and there are striking, white, crescent-shaped marks on the wings.

All pigeons are fast and powerful fliers and this one is no exception. When disturbed it explodes from trees or from the ground with an audible clatter of its wings. It also has a distinctive, short display flight in which it towers upwards, clapping its wings together abruptly, and then planes down again. The well-known song is a deep, almost muffled phrase of five cooing notes, usually repeated, with the accent on the first syllable and the final one rather clipped and abrupt.

Woodpigeons are widespread and common over much of Europe, being mainly associated with trees and open, usually agricultural country. They are common in many towns and cities, having adapted well to living alongside man, and where necessary, even nesting on buildings instead of in the more normal tree sites. They are frequent nesters in gardens with trees, and come readily to food put out on the ground (or, not infrequently, on bird tables). They are mainly vegetarian, eating seeds and grain, the stems and leaves of many plants—including crops and vegetables—and a variety of nuts (including acorns), fruits and berries. Woodpigeons are a mixed blessing in the garden, and standard scaring or deterrent techniques are often necessary to keep them off vegetable plots.

Originally a woodland species, the woodpigeon spread rapidly into farmland in the wake of the Agricultural Revolution, directly as a result of a greatly increased food supply. It adapted quickly to nesting in copses shelterbelts and even large bushes, and ultimately around human habitations. It also soon became a serious agricultural pest in Britain and remains so to this day. None of the forms of control used so far has made any significant inroad into the large population (swollen by migrants in winter), or the amount of damage caused to crops—estimated to run to over £1,000,000 per year.

## FACTS AND FEATURES

40.5 cm/16 in

**Plumage** Back and inner wings grey, outer wing black, white crescent-shaped mark between. Head and black-tipped tail greyish blue. Glossy, greenish-purple and white patches on neck. Breast purplish-pink.
**Habitat** Widespread: gardens, farmland, woodland and sea coasts.
**Food** Grain, seeds, vegetables, plants, acorns and berries.
**Nest** A flimsy platform of thin twigs in trees or bushes.

*The woodpigeon is the largest pigeon in Europe, and possibly the most attractive. It is mainly grey above with black primaries and terminal band, and a breast washed with pink. Nests are usually flimsy platforms of sticks placed in a tree.*

# TURTLE DOVE *Streptopelia turtur*

WIDESPREAD OVER MUCH OF EUROPE, except in the far north, the turtle dove, one of our smallest pigeons, is a summer visitor. In Britain it nests mainly in the south, but appears to be increasing in the north, where it is colonizing new areas, and expanding to Scotland and Ireland. Adults are delicately marked having a greyish brown back and grey-edged chestnut wings with black chequering. The breast is pinkish and the belly white. The greyish head with the fine black and white neck patches make the adult distinctive; juveniles have a duller plumage overall and lack these patches. The flight is fast and swinging with very clipped wingbeats, and the long, graduated black tail with its white tips, and the greyish underwings are characteristic.

The turtle dove's presence is usually first detected by its deep, purring-like cooing, a soft, often repeated *rooo-or*. Basically a bird of open country favouring small copses, overgrown hedgerows, orchards or large, scattered, bushy areas to nest, it is also found at the edges of large wooded areas. The nest is usually low down, lower than in most other pigeons, and often in hawthorn or blackthorn where this is present. The nest is a scanty affair consisting of a thin, frail platform of fine twigs lined with grass and root material (although instances have been recorded of birds utilizing former rooks' nests or squirrels' dreys).

Being fairly shy, the turtle dove is not a common garden bird in Britain, unless large trees or dense bushes occur on the fringes, but it is seen more often in or around gardens in southern Europe. However, if a pond or drinking area is provided, especially if placed in a secluded, sheltered spot, the average garden has a fair chance of attracting them. More commonly they are seen in farmyards near grain stores or, more especially, where chickens are present, as they are predominantly seed eaters. In open areas they concentrate largely on corn, many species of weed and grass, with a special preference for the seeds of fumitory. Although their diet is almost entirely of vegetable matter, small molluscs may also be taken.

*The turtle dove prefers low perches on trees and bushes and is also seen frequently on telegraph wires. Arriving from Africa in the spring, it is usually seen singly or in pairs, but in autumn small flocks can occur. The chestnut back and black and white neck patches differentiate it from all other European doves.*

## FACTS AND FEATURES

**Plumage** Brown upperparts speckled with black. Grey head, black and white neck patch, pink breast, white tip to tail.
**Habitat** Wood edges, bushes and copses.
**Food** Seeds.
**Nest** In thorn bushes or in old rooks' nests.

27 cm/10¾ in

# COLLARED DOVE *Streptopelia decaocto*

ONCE A VERY RARE BIRD IN EUROPE, the collared dove began a sudden range expansion in the 1930s: from its, then only European home in the Balkans it swept north-west very rapidly and began breeding in Britain in the mid-1950s; it continues to spread north and westwards. Larger and stockier than the turtle dove, it is distinguished by its almost uniform, pale, greyish brown plumage with pinkish breast, blackish wingtips and blue grey coverts. Its most distinctive feature is the narrow, white-bordered black, half collar around the back of the neck. This is less noticeable, or almost absent, in juvenile birds. It is not to be confused with the Barbary dove, a common 'escape bird', which is similar, but smaller and much creamier in coloration, and lacking the black wingtips. In flight, which is fast and direct, the collared dove shows from below a distinctive tail pattern, the outer half being white, while the basal half is black.

The song, a deep *coo-coooo-coo*, although pleasant for a while, is uttered with such persistence and for such long periods, that it soon becomes monotonous and irritating, especially first thing in the morning outside a bedroom.

The nest is built in trees, usually conifers or fruit trees, or in ivy, where this is dense around the trunk. It is rare on buildings. Like most pigeons, the nest is a thin, flimsy platform of twigs, sometimes lined with roots or grass stems and can be anything from 1.5–15 m (5–50 ft) off the ground.

The collared dove is very tolerant of humans and is often found in gardens. Indeed, it seems to prefer areas of human habitation rather than open country, and in some areas it is now regarded as a pest, especially where it congregates on large farms, chicken runs or grain stores, where it can form large flocks in winter. Its main diet consists of grain and seeds, but it will also eat small fruit such as elderberries, and scraps from the garden.

Collared doves will always visit gardens where large trees are present for breeding sites, and also when seed and scraps are put out. Like all pigeons, they drink frequently and, if water is provided, this will encourage them even more.

## FACTS AND FEATURES

**Plumage** Uniform, pale brown and grey, black half collar at back of neck.
**Habitat** Farmyards, gardens, parks.
**Food** Grain, seeds, fruit.
**Nest** Fruit or conifer trees, in ivy.

30.5 cm/12 in

*Juvenile collared doves are much greyer than the adult shown here, and they lack the neck collar. The Barbary dove is similar but paler overall with greyish brown, not black, primaries. Water provided for drinking, and seed for food will entice these birds into most gardens.*

73

# BARN OWL *Tyto alba*

*A barn owl at the entrance to its nesting hole (right) with one of its main prey items, a vole. It is most often seen at night or at dusk, but it can be observed during the day in winter, or when busy feeding hungry young.*

## FACTS AND FEATURES

**Plumage** Western form: heart-shaped face, underparts and feathered legs white; upperparts including crown, sandy buff, delicately marked with grey and white. Eastern form: darker, greyer upperparts and buff underparts.
**Habitat** Parks, fields, farms and ruins.
**Food** Small mammals including mice and voles; small birds and insects.
**Nest** In holes in old trees, in farm buildings and outhouses.

34 cm/13½ in

WHILE BARN OWLS MAY HUNT over large gardens, and even nest there, if there are suitable old trees with holes, or deserted or little-used outhouses, they are mostly associated with farms, ruins and churchyards.

Barn owls have a very characteristic appearance: long, slightly rounded wings, long, feathered legs and a heart-shaped face. They hunt over open country and field edges (often at the roadside) with a light, buoyant flight action. They hover and pause frequently on all sorts of exposed vantage points, from which they pounce on their prey. Most barn owls feed mainly on mice, rats and voles, but some also kill quite a lot of small birds. Their presence is often revealed by the numerous black, sausage-shaped pellets which accumulate at roosting and nesting-sites.

The barn owl breeds throughout most of Europe except for most of Scandinavia and Finland. The typical form is pure white on the face and underparts, with very pale, sandy-coloured upperparts beautifully marked with grey and white. The whole impression, especially in flight, is of a ghostly white bird. In northern and eastern parts of the European range, the upperparts are considerably darker and the face and underparts are rich buff—this is the so-called 'dark-breasted barn owl'. Various hissing, snoring and yapping noises are heard at the nest, but otherwise the only call likely to be heard is an unearthly shriek, often uttered in flight.

Barn owls have declined markedly in Britain, probably through a combination of factors associated with changes in agriculture. There has been a loss of habitat for hunting (and therefore less available prey) and, in some areas at least, loss of traditional nest-sites, as old trees are felled and farm buildings are replaced or modernized. Nestboxes can help; these can be erected in outhouses or barns (see page 45).

# TAWNY OWL *Strix aluco*

TAWNY OWLS ARE MEDIUM-SIZED, chunky-looking birds with fairly long, broad wings and large round heads. Apart from the much larger Ural owl of northern Europe, they are the only species with wholly dark eyes. The upperparts vary in tone from grey-brown to a rich chestnut brown (but nevertheless birds fall quite distinctly into grey or brown phases), with dark streaks and lines of creamy marks on the wing-covers, which are very conspicuous on perched birds. The paler underparts are streaked darker.

Although sometimes seen in the daytime, tawny owls are usually strictly nocturnal. While not too difficult to observe, with patience and practice, they are far more often heard than seen. Theirs is the high, ringing *kee-wick* call one hears so frequently—and also the familiar song, a loud and far-carrying hooting, beginning with a single, wavering *hoooo!* and followed by a musical *oo-oo-oo-oo*.

This is much the most widespread of all European owls and generally the commonest, although, curiously, it is entirely absent from Ireland. It is basically a bird of mature woodland, but has shown great adaptability to changes wrought by man and is as much at home in parks and gardens, including those in villages and towns and even in the middle of large cities. Indeed, it may occur almost anywhere if there is reasonable tree cover. Rural tawny owls feed mainly on mice and voles, but those in urban situations eat a large proportion of small birds. It is this great versatility which has enabled them to live cheek-by-jowl with man and is of course, the reason for their success as a species.

Large gardens with mature trees may have nesting tawny owls if there is a suitably large natural hole available. Artificial sites can be provided in the form of purpose-built nestboxes (see page 44); other possibilities include wooden crates or tea chests and even wooden or plastic barrels with an opening at one end. Generally, though, if owls are present regularly, and heard frequently, it is a fair bet that they have a perfectly good natural site nearby and require no help. In any case, tawny owls can be aggressive at the nest (see page 45) and caution must be exercised in siting nestboxes for them.

*The presence of a tawny owl quietly roosting is often indicated by chattering alarm calls from several small birds nervously flicking in the tree branches. Because of their nocturnal behaviour, their presence is only otherwise revealed by the deep 'hoo-hoo-hoo' call.*

## FACTS AND FEATURES

**Plumage** Greyish brown or chestnut brown upperparts, streaked and mottled with darker brown. Creamy white marks on wings. Underparts buffish, streaked and barred darker brown. Tail barred, Buffish grey face with large, blackish eyes.
**Habitat** Parks, large gardens, woodland.
**Food** Rats, mice, voles, small birds, frogs and worms.
**Nest** In holes or crevices in trees or rocks.

38 cm/15 in

# LITTLE OWL *Athene noctua*

BECAUSE IT IS SO OFTEN ACTIVE IN DAYLIGHT—and often sits out in exposed places by day—the little owl is familiar to many people in many parts of Europe. It is likely to appear (and breed) around farms, on factory or works sites and in and around large gardens; it has a marked preference for semi-open country, with scattered trees, but also occurs on all sorts of wasteland, in quarries and on stony and scrubby hillsides. Little owls are found throughout Europe, except in Scandinavia and Finland; in Britain they are introduced birds, this presence resulting from releases in the wild in the mid- and late 19th century. They are commonest in the southern two-thirds of England, rare in northern England and around the Borders and absent from Ireland. In some areas they are scarce, however, possibly due to agricultural change and the loss of natural nest-sites.

Little owls present no identification problems. Their small size and squat, flat-headed appearance is in itself very distinctive. Unlike other European owls, they fly with rapid wingbeats and a noticably bounding action. The upperparts are a rather light brown, with copious whitish spots and blotches, and the underparts are pale with dark streaks; the brown crown is streaked with lines of whitish spots, and above frowning whitish 'eyebrows' are yellow-rimmed eyes. Little owls are often extremely noisy, the commonest note being a yelping far-carrying *werrow*. The song consists of a plaintive, single note, with a slightly rising inflection, repeated in long series.

The main food is insects, especially larvae, caterpillars and beetles, and small rodents; few small birds are taken and (as a famous pre-war study showed all too clearly) the little owl very rarely takes gamebird chicks, contrary to popular opinion. Old trees with natural holes, particularly those in hedgerows, provide nest-sites, and leaving dead or dying treees around the edges of large gardens could help little owls. They will also nest in lofts in little-used buildings and, on the Continent, have also used nestboxes successfully. See page 44 for details of nestbox design.

## FACTS AND FEATURES

**Plumage** Upperparts brown, blotched and spotted with white; dark brown crown spotted with white; underparts pale whitish buff with dark streaking. Feathered legs white. Facial disc whitish with brownish cheeks, yellow-rimmed eyes.
**Habitat** Parks, cliffs, wasteland, gardens, farmland and open country.
**Food** Insects, worms, small mammals and birds.
**Nest** In holes in trees, rocks, cliffs, or in a burrow on the ground.

21.5 cm/8½ in

*This species can often be seen during the hours of daylight sitting in quite open situations such as telegraph poles and fence posts. The flight is usually low, swift and strongly undulated. Many nesting situations may be used, and these include holes in trees (above), buildings, under chicken hutches and nestboxes.*

# SCOPS OWL *Otus scops*

VERY RARE IN BRITAIN and northern Europe, the Scops owl is largely confined to France, Spain and the southern half of Europe, where it is normally a summer visitor only, with a very scattered distribution. The second smallest owl in Europe, it is distinguished by its diminutive appearance (it is smaller than a starling), and its ear tufts, although these are not always raised and, therefore, not conspicuous. It has a thinner, more tapered body than the little owl, but it has a longer tail. The plumage is grey and brown, delicately vermiculated and spotted, making it very difficult to see. The eyes are lemon or orange yellow and the feet are unfeathered. Although a strictly nocturnal owl, it can be seen during the day roosting in cover or, more often, sitting close to the trunk of a tree. When alarmed it freezes, slimming itself into an elongated upright posture.

This owl is most often detected by its monotonous call, a soft whistled *pew*, which is constantly repeated. This call, however, is easily confused with the similar note emitted by the midwife toad, which also occurs in France and Spain and also calls at night. Whereas the little owl has a bounding or undulating flight, the scops owl has a more wavering flight.

The scops owl's favourite habitat is anywhere where there are large broad-leaved trees, in gardens, parks, tree-lined avenues, orchards, hedges and open woodland. The nest is usually in a cavity in a tree, though holes in buildings, ruins or walls are also used. Occasionally the old nest of another bird is utilized.

The diet of the scops owl is mainly insectivorous,

## FACTS AND FEATURES

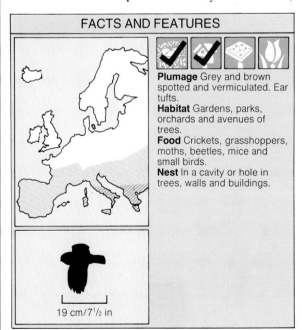

**Plumage** Grey and brown spotted and vermiculated. Ear tufts.
**Habitat** Gardens, parks, orchards and avenues of trees.
**Food** Crickets, grasshoppers, moths, beetles, mice and small birds.
**Nest** In a cavity or hole in trees, walls and buildings.

19 cm/7½ in

*The scops owl prefers the warmer regions, especially those countries which border the Mediterranean where larger insects are more readily available for food. Where they are common, they can be quite difficult to see; the plaintive call is usually the only indication of their presence.*

largely consisting of bush crickets and moths, but it will also take beetles, grasshoppers, small rodents such as mice and shrews, and even reptiles, amphibians and small birds at times. The indigestible items of its prey are coughed up in the form of a pellet some 20 mm ($^4/_5$ in) long and 10 mm ($^2/_5$ in) wide which, if found on the ground, can indicate a favoured roosting site.

There is no guaranteed way of attracting the scops owl to your garden, but large trees with holes should be left as possible breeding sites—an outside light to attract moths, which in turn will attract the owl, may help, and provision of a suitable nestbox may also encourage them.

# Ring-Necked Parakeet *Psittacula krameri*

PARROTS ceased to be part of the European birdlife many millions of years ago, when, through climatical and environmental changes, and, probably, competition with other species, this group of birds became more characteristic of the warmer regions of the world. Therefore, the direct descendants of the ring-necked parakeet we see in Europe are the result of escapes from captivity, rather than any extension of range. Its natural breeding area includes much of the Indian sub-continent, eastwards to China and westwards to Arabia. They have been able to survive the cold winters of Europe because of two factors: firstly, certain populations in India have managed to adapt to the colder climate of the Himalayan foothills, therefore they do have the ability to withstand a less tropical climate, and secondly, by the provision of food on bird tables. The latter has certainly been a major factor in enabling this parakeet to survive in Britain, even in the hardest of winters. In fact, over the past 10 years or so, their numbers have increased through natural breeding to such an extent that, in the fruit-growing regions, they are regarded as a pest. The selected habitats are remarkably similar to those of the wild populations and include open woodland, orchards and around human habitation.

In appearance this parakeet presents itself as a long, slim-winged and long-tailed bird, which, in flight, has shallow wing beats. The male is all grass-green with a rose-pink and black collar, black chin and hooked, red bill. The female is similar, but lacks the collar and black chin, and displays an emerald-green ring around the neck. Young birds are all green and have brown bills. Like all parrots, this species is extremely vocal and produces a shrill, screaming *keeo-keeo-keeo*.

They nest in natural holes in trees, which are normally enlarged to the bird's size, other species' old nesting holes, or even in crevices in rocks or old buildings. In the latter locations they sometimes form loose colonies. They will also readily use nestboxes placed high up in a tree.

In winter they will readily come to bird tables, especially if peanuts are provided.

*The ring-necked parakeet is unmistakable — it is almost entirely green with a long, pointed tail. Its occurrence in Europe is due entirely to escapes from captivity.*

## FACTS AND FEATURES

**Plumage** Bright green; flight feathers darker; bluish nape; black chin and rose-pink and black collar. Long, graduated tail bluish-green. Bill red. Female lacks the black chin and collar.
**Habitat** Parks, gardens and open woodlands, near habitation.
**Food** Fruit, berries, seeds and nuts, especially peanuts.
**Nest** A natural hole in a tree; crevices in rocks and buildings.

40.5 cm/16 in

# CUCKOO *Cuculus canorus*

CUCKOOS OCCUR THROUGHOUT EUROPE as summer migrants. In Britain, the first birds do not usually appear in the south until well into April, and in many areas the male's characteristic song is not heard until the middle of the month or even later. Numbers seem to fluctuate from year to year and from area to area, giving rise to rumours of decline, but although there was an apparent decrease in the 1950s there is little hard evidence of the bird becoming rarer in recent years.

There is a rare, rufous form of the female cuckoo, but essentially the sexes are alike. The cuckoo is a long-winged bird, with a long and ample tail, grey all over except for whitish underparts finely barred with grey, white undertail coverts and a dark, slate-grey tail tipped and spotted with white. Juveniles vary in appearance from reddish-brown above with strong dark barring, to greyer-brown with much less obvious bars; their underparts are buffish, barred darker, and there is a fairly prominent white spot on the nape.

In flight, cuckoos suggest a small hawk or falcon, with their pointed wings and long tails, but they have much smaller, rounded heads and a steady, direct flight unbroken by glides. At rest, they appear very small-headed and long-tailed; males in particular perch untidily, especially when calling, with drooping wings and spread tails. The song is a rhythmic *cuc-koo cuc-koo . . .*, replaced by a three-note version later in the season; females emit a loud, long, bubbling call.

Cuckoos occur in virtually every imaginable habitat, except heavily built-up areas, and they are not at all infrequent in gardens; they are insectivorous. They are brood parasites, building no nest of their own but removing one egg from the host species and replacing it with one of their own, which usually mimics that of the host. A wide range of birds is used in this way, ranging in size from blackbirds down to wrens. Pipits and reed warblers are the commonest hosts, and among garden birds the dunnock; each cuckoo is specific to one host only and this will usually be an insectivorous bird.

The young cuckoo expels the remaining eggs of the host species—or the young if they hatch first—and then has the nest and its foster parents all to itself. One of the strangest sights in nature is that of a huge, very hungry baby cuckoo, in or out of the nest, being fed by its relatively tiny, hard-pressed foster parents. This all seems very unfair to us, but brood parasites are not uncommon among birds around the world; cuckoos may have what appears to be bad habits, but they do not affect small bird numbers in any way.

## FACTS AND FEATURES

**Plumage** Adult: grey overall, wingtips darker; underparts, whitish barred with grey. Tail slate-grey tipped with white. Juveniles: grey or rufous brown above, with darker barring and buffish below.
**Habitat** Farmland, woodland, moorland, reedbeds and gardens.
**Food** Insects, especially caterpillars.
**Nest** Does not build a nest, uses nest of another species.

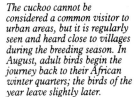

33 cm/13 in

*The cuckoo cannot be considered a common visitor to urban areas, but it is regularly seen and heard close to villages during the breeding season. In August, adult birds begin the journey back to their African winter quarters; the birds of the year leave slightly later.*

# SWIFT *Apus apus*

SWIFTS ARE SUMMER MIGRANTS, arriving in late April and early May, usually some time after swallows and martins. They are among the first migrants to depart—most have gone by the end of August or early September.

Since their habitat is really the air itself, swifts occur virtually everywhere. Their distribution is governed by the weather and the availability of the flying insects on which they feed exclusively. They feed at all sorts of altitudes, not infrequently at low level on warm, humid summer evenings when food is plentiful, especially around or over water. They show scant regard for humans at such times, often passing very close and at great speed, with audible snaps of their mouths as they feed. They are strongly gregarious when feeding and may appear in large flocks. They also often travel considerable distances to find suitable feeding areas.

Swifts differ from swallows and martins (to which they are not closely related) in several ways. They have much larger gapes and even smaller bills and much longer, narrower and less flexible wings; they are even faster and more manoeuvrable in flight. Their small feet are virtually useless, except for clinging on to walls near their nest. Indeed, they almost never perch and, except when visiting the nest, spend their lives flying. They even sleep and copulate on the wing. The plumage differs from that of swallows and martins too: swifts are sooty-black all over, apart from a small and often indistinct whitish patch at the throat.

They are garden birds only in the sense that they feed around and over gardens—but they also nest in buildings of all kinds, including older houses, under eaves where they can enter suitable holes or crevices, or in any kind of holes which are large enough. They are loosely colonial and usually occupy traditional sites year after year. In Britain, a minority nest in crevices in sea-cliffs, inland cliffs and quarries, but nesting in holes in trees is very rare, although commonplace in eastern and parts of northern Europe. Specially constructed nestboxes (see page 46) can be erected for swifts.

*Long, scimitar wings and a short, forked tail separate swifts from swallows and martins. The all dark appearance also makes them distinctive. They are often seen in groups on the wing, especially when the young leave the nests, screaming as they chase each other over the skies.*

## FACTS AND FEATURES

**Plumage** Long, scimitar wings; short, forked tail and body all dark, sooty brown. Indistinct whitish throat. Juveniles: usually browner with a larger throat patch, but difficult to separate from adults.
**Habitat** Almost anywhere, but especially near water and over towns.
**Food** Insects caught on the wing.
**Nest** Under eaves of houses, or in crevices on cliffs.

16.5 cm/6½ in

# KINGFISHER *Alcedo atthis*

THERE CAN BE FEW GARDEN VISITORS as delightful as the kingfisher: even though it may eat the smallest ornamental fish in your garden pool you will forgive it. It is probably the only bird in this book which can accurately be described in one word: unmistakeable. It is tolerably common and widespread in areas with lakes, ponds, ditches and slow-moving streams and rivers (and canals) and is likely to appear in any garden with pools or water frontage—although not in areas away from other waters.

## FACTS AND FEATURES

**Plumage** Back and tail brilliant cobalt blue; crown, wings and moustache greenish blue, with bluish barring on crown. White on chin, throat and sides of neck. Cheeks through to base of bill and also underparts bright orange chestnut.
**Habitat** Lakes, ponds, rivers and streams with slow-moving water.
**Food** Small insects, but mainly small fish.
**Nest** In a chamber at the end of a tunnel excavated in banks near water.

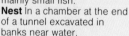

16.5 cm/6½ in

Kingfishers are small, bumpy, short-tailed birds with disproportionately large heads and big, dagger-shaped bills. The predominant colour is the bright blue or blue-green of the crown and upperparts—especially the vivid cobalt splash of colour down the back—but the bird also has a white chin, chestnut and white markings on the side of the head and chestnut underparts. The bill is blackish and the tiny feet are sealing-wax red. Kingfishers fly low and fast, often giving a high-pitched piping call as they go. They fish from exposed perches above the water, plunging in with a headlong dive, or sometimes by hovering.

Since they eat small fish and a variety of small invertebrates, appearances at pools are always likely. The provision of a few simple perches may encourage them to stay, or come again—a branch or stick, firmly placed and angling out over the water, is all that is required. Place the branch where you can see it from a window, but remember to keep very still if a kingfisher comes, as they are normally very shy and easily disturbed.

Kingfishers nest in long tunnels which they excavate in banks above or close to water. It is not feasible to provide artificial tunnels for them, but a suitable bank (ideally with an open 'face' at least 1.2 m [4 ft] high) could be engineered in a large garden or along a water frontage. The most important consideration is that the site must be as little disturbed as possible; this is also important if you find birds nesting near your garden. In Britain it is an offence under the Wildlife and Countryside Act, 1981, wilfully to disturb nesting kingfishers without a licence.

*The jewel of the waterside, the kingfisher is very shy, and views of its vivid, cobalt back as it flies away are often all that are seen. When it catches a fish, the kingfisher holds it by the tail and beats its head on a suitable perch (above) to kill it. The fish is carried head outwards in the bill ready for presentation to the young.*

# HOOPOE *Upupa epops*

MOST BRITISH BIRD GARDENERS dream of the day when a hoopoe will visit their garden. For most, it remains just a dream, but hoopoes do turn up every spring and autumn, and most come to gardens and often stay around for days at a time. In exceptional cases they may even breed somewhere nearby. On the Continent they are much more familiar and widespread.

On the ground, a feeding hoopoe can be surprisingly inconspicuous—it is a curiously low-slung, long-bodied bird with short legs, a long, decurved bill and a long, backwards-raking crest. The predominant colour is a pale pinkish-brown, with black and white stripes across the closed wings, the back and the tail. The crest is erectile and is often flicked up suddenly and then lowered, especially if the bird is excited or alarmed; it is often raised just as the bird alights. When it flies, the hoopoe is suddenly transformed into a spectacularly pink, black and white bird, with big, rounded wings and a characteristically floppy, open-and-shut flight action. The song is a quiet, but surprisingly far-carrying *poo-poo-poo-poo* . . .

Hoopoes are ground-feeders, eating mainly insects and small invertebrates, but also lizards and even, occasionally, small mammals. They feed on all sorts of open ground or in low cover, but are also particularly fond of large lawns—or a whole series of smaller ones in one area. It should be added that they can be exceptionally wary and are easily disturbed—it is best to watch them from inside a house, or at a distance using binoculars. Other than maintaining your lawn and hoping, there is little you can do for the hoopoe, although in Europe (where they are hole-nesters) they have been attracted successfully to standard-type, large-size nestboxes.

One word of warning: a hoopoe in your garden could attract dozens of birdwatchers from miles around. Before you announce that it is around, think carefully about whether you could cope with the likely invasion, or whether you might be prepared to lay on viewing facilities from your house . . ..

## FACTS AND FEATURES

**Plumage** Head, neck and body pinkish brown. Wings, lower back, rump and tail have bold black and white stripes. The crest is pink with black tips.
**Habitat** Orchards; open grassy areas in woodland; parks; gardens.
**Food** Chiefly insects and their larvae; worms, lizards and small mammals.
**Nest** Holes or crevices in trees, buildings, stone walls or nestboxes.

28 cm/11 in

*One of Europe's more exotic birds, the hoopoe, with its pinkish brown plumage, fan-like erectile crest and black and white wings and tail is unmistakable and unlikely to be confused with any other bird, except perhaps the jay.*

# WRYNECK *Jynx torquilla*

ALTHOUGH TOLERABLY COMMON in many parts of Europe, the wryneck has all but vanished from Britain as a breeding bird. A few still turn up in spring in southern England, but otherwise they chiefly occur as autumn migrants, usually at or near the east coast, but also sometimes inland. The reasons for their decline are unknown, but are probably connected to long-term climatic change. These might also explain the relatively recent, small-scale colonization of a few parts of Scotland, by birds of southern Scandinavian origin.

Technically, wrynecks are woodpeckers, although they are much less tied to life in the trees than the other typical species featured here. They are sparrow-size and, indeed, could be mistaken for sparrows at a quick glance. The upperparts are beautifully patterned in brown, greys and buffs, the crown is grey and, in a rear view, there are noticeable pale 'braces' on the upper back; the underparts are buffish with fine dark barring. The bill is dark, rather short and unlike those of the typical woodpeckers.

While wrynecks feed in trees, they are particularly fond of ants and, for this reason, feed regularly on lawns, in flowerbeds and on other open areas—including paths. In Europe, gardens and orchards are typical wryneck habitats and that is where many bred in southern England when the species was more common. Autumn birds regularly frequent gardens and may stay for days.

Wrynecks do not excavate nest-holes like other woodpeckers, but use natural holes or cavities in trees, walls, buildings, etc. In spring, males find and select a suitable hole and may even sing from it, with just the head poking out—although they also sing from all sorts of other perches. The ringing and monotonous *quee-quee-quee-quee* . . . has a curiously ventriloquil quality and this can make the bird exceptionally difficult to spot, even when you have pinned it down to a small area. Sadly, singing and nesting wrynecks are virtually a thing of the past in southern Britain, but where they occur, they will certainly use standard-type nestboxes (hole size as for nuthatch) if provided.

## FACTS AND FEATURES

**Plumage** Upperparts marked with browns, buff and grey. Usually shows two pale braces on back and dark blackish, curving line from nape to lower back. Underparts buffish with fine, dark barring; throat more yellow with dark barring.
**Habitat** Orchards, open woodland, gardens, and heathland with trees.
**Food** Insects, especially ants.
**Nest** In natural hole or cavity in trees, buildings and banks.

16.5 cm/6¹/₂ in

*Cryptically camouflaged, the wryneck is difficult to pick out from surrounding vegetation. So called because of its habit of twisting and turning its neck in display or when alarmed, it is also known as 'snake bird'.*

# GREEN WOODPECKER *Picus viridis*

A LARGE WOODPECKER common throughout Europe except in the north, the green woodpecker has a distinct plumage, and could be confused only with the grey-headed woodpecker in the central and eastern parts of its range. The adults have green upperparts with a contrasting yellowish rump and dark tail. The underparts are a pale greeny grey. The head in both sexes has a bright red crown, the rest of the face being black with greyish cheeks and large black moustachial stripes, which, in the male only, have a red centre. The bill is long, straight, strong and pointed. Juveniles are much duller, with streaks and speckles over the entire plumage. The yellowish rump shows clearly when the woodpecker is in flight, which is bounding or undulating, the wings being closed on the downward sweep.

It is known in Britain as the yaffle because of its loud, ringing, laughing call, a *pueu-pueu-pueu*. Unlike most of our other woodpeckers it rarely drums.

The green woodpecker is common in large open woodland, parklands, orchards and also on heaths and meadows where scattered trees occur. The nest is excavated by both adults, and consists of a hole leading to a chamber, which is unlined save for a few woodchips.

The green woodpecker is often seen hopping vertically up tree trunks in short jerks, its stiff tail pushed against the trunk as a support. Part of its diet consists of the larvae of wood-boring beetles and insects, which it extracts by using its bill as a chisel, and inserting its very long tongue into the larval burrow or chamber. A much favoured food is ants and, for this reason, the green woodpecker is often seen on lawns in gardens, searching for ants and their nests, from which the grubs are extracted with its long sticky tongue. They will also eat seeds and some fruit.

Green woodpeckers like water and you can attract them into your garden by providing a pond or bird bath. In winter, they will visit bird tables if fat or mealworms are provided; they have sometimes been known to attack beehives to get at the grubs. Nestboxes can also be provided as a further enticement.

♂

*The green woodpecker is the woodpecker most likely to be seen on the ground. Its favourite food is ants, which it collects by thrusting its very long sticky tongue into ants' nests. Unlike other species it rarely drums.*

## FACTS AND FEATURES

**Plumage** Green upperparts with yellow rump; pale greyish underparts. Bright red crown and black moustachial stripes.
**Habitat** Open woodland, parkland, orchards and heathland.
**Food** Larvae of wood-boring beetles and ants.
**Nest** A chamber excavated in a tree.

31.5 cm/12½ in

# GREAT-SPOTTED WOODPECKER *Dendrocopos major*

THE COMMONEST black and white woodpecker in Europe,missing only from Ireland. Intermediate in size between the smaller lesser-spotted and the larger green woodpecker, it is becoming more frequently seen in gardens, especially in winter. The adults have largely black upperparts with a white patch on each wing, and some white spots across the primaries and secondaries; the tail is also black, but with white barring on the outer feathers. The underparts are creamy white, except for the undertail coverts which are bright red. The head has a glossy black crown and nape, whitish cheeks separated from a buffish white throat by a black moustachial stripe, and there is a white patch on either side of the neck. There is also a buff patch on the forehead. The male has a small red patch on the nape which is lacking in the female. Juveniles, for a short time, have a totally red crown, but are otherwise similar.

The great-spotted woodpecker's presence is usually first detected by its drumming, which lasts only for a second, being shorter in duration than that of the lesser-spotted. It also has a distinctive *tchick* note in flight.

Favoured habitats are woods and copses and, in some areas, it shows a marked preference for coniferous trees. The nest is a small chamber, excavated by both sexes, in a suitable tree. The chamber is unlined except for a few wood chippings.

Unlike the green woodpecker, the great-spotted spends little time on the ground, preferring to feed almost solely on the tree trunk or in the canopy, searching for wood-boring larvae and insects, spiders, nuts and berries. They are also known to take small nestlings of other birds and sometimes attack nestboxes to get at the young inside. In some countries a favourite food is the seed of pine cones. It can obtain the seeds by jamming the cone in a suitable crack in a tree and then hammering it open, extracting the seed as it goes. The ground below a favourite anvil can be littered with hundreds of cones.

The great-spotted woodpecker is a regular garden visitor, especially in winter, if nuts, suet and oats are there.

♂

*The great-spotted woodpecker is distinguished from the smaller lesser-spotted by the large, white patches on the wing and its red undertail coverts. It is a common visitor to gardens particularly where fat has been hung out to attract it.*

## FACTS AND FEATURES

**Plumage** Black upperparts with large, white patch on each wing; underparts creamy white, undertail coverts bright red; black crown with nape red on male, no red on female.
**Habitat** Woods and copses— both mixed and coniferous.
**Food** Larvae of wood-boring beetles, spiders, nuts and berries.
**Nest** A small chamber excavated in a suitable tree.

23 cm/9 in

# LESSER-SPOTTED WOODPECKER *Dendrocopos minor*

THE SMALLEST WOODPECKER IN EUROPE, the lesser-spotted is only the size of a sparrow; it is found over almost all the area except for northern England, Scotland, Ireland and Denmark. It is also, perhaps, the rarest woodpecker in Britain. The upperparts and wings are barred black and white and have no shoulder patches; the forehead and cheeks are whitish, with a black nape, black moustachial streak and black line through the eye. The male has a red crown, while the female has a brownish white crown, sometimes speckled faintly with red. The female has a small, sharply tapering bill, the underparts are whitish, streaked faintly with black, and the short, stiff tail is black. Juveniles are more brownish below and the forehead has blackish streaks.

The lesser-spotted is a very shy and retiring woodpecker, keeping largely to the higher branches and twigs to feed, and rarely coming down to the ground. Its presence is often overlooked and it is really only noted by its call, a shrill *pee-pee-pee-pee*, similar to the wryneck, but less strong, or by its rather feeble drumming, which although much fainter than that of the great-spotted, lasts longer. It also utters a weak *tchick* call. The flight is slow and undulating, but it can be seen fluttering around the upper branches of trees in search of food.

The lesser-spotted woodpecker's favourite habitats are large open woods, parkland, orchards, avenues of trees, and lines of alders beside rivers and streams. The nest, as in all woodpeckers, is a chamber excavated by both adults and is usually situated on the underside of a branch or in the more soft, decaying wood of the trunk of a tree. The entrance hole is small and often high up in the tree. The chamber is unlined, or sometimes has a few woodchips.

As with other woodpeckers, the lesser-spotted's main food items are the larvae of wood-boring beetles and insects, spiders and small berries. It visits gardens with less frequency than the great-spotted, but is attracted by old fruit trees, in which it may breed, especially if they are in a secluded, quiet area. It rarely visits bird tables but may occasionally take nuts, fat or fruit.

## FACTS AND FEATURES

**Plumage** Upperparts black, barred with white; underparts creamy white. Male has red crown, female has brownish white crown.
**Habitat** Large open woodland, orchards and parkland.
**Food** Larvae of wood-boring insects, spiders and berries.
**Nest** Small chamber excavated in the underside of a branch or in soft wood.

14.5 cm/5¾ in

*This male with a billful of insect larvae (above) is at the entrance to the nest cavity. The female lacks the red crown. As the young get older they will look out of the nest hole for the adults returning with food, and call excitedly.*

# HOUSE MARTIN *Delichon urbica*

WIDESPREAD THROUGHOUT EUROPE the house martin, like the swallow, is a summer visitor which also spends much time on the wing. Differing in its shorter, browner wings and forked tail without streamers, it is readily distinguished by its pure white rump. The upperparts, including the head, apart from the rump, are a dark, steely blue; the flight feathers and tail are browner; the underparts, throat and lower cheeks are pure white, as are the legs and feet, which are also feathered. Juveniles

are much less blue, being browner on the back. Its infrequently uttered song is no more than a soft twitter and the most common note is a strong *tchirrip*.

Like the swallow, much of its time is spent on the wing hawking for insects, and although it can be found in open country, especially where cliffs or rocky outcrops occur, most house martins are found in towns and villages, where they nest on manmade structures. The nest, which is a half cup of mud and grass fibres, is stuck to a suitable vertical surface under an overhang (on houses usually under the eaves), leaving a small entrance hole at the top; this is then lined with plant stems and feathers. It is colonial, and many nests may be seen close together.

The diet consists entirely of insects caught on the wing—when house martins are seen on the ground they are not feeding, but collecting mud for their nests.

In autumn, when the birds are returning to their winter quarters in Africa, the migrating birds moving south often take over nests left behind by other house martins to roost in overnight. They will also roost in reedbeds, but not to the same extent as swallows. On the south coast of Britain on suitable days in the autumn, many thousands of these birds can be seen migrating.

To attract house martins to the garden, you can buy artificial nests which can be screwed up under the eaves—several together will have more effect and ideally an existing colony should be nearby. It is best not to place the nests over windows, which can get streaked with droppings. Provision of a muddy patch in the garden will also entice them to build their own nests.

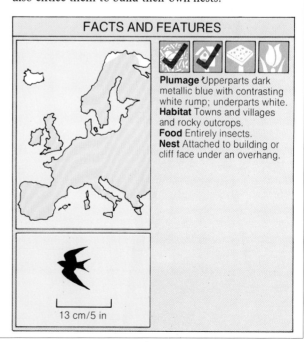

The house martin's white rump is the main feature distinguishing it from the swallow. The house martin rears two to three broods a year, and young birds from the first brood may stay and help feed birds in the later broods.

## FACTS AND FEATURES

**Plumage** Upperparts dark metallic blue with contrasting white rump; underparts white.
**Habitat** Towns and villages and rocky outcrops.
**Food** Entirely insects.
**Nest** Attached to building or cliff face under an overhang.

13 cm/5 in

# SWALLOW *Hirundo rustica*

COMMON THROUGHOUT EUROPE except in the far north, the swallow is a summer visitor migrating to Britain from Africa, where it spends the winter. Spending much of its time in flight, it is built for the aerial pursuit of insects, having long, pointed wings and a slender body. the plumage above is a deep, steely, metallic blue and the underparts are creamy with a contrasting deep, bluish, upper breast band. The throat and forehead are a reddish chestnut. The most characteristic feature of the adult is the long tail streamers, which are longer in the male than the female. The juvenile birds are duller overall and have shorter streamers. The song is a pleasant twittering, interspersed with trills, uttered mostly on the wing.

The swallow spends much of its time hawking for insects over farmland, towns, villages, meadows and especially over water where it catches the emerging flies and other insects. It can be seen drinking while on the wing, flying just above the water surface and scooping up water in its bill. Many insects are also picked up from the water surface. When resting between feeding, its favourite perches are telegraph wires and rooftops where it spends much time preening and twittering. In autumn, large flocks gather together prior to their return to Africa, forming long lines on suitable perches, and, in the evenings many hundreds can be seen flying into reedbeds, a favourite site for roosting at night.

Originally, swallows must have nested in caves and under rock ledges, but now they build their nests mostly in association with manmade structures—often in sheds, bridges, house eaves and in farm buildings. The nest is constructed of straw and other plant fibres, mixed and stuck together with mud and then lined with feathers, forming a shallow, saucer-shaped platform, open at the top and supported from below by a beam or rafter, and against an upright of some description. The period of nest-building is one of the only times the swallow will be seen on the ground, collecting the mud for its nest.

Swallows are common garden birds, seen flying overhead and around the houses. One way to encourage them is to leave a window open in a shed or to put up shallow trays on joists and rafters in open-ended outbuildings to encourage breeding.

*The long tail streamers and glossy metallic blue plumage with red forehead and throat are the characteristics of the adult swallow. Note also the white spots on the tail (left).*

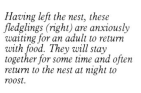

*Having left the nest, these fledglings (right) are anxiously waiting for an adult to return with food. They will stay together for some time and often return to the nest at night to roost.*

*Swallows and house martins often congregate in late summer forming large flocks prior to migration. Most of these are young birds, and telegraph wires (above) are a favourite perch for preening.*

*These young swallows (left) are about to leave the nest; note the pale yellowish gape around the bill. The adult is keeping its balance by half perching and flapping its wings.*

## FACTS AND FEATURES

**Plumage** Deep, steely blue upperparts; creamy underparts with bluish breastband; throat and forehead reddish chestnut.
**Habitat** Farmland, meadows, towns and villages.
**Food** Solely insects.
**Nest** Of straw and mud, in sheds, farm buildings and bridges.

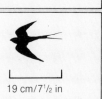

19 cm/7½ in

# Meadow Pipit *Anthus pratensis*

IN SUMMER the meadow pipit is commonly found in northern Europe, but is absent from southern France, Iberia, much of Italy and Yugoslavia, and is present in these countries only during the winter, when the northernmost populations migrate southwards. In Britain and France it can be found all the year round. Not to be confused with the very similar tree pipit, which is also found over most of the area, the meadow pipit has more olive underparts and paler underparts. The upperparts are olive-brown with distinct black streaking (lacking on the rump), the underparts are whitish, with some yellowy buff on the breast, and heavy dark streaks on the breast and flanks. The outer tail feathers are white and the hind toes have very long claws. Juveniles are darker above and their underparts are very yellow. The surest way to distinguish between a meadow and a tree pipit is to listen for the call: a thin *tsisip* in meadow, a hoarse *teeze* in tree. The song, typically delivered while the bird is fluttering upwards and then gliding down on outspread wings, is a thin accelerating trill.

It is a bird of open country; the favoured habitats are moorland, rough pastures, alpine meadows, marshland and dunes. It seldom perches in trees (except on migration), usually keeping to the ground or sitting on tops of bushes, posts etc. Its diet consists mainly of insects, especially flies and mosquitoes, earthworms and spiders; seeds are also taken, mainly in winter.

The nest is on the ground, well concealed in a tussock, in heather, or in dense plants. It is frequently placed in a depression, and is made up of dried plant stems and grasses, and lined with hair. Meadow pipits are one of the commonest species to be parasitized by the cuckoo.

On migration in the autumn, the meadow pipit often occurs in large flocks on farmland and also, at this time, on the sea coast. They are relatively tame, and if you come across a large flock you can approach quite closely—they will depart only a short distance in ones or twos, rather than as a whole group, uttering a clear *tsisip* alarm note.

It is not at all a common garden bird, unless the garden is a large tract of open land, but some do alight in even the smallest gardens on autumn passage.

## FACTS AND FEATURES

**Plumage** Olive-brown upperparts streaked with black; white outer tail feathers; underparts buffish with dark streaking.
**Habitat** Open country, alpine meadows and marshland.
**Food** Insects, worms and spiders.
**Nest** On ground in a depression, concealed by vegetation.

14.5 cm/5¾ in

*Pipits are difficult species to identify by plumage alone; the calls and songs are the most reliable features.*

# PIED/WHITE WAGTAIL *Motacilla alba*

*This wagtail breeds regularly in holes in buildings, especially those in and about farmyards. During the winter, large numbers often congregate in roosts in trees and reedbeds.*

COMMON THROUGHOUT EUROPE, these birds from the northern populations migrate south in winter. There are two distinct forms with quite different plumages: the pied, commonly occurring in Britain, and the white, which is the race found in the rest of Europe. In summer, the pied wagtail has black upperparts, including the rump, crown, throat, breast and tail; the forehead and sides of the head, the belly, vent, outer tail feathers and the two wing-bars are white. The sexes are similar, although the female is dark grey on the back and has less black on the breast. In winter, adults have a white throat and a back more grey than black. Juveniles are brown grey, with buffmarks on the head, throat and breast. The white wagtail has pale grey upperparts, including the rump; the crown and nape are black; the throat and breast are also black and clearly separated from the black on the head. The pale grey rump is the main distinguishing feature. In both species, the long tail is often wagged up and down and the head moves in a curious backwards and forwards motion. The call is a sharp *chissick* usually uttered in flight.

Favoured habitats are open countryside, towns, parks, farms, gardens, alpine meadows and tundra, where it can be seen running across the ground picking up insects or suddenly springing up into the air to catch passing flies. In Britain and elsewhere in Europe, changes in farming practice have not been to the birds' advantage.Farm yards are now more sterile with fewer open ditches in use, as more water is piped underground.

The nest of the pied or white wagtail is usually well-concealed and often near water. Built of grass stems, twigs, moss and leaves and lined with wool or hair and feathers, it is placed in a hole or recess in grassy banks, walls, buildings, or in ivy. It occasionally uses old nests of other birds including the house martin. The nest-building and most of the incubation is done by the female alone. Communal roosting is well-known with these birds, choice sites being trees, reedbeds and, most recently, glasshouses in large commercial market gardens.

This wagtail is a frequent visitor to the garden and can be encouraged by putting out crumbs and also by erecting open-fronted nestboxes in dark, secluded places, such as in a stone wall or behind ivy on a tree.

## FACTS AND FEATURES

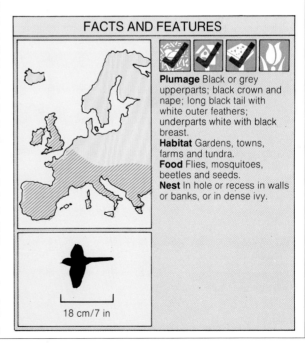

**Plumage** Black or grey upperparts; black crown and nape; long black tail with white outer feathers; underparts white with black breast.
**Habitat** Gardens, towns, farms and tundra.
**Food** Flies, mosquitoes, beetles and seeds.
**Nest** In hole or recess in walls or banks, or in dense ivy.

18 cm/7 in

# YELLOW WAGTAIL *Motacilla flava*

OCCURRING THROUGHOUT MOST OF EUROPE, but now absent from much of Scotland and Ireland, the yellow wagtail has several different forms or races, all of which are fairly distinctive. Space precludes thorough descriptions of them all, but the following is a basic summary. For the most part these long-legged, long-tailed, brightly coloured birds have yellow underparts (the British race being the brightest yellow) and the upperparts are a greenish yellow. The tails are black with white outer feathers. It is the head markings which are the most important for separating the males of the different races. The British race, the yellow wagtail, has a bright yellow forehead and supercilium; the crown and cheeks are yellowish green. The Central European race, the blue-headed, has a bluish grey crown and cheeks, the latter being slightly darker, with a white supercilium. The Scandinavian race, the grey-headed, has a dark grey crown and almost black cheeks. In Italy, the ashy-headed occurs—this is similar to the blue-headed, but with darker cheeks and a less noticeable supercilium. In Spain and the south-east of France the Spanish race is found, again similar to the blue-headed, but with a white supercilium only behind the eye, and a white throat. Other races do occur and interbreeding between races produces yet more variations! A most complex group. Females and juveniles are virtually indistinguishable in the field.

It is a water-loving bird preferring marshland, wet meadows, gravel pits, moorland, sewage farms and river valleys. Often found in association with grazing cattle or sheep, it runs on the ground between the animals picking up insects disturbed by their feet, sometimes even resting on the animals' backs between snacks. Its diet is almost entirely of insects, although small molluscs are also eaten.

The nest is usually on the ground, in a hollow, and is constructed of grasses and roots, and lined with hair.

Like other wagtails this species moves its tail up and down in a wagging motion, the call, uttered mostly in flight, is a shrill *tsweep* or *tswee-ip* and the song is a short warble. The flight is strong and undulating.

The yellow wagtail is not usually found in gardens unless the grounds are large or contain a pond, or a marshy area with reeds—their favourite communal roosting site.

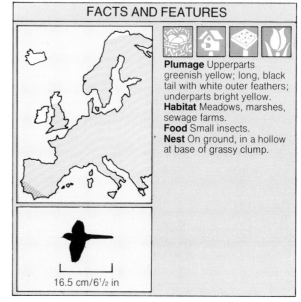

## FACTS AND FEATURES

**Plumage** Upperparts greenish yellow; long, black tail with white outer feathers; underparts bright yellow.
**Habitat** Meadows, marshes, sewage farms.
**Food** Small insects.
**Nest** On ground, in a hollow at base of grassy clump.

16.5 cm/6½ in

*Several races showing different head colourings occur in Europe. These vary from entirely black to combinations of blue and grey, with or without white stripes above the eye. The British race has a greenish yellow head.*

# GREY WAGTAIL *Motacilla cinerea*

A PARTIAL MIGRANT, the grey wagtail occurs in most of Europe with the exception of Scandinavia, where it is present only in the south: in much of Denmark and the Netherlands it occurs only in winter or on passage. It is longer-tailed than other wagtails in the region and its wagging motion is more accentuated. Despite being called the grey wagtail, indicating a drab bird, it is very similar to the yellow wagtail, with which it is frequently confused, and any winter records of a yellow wagtail will certainly refer to this species. Upperparts, including crown and cheeks, are bluish grey, the rump greenish yellow, the wing feathers blackish and the supercilium white. In the male, during the summer, the throat is black with a white moustachial stripe either side, while in the female, and the male in winter, the throat is white. The rest of the underparts are yellow—noticeably on the breast and vent, but paler on the belly and flanks. The tail is black and the outer feathers white. Juveniles are grey above, the rump is dull greyish green and buff below with a yellow vent. The call is a shrill *tsizee*, and the song is a trilling warble.

Almost always encountered near fast-flowing water, its favourite habitat is in mountain streams, or where there is tumbling, turbulent water, but it also frequents lakes, slow-moving rivers and, in winter, small ditches, ponds and cress beds.

It runs or walks along the water's edge, or perches on boulders and flits into the air to catch passing insects; it also picks food from or near the surface of the water. Its diet consists of insects and their water-borne larvae, and small crustaceans.

The nest, a cup of grasses, roots and moss, lined with hair, is seldom far from water. It is usually on a ledge, or in a crevice or hole in the river bank. Grey wagtails can be encouraged to breed by providing an open-fronted nestbox or ledge under a bridge, or in thick ivy on stone, or walls, near weirs or mill races.

This most attractive bird is encountered in gardens only if a river or stream runs nearby, or a pond is present, but it may be heard flying over, especially in winter, when going to roost—this is the only time these birds are gregarious, gathering together in trees by the water's edge.

## FACTS AND FEATURES

**Plumage** Upperparts bluish grey with black wings; underparts white with bright yellow on breast and undertail coverts.
**Habitat** Fast-flowing rivers and streams, mill races, cress beds.
**Food** Insects, larvae, small fry.
**Nest** On a ledge, or in a crevice in river bank or in thick ivy on stone.

19 cm/7½ in

*The grey wagtail has the longest tail of this family, and so its movements are very pronounced. It favours fast-flowing, shallow streams with rock or gravel edges. Nests are often placed on a ledge or in a crevice in the river bank.*

# STARLING *Sternus vulgaris*

THE STARLING is one of the commonest birds of Europe, and is found in all areas in the breeding season, except in Iberia, where it is replaced by the spotless starling. Familiar to all, the starling is a stocky bird with a long, pointed bill. In summer, adults are blackish overall, with a green and purplish gloss, with brownish edgings to the wing feathers. In late autumn and winter, adults change into a more speckled appearance, being heavily spotted with white below and buff spots on the back; the yellow bill changes to brown. Juvenile birds are greyish brown overall with a whitish throat, becoming very patchy with darker adult plumage appearing in late autumn.

The starling has no clearly defined song, but utters various grunts, whistles, clicks and warbles, and is a marvellous mimic often imitating other bird calls including chicken noises.

Its diet consists mainly of earthworms, insects, spiders and snails; it will also eat seeds, fruit, berries and cereals. Starlings will also eat practically anything put out in the garden in the way of scraps, and they can take over the feeding area, chasing smaller birds away. They hawk for flying ants and other insects in the air rather like a swallow. The nest is almost always in a cavity or in holes in trees, buildings or rocks—sometimes in ivy. The nesting holes are conspicuous by the accumulation of droppings outside. The nest itself is very untidy, made of straw and lined with leaves, wool and feathers.

After the breeding season, starlings gather in huge flocks to roost communally, with birds flying quite long distances to join in. Willows, pine plantations and copses are favoured, as well as buildings in towns and cities—London is famous for them. Flocks perform aerial convolutions and chirp vociferously before suddenly diving into the roost, and then silence falls. Many of the birds of the northern and eastern populations move south and west in winter to swell the numbers of birds in the south.

Despite being a common garden visitor, the starling remains remarkably shy in most areas, so if food is put out for them and for smaller birds it is best to separate it, some close to the house for the smaller birds and some further away for the starlings. They may also investigate any nestboxes in the garden and often nest in the roofs of houses where holes will allow them entrance.

*In winter plumage, the starling is heavily spotted and the bill is not completely yellow. At other times, both sexes are almost entirely glossy black shot with purple and green. Young birds are mousy brown, but attain darker feathers gradually through the summer.*

## FACTS AND FEATURES

**Plumage** In summer, blackish overall with purple, green and blue sheen and yellow bill. In winter, becomes spotted above and below; bill becomes brown.
**Habitat** Gardens, towns, villages, parks, farmland, woods and cliff faces.
**Food** Worms, spiders, insects, seeds, fruit and berries.
**Nest** In a hole or cavity in buildings, trees or rocks.

21.5 cm/8½ in

# GOLDEN ORIOLE *Oriolus oriolus*

ONE OF THE MOST SPECTACULAR of European birds, the golden oriole is a summer visitor which winters in Africa. The body of the male is a beautiful, golden yellow contrasting with the almost solidly black wings. The tail is also black with yellow corners, and there is a blackish stripe immediately behind a reddish-brown bill. Females are similarly patterned, but the yellow is replaced by dull greenish above, and off-white below, slightly streaked with brown. Old females, however, can resemble the adult male, but the yellow is less intense. Young individuals recall the plumage of the normal female, but are speckled yellow above and less streaked below. The flight is heavily undulating and ends in a characteristic upward sweep into the tree canopy.

With such bright colouring, and marked patterning you would expect to be able to see this bird easily, but this is not the case, for it is particularly secretive. Furthermore, the colouration, although startling in open situations, acts as a superb camouflage when the bird is sitting in a heavily-leaved tree. The song, therefore, will probably be the only indication of the presence of this species. It consists of an unmistakable, loud fluty whistle of *weela-whee-oh.* Calls include harsh jay-like notes.

This species breeds throughout much of Europe, except Scandinavia, but there have been recent indications of some range extension, for several pairs are now breeding regularly in Britain. It is very much a bird of broad-leaved, mixed woodland, riverine forests, parks and orchards, but it has a particular liking for poplar plantations. The nest is located in the fork of a branch,

and is suspended from it by the rim. The female makes the construction out of grass, strips of bark and wool, and lines it with hair.

The diet of the golden oriole consists of large insects including beetles and their larvae, caterpillars and fruit and berries. It obtains its food mainly from the tree canopy, and rarely descends to the ground. With its liking for tree-lined avenues and orchards, it is possible that it will visit gardens bordering on such areas.

## FACTS AND FEATURES

**Plumage** Male: bright yellow; wings and tail mainly black with some yellow. Female: yellow green with some streaking on the underparts; older females become yellower with age.
**Habitat** Parks, mixed broad-leaved woodland, riverine forests and poplar plantations.
**Food** Large insects, caterpillars, fruit and berries.
**Nest** Placed in a tree fork.

24 cm/9½ in

*The golden oriole has extended its range as a breeding bird northwards to Britain. However, it is commoner in the Mediterranean area. Although brightly coloured, it is difficult to see because of its secretive habits.*

# JAY *Garrulus glandarius*

A SECRETIVE, THOUGH NOISY BIRD, the jay is widely distributed throughout Europe, missing only from parts of Scandinavia, Scotland and Ireland. Its range appears to be increasing in Scotland and Ireland due to afforestation. The plumage is distinctive: the back and nape are brownish, contrasting with black wings, which have a large white patch across the inner secondaries, and a blue, black and white patch on the coverts. It has a white rump, which is especially conspicuous in flight; the underparts are a delicate brownish pink, and the vent and throat are white. Black and white crown feathers can be raised to form a thick crest; and there are heavy, thick, black moustaches on the face. The bill is heavy and blackish; the tail is also black. The call is a harsh *kraaag* or *kahk*. The flight is slow and heavy, with jerky beats of rounded wings; it also hops on the ground.

The jay is largely dependent on the oak for its main food source, the acorn, and it can be found in any wooded habitat including mixed deciduous woodland, coniferous forests, orchards, parks and gardens. It will eat pine seeds, acorns, beechnuts, fruit, large insects including beetles, caterpillars, slugs and spiders, and is not averse to stealing eggs, or young birds, from the nests of smaller, woodland bird species during the breeding season. The jay is well-known for burying acorns in the ground in autumn, as a reserve supply for the winter, coming back and unearthing them when food is scarce. Thus jays play an important role in spreading the oak to new areas.

The untidy nest, usually situated in a tall bush or tree, is constructed of twigs, sticks and earth, and then neatly lined with roots and hair.

Most often seen in pairs or small parties, large movements may occur in autumn, when sizeable flocks of jays migrate south and westwards, searching for food after the crop in their own country fails.

A shy, wary bird, in most areas it will, however, visit gardens in well-wooded situations, especially if thick hedges are present. It can then become very tame and a frequent visitor to the bird table.

## FACTS AND FEATURES

**Plumage** Brownish pink overall, browner on back; black wings with blue, black and white patch; white rump. Black tail, streaked crown and large, black moustachial streaks.
**Habitat** Deciduous woodland, preferring oak, parks, gardens and orchards.
**Food** Acorns, beetles, fruit, nuts, eggs and nestlings, small mammals.
**Nest** Tall bush or tree.

34 cm/13½ in

*During the autumn, parties of jays occasionally visit urban gardens to provide observers with spectacular views of this handsome crow (below). In the breeding season, however, it is very secretive and rarely allows close inspection; the most that can be expected is a fleeting glimpse of a white rump as it moves through the tree canopy.*

# MAGPIE *Pica pica*

*In the more urban areas, the magpie has increased dramatically and is in danger of becoming a serious threat to many garden-nesting birds because of its nest-robbing habit. The reason for the increase is due in part to the bird's ability to utilize the natural habitats found along railway embankments and canals which lead into the hearts of towns.*

THE MAGPIE is widespread throughout Europe, though rare in parts of Scotland. Its pied plumage and long tail make it very distinctive. The head, breast, back and rump are black while the belly, flanks and scapulars are white. The wings and back are glossy black, with bluish green and reddish purplish sheens. Juveniles are duller, with no gloss and a short tail. In flight, the wedge-shaped tail is obvious, and some white shows in the primaries. The call is a loud *chak-chak-chak* or *cha-har-ack*. The tail is often held up at an angle when the bird is strutting along; it also has a curious sideways hopping movement, and it is wary, though inquisitive.

It is a bird of open country and farmland, in particular moorland and parks, but it spreads into urban areas where suitable large trees for nesting are evident. In some southern counties of England it appears to be increasing in numbers. In the past many people persecuted the magpie through superstition; gamekeepers in particular persecuted it because of its habit of eating the eggs and young of pheasant and partridge. The magpie is still considered by many to be vermin and it is generally discouraged.

The magpie builds its bulky nest on the edge of woodland, in trees, in hedges, in bushes, and, in some parts of Europe, on electricity pylons. The nest is a domed structure, with a small side opening; it is made of sticks, twigs and earth, and lined with roots and hair.

Its diet is broad, ranging from large insects and small mammals, to eggs and birds. It will also eat carrion, frequently being seen eating birds and mammals killed by road traffic, as well as cereals, fruit, berries, slugs and worms. It is often seen near human habitation looking through garbage for anything edible. Like the rest of the

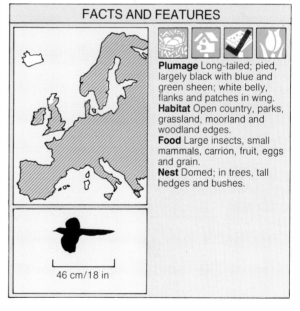

## FACTS AND FEATURES

**Plumage** Long-tailed; pied, largely black with blue and green sheen; white belly, flanks and patches in wing.
**Habitat** Open country, parks, grassland, moorland and woodland edges.
**Food** Large insects, small mammals, carrion, fruit, eggs and grain.
**Nest** Domed; in trees, tall hedges and bushes.

46 cm/18 in

crow family, the magpie hides and stores food, and has been accused of stealing bright objects and hiding them, but this is probably only folklore.

The magpie is becoming a more frequent visitor to gardens and will visit feeding stations, usually picking up scraps and taking them away. It attacks milk bottle tops to drink milk and birds have been known regularly to open egg cartons delivered to the doorstep and to devour the contents. It is not to be encouraged, because of its habit of eating the eggs and young of other birds that may be nesting in the garden.

# JACKDAW *Corvus monedula*

THIS SMALL MEMBER OF THE CROW FAMILY has steadily been increasing in numbers and increasing its range in Europe during the last century—this is probably due to the extension of cultivated land. It is common in most areas except northern Scandinavia, from where it is absent. The back, wings and tail are glossy black with a bluish and greenish sheen, and separated from a glossy black cap and throat by a grey nape and sides of head. The underparts are greyish black, the eyes pearl-grey, and the short, stubby, dark bill is feathered at the base. Juveniles are browner, without the gloss, and the eye is brown. A slightly different race occurs in Scandinavia: it has a paler nape and a small white patch on either side of the neck. In flight it is more pigeon-like than other crows, being smaller, with a short bill and quicker wingbeats. It is also very agile—swooping on closed wings and performing various aerial acrobatics. The call is a familiar *tchak* or *tchak-ak* and *kaarr*.

Jackdaws inhabit villages, towns, farmland, woodland, sea cliffs and old quarries. Highly gregarious, they are often seen feeding with starlings and rooks on the ground. They are also opportunists, feeding on rubbish from litter bins in many towns and parks. They are commonly seen in gardens, where they will take scraps and fly off to eat them. The jackdaw's main diet consists of insects, grubs, fruit, nut, berries and, like the magpie, eggs and nestlings. It has been known to bury food.

It is a colonial nester, and birds choose to build in holes or crevices in trees, walls, rock faces and buildings, especially ruins. The nest is built of sticks and twigs, and is lined with earth, hair and wool—jackdaws can be seen sitting on the backs of sheep and cows plucking the wool or hair from them. They will also nest in the bottom of rooks' or herons' nests, or in chimneys, where the accumulation of twigs and sticks over a period of years can cause problems.

Jackdaws roost communally at all times of the year, and you can meet flocks of several hundred in woodlands or on cliffs.

If scraps are put out in the garden, the jackdaw is likely to come—they are said to be very fond of macaroni cheese! Nestboxes in old trees may also entice them.

*The smallest of the black crows to be found in the region, the jackdaw is separated from all other species by its greyish nape, sides of head and eyes. It commonly breeds in buildings.*

## FACTS AND FEATURES

**Plumage** Glossy black overall, with blue and green sheen; sides of head and nape grey. Short bill, feathered at base to upper mandible.
**Habitat** Towns, villages, sea cliffs, farmland, woods and ruins.
**Food** Large insects, fruit, nuts, berries and eggs.
**Nest** In holes or crevices in cliffs, ruins, trees and walls.

33 cm/13 in

# ROOK *Corvus frugilegus*

EVERYONE HAS SEEN A ROOKERY, a noisy, busy colony of these sociable birds, which can be found anywhere near suitable agricultural land. The rook is found in much of Europe, from central, southern France northwards to southern Scandinavia. Since they obtain food from the ground, northern populations move south to Iberia and the Mediterranean when the ground is frozen.

The plumage is black glossed with purple, green and blue sheens. The bare face and chin, at the base of the bill, are pale grey in colour and denote the adults. The long, pointed bill is black. Juveniles are duller, lacking the glossy sheen and they have a fully feathered face. The calls are varied—the best known is a *caw* or *kaa*, with a higher *kaaa-ah* note during bowing and tail-fanning.

The flight is similar to that of the crow, but the wingbeats are more rapid. In late autumn and early spring, flocks or pairs perform a pursuit display flight: they also indulge in tumbling, rolling and diving.

A bird of open country, the rook prefers open, agricultural land with stands of large trees and woods, riverine forests, marshy grassland and parks.

They probe for worms, caterpillars, beetles and various insect larvae, especially leatherjackets, but they also rely on grain to form the staple part of their diet. Other items of food include acorns, molluscs, potatoes and roots. Like other members of the crow family, they store or hide food, usually acorns, in the ground.

Rooks nest communally. Rookeries containing just a few nests are not unusual, and most are under 50 pairs, but some contain hundreds or even thousands of nests.

One rookery in Scotland has had 6,000 nests present. Consisting of a bulky cup of sticks, twigs and earth, the nest is lined with grass, leaves, roots, hair and moss.

In winter, rooks form roosts with birds from several rookeries, often with jackdaws—these can be enormous, containing tens of thousands of birds.

Rooks will visit gardens, though mainly in winter, and they will eat almost anything in the way of scraps, such as meat, bread, potatoes and fruit, cooked or otherwise.

## FACTS AND FEATURES

**Plumage** Black, glossed with green, blue and purple sheens. Bare face and chin at base of long, pointed bill greyish white. Baggy, loose feathered thighs.
**Habitat** Agricultural land, riverine forests, parks and grassland with stands of large trees.
**Food** Worms, caterpillars, leatherjackets, acorns and grain.
**Nest** Communal; in rookery high up in trees.

45.5 cm/18 in

*The rook is distinguished from the similar sized carrion crow by its bare, white face (feathered in juveniles), its glossy black plumage and elongated thigh feathers. They often form large flocks numbering several thousands of individuals and are thought by many to be a pest.*

# CARRION/HOODED CROW *Corvus corone*

*In the foreground is the carrion crow with the hooded crow behind. As these two interbreed, plumages in between the two occur. Note that the bill is heavier than the rook's and that it has bristles at the base.*

THESE ARE TWO DIFFERENT RACES of the same species. They are geographically separated, although overlaps in distribution do occur, and they do interbreed. The carrion crow is all black, the hooded crow is black and ash-grey. Found throughout Europe, both races migrate south, like the rook, when feeding becomes difficult, in winter. Most of the British population is resident throughout the year. The hooded crow is found in the north and east of Europe, the carrion crow is confined to western, central and southern Europe. The plumage in the carrion crow is entirely black with a glossy blue and green sheen; in the hooded crow, back, rump, scapulars, lower breast, belly flanks and undertail coverts are ash-grey, and all the rest is black. In both races, the sexes are similar. The bill is stout and black, and the base of the upper mandible is covered with bristles. Juveniles are browner than adults and lack the glossy sheen. Hybrids usually show grey, blotched with black or brown.

The usual call is a croaking *kraa-kraa-kraa*. The flight is similar to the rook's, but slower, rarely indulging in aerial acrobatics.

Both crows inhabit similar terrain, preferring farmland, moorland, sea coasts, villages, towns, parkland and open woodland. Their habitats are more varied than those of rooks or jackdaws.

They are ground-feeders, picking up or probing for worms, insects and their larvae, frogs, small mammals, birds including nestlings, eggs and carrion. On the sea-shore, they select crabs and various molluscs, picking them up and gaining height, then dropping them to break them open. They sometimes repeat this process several times. They also take cereals, fruit and potatoes.

The nest, although usually in a tree, can be built in bushes, on cliff ledges or in buildings, if no tall vegetation is available on the ground. It consists of an outer layer of sticks, plant stems or seaweed, bound with earth and grass, and lined with moss, hair and wool.

One of their activities which is difficult to explain is that they will pick up an object, such as a stick, fly up and drop it, only to pick it up again and repeat the action, which is similar to the method for breaking open food items. No rational explanation has yet been put forward other than that it is a form of play.

These crows are very wary, but they will visit gardens for bread, scraps and fruit, especially in winter.

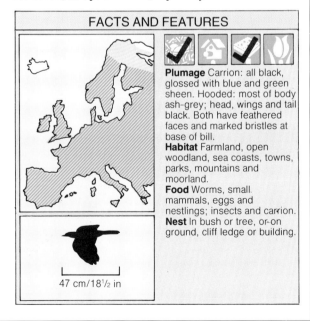

## FACTS AND FEATURES

**Plumage** Carrion: all black, glossed with blue and green sheen. Hooded: most of body ash-grey; head, wings and tail black. Both have feathered faces and marked bristles at base of bill.
**Habitat** Farmland, open woodland, sea coasts, towns, parks, mountains and moorland.
**Food** Worms, small mammals, eggs and nestlings; insects and carrion.
**Nest** In bush or tree, or on ground, cliff ledge or building.

47 cm/18½ in

# WAXWING *Bombycilla garrulus*

IT IS QUITE DIFFICULT to describe the colours of a waxwing correctly—many bird books fail to do justice, either in words or pictures, to this subtly attractive bird. It is basically a rather pale pinkish-brown and darker on the upperparts. There are, however, a number of obvious distinguishing features: a fairly long and conspicuous crest, a short, slightly decurved bill, a black mask to the face (giving the bird a slightly severe expression), a short black bib narrowly edged with white at the base of the bill and, often, a long-necked appearance. The lower back and rump are grey, shading down to a black tail with a broad yellow tip; the undertail coverts are a rich, dark chestnut brown. Most striking of all, at close quarters, are the wings, with their white and bright-yellow markings and waxy red tips to the secondaries. Juveniles are much duller, lacking the black throat, and with streaked underparts.

Waxwings will perch high in trees, or sit on television aerials and wires, and sometimes remain immobile for long periods. When feeding, they are often very mobile and aerobatic, and at all times are likely to be calling—a very characteristic thin, rather feeble, trilling *sirrr . . .* note. Their flight is strong and direct and, on the wing, they have an outline and flight-action which strongly recalls a starling.

They are winter visitors to most of Europe (mainly the northern half), but irregular in most places and in varying numbers. Periodically when a failure of their winter food supply in the north follows a good breeding season, they erupt in large numbers. Singletons, small parties and sometimes large flocks may then appear almost anywhere.

Since berries are their main food, they frequently appear in gardens and feed on berberis, cotoneaster, pyracantha, rowan and many others; they will also come readily to apples left on the tree. They can be ridiculously tame and many are killed by cats, or become traffic victims on busy roads.

On their breeding grounds, in the forests of the far north, they are largely insectivorous and, indeed, on mild winter days will sometimes catch insects on the wing.

## FACTS AND FEATURES

**Plumage** Breast and crest pinkish, upperparts brownish chestnut. Rump grey; tail blackish with yellow tip. Vent and undertail coverts rusty chestnut. Black throat patch and thin black line through eye; bill black, crest very soft and light.
**Habitat** Coniferous forests, trees alongside rivers, gardens with berry-bearing bushes.
**Food** Chiefly insects, berries, buds and fruit.
**Nest** In trees—a cup of twigs and grass.

19 cm/7½ in

*Unmistakable, except perhaps in flight when it may resemble a starling, the waxwing derives its name from the waxy red tips to the secondaries. It is very acrobatic when feeding on berries in tree tops and, from below, the yellow tip to the tail and the chestnut undertail are obvious.*

# WREN *Troglodytes troglodytes*

COMMON THROUGHOUT EUROPE, except in the far north of Scandinavia, this tiny, stumpy little bird, with a short tail is a frequent visitor to gardens. The upperparts are a rufous brown with fine dark barring, the wings are more heavily barred and the outer wing feathers have pale buff spots. The head has a pale buff eye stripe and a shortish slightly decurved bill. The underparts are buff, the flanks barred darker and the undertail coverts are brownish spotted with white. The short tail, often held cocked up, is brown with darker barring. The call is a sharp, hard *tick tick* and a harsh *churr*. The song, a rattling trill, is explosive and very loud considering the size of the bird.

The short flights made on whirring wings are fast and direct. The wren's favourite habitats are in dark, tangled cover, often in swampy ground, especially reedbeds, woodland and forests with dense undergrowth, brambles, rocks and crevices along streams and on cliff faces, gardens and parks. The wren is found from the sea-shore to high altitudes, and is constantly on the move, like a small mouse, usually low down in vegetation, searching in all cracks and crevices for its food, which consists of spiders, small beetles, mosquitoes, caterpillars, ants, earwigs and millipedes. It will often enter open windows of houses and search in rooms for insects.

The nest, usually situated low down in ivy, hedges, or in holes in walls or trees, is a domed structure. The male will make several nests of leaves, grass, plant stems and moss, and the female will then make her choice. When a suitable one is selected the nest is then lined with feathers.

The male, however, is polygamous and will try to entice other females to use the other nests. It is unlikely to be attracted to nestboxes, but will often build in sheds and outhouses, even those in constant use. It sometimes chooses odd places such as old boots or coat pockets.

The wren is not a frequent visitor to the bird table, but may be seen on lawns pecking up crumbs. In cold weather wrens may roost communally: nestboxes and old house martin nests seem to be favourite places.

## FACTS AND FEATURES

**Plumage** Rufous brown with dark barring, pale buff eye stripe, undertail coverts tipped white.
**Habitat** Swampy ground, undergrowth in woodland, parks and gardens, tangled cover.
**Food** Flies, small beetles, spiders, ants and earwigs.
**Nest** Domed; in ivy, holes in walls or bases of trees.

9.5 cm/3¾ in

*The wren's short, cocked tail and rufous-brown, barred upperparts are very distinctive, but their presence is obvious only during the breeding season. At this time, they may be seen delivering their loud, explosive song from an exposed perch, especially early in the morning.*

# DIPPER *Cinclus cinclus*

*Although the dipper may be seen in lowland areas during the winter months (especially in coastal situations), it is a species which prefers fast-flowing, moorland streams. Nests are usually placed on rocky ledges in river banks in hanging vegetation (above) or under bridges and sometimes behind waterfalls.*

UNLESS YOU HAVE A SWIFT-FLOWING, river stream actually running through your garden, this remarkable hill-stream bird will not be a garden bird in the true sense. It may, however, be a regular neighbour if your garden adjoins such a stream—a common enough situation in many upland areas in Britain and Europe. As suggested elsewhere, strategically placed stones or perhaps a suitably contrived stretch of stony 'shore', might encourage dippers to stop where you can watch them—and few birds are as much fun to watch.

Dippers are stocky birds with short tails and rather sturdy legs—not unlike giant wrens in appearance. They are basically black-brown with a prominent white breast, bordered with dark chestnut below (but this chestnut is absent in some northern areas); another immediately noticeable feature is the bird's white eyelids. Juveniles are much greyer, with pale markings on the upperparts and mottled grey and white underparts. The flight is fast and direct, usually low over the water and often with the accompaniment of a sharp, distinctive *zit-zat* call. Dippers sing loudly and quite musically, usually from a rock or similar vantage-point in midstream.

The really remarkable thing about dippers is the way they are at home in the wildest and most turbulent streams. They perch on stones and boulders and commonly seek their insect and invertebrate prey on or around these, or by wading in the shallows—but they are equally likely to wade into deep rushing water (or to plunge into it) and disappear. They can actually walk on the stream bed, using their powerful feet to grip the stones as they search for food! They swim well, though usually

## FACTS AND FEATURES

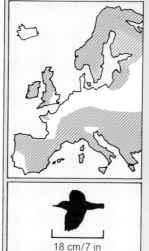

**Plumage** Adult: upperparts blackish brown, head browner; breast, throat and chin white; chestnut band below; rest of underparts blackish. Northern races lack the chestnut band. Juveniles: greyish; off-white breast scaled with grey.
**Habitat** Streams and rivers, lakesides.
**Food** Small, aquatic insects and their larvae; molluscs and small fish.
**Nest** Domed; built in a hole in banks near water.

18 cm/7 in

only for short distances.

Dippers build a big domed nest, with a side entrance, in recesses under old stone bridges, in walls and banks, or under boulders, invariably above or very close to the water. They also often find a suitable site among the girders or wooden beams and supports of bridges. With a little ingenuity, suitable cavity sites could be provided for them in many situations, or a wooden framework engineered under a bridge. Unfortunately, most modern, concrete bridges on dipper streams are totally unsuitable.

# DUNNOCK *Prunella modularis*

COMMON THROUGHOUT EUROPE, except in parts of Sweden and a large part of Spain, the dunnock, often called the hedge sparrow in Britain, although it is not at all related, is frequently seen in gardens. In adults the head, throat and breast are grey with brownish crown and ear coverts; the back is a dull rufous brown streaked with black; the flanks are also dull rufous with darker streaking; the tail is brown, and there is a thin pale wing-bar. The eye is reddish brown, and the bill is slender and

dark. Juveniles are browner, less rufous on the back and their buffish grey underparts are heavily streaked. They have a muddy brown eye. Often described as a drab bird, on closer inspection it is well marked and quite attractive. The call is a shrill, clear *tseeek* and the song, usually delivered from the top of a bush or hedge, is a repeated short, high, warbling jingle similar to the wren.

It is found in many habitats including gardens, parks, hedges, mixed woodland, young coniferous plantations and moorland scrub, where it may be seen unobtrusively flicking among the low cover, or making short undulating flights, usually low over the ground. It walks, hops and shuffles across open ground, occasionally flicking its wings in the process.

In summer, the dunnock's diet consists of various small insects and spiders; in winter, it lives mainly on seeds of grasses, chickweed and plantains.

The stout, deep, cup-shaped nest, made of plant roots, grass stems, leaves and moss on a foundation of twigs, is built by both adults, lined with wool or hair, and is usually situated in thick hedges, scrub, or low, dense cover, especially in evergreens and conifers. Occasionally old nests of other birds are used. The cuckoo frequently chooses to lay its egg in a dunnock's nest.

The dunnock, although a common garden bird, is usually solitary and is not always obvious. It spends a lot of time at the bottom of hedges picking through the dead leaves for food, but it will appear at tops of hedges to sing, before diving into cover again. It will come out into the open for seeds and crumbs, but rarely visits bird tables.

## FACTS AND FEATURES

**Plumage** Upperparts dull brown with black streaking; head, throat and breast grey; flanks streaked with rufous and black; thin, pale wing-bar.
**Habitat** Parks, gardens, moorland scrub, hedges and mixed woodland.
**Food** Small insects, spiders and seeds.
**Nest** In thick cover, hedges or conifers.

14.5 cm/5³/₄ in

*The dunnock's grey head and underparts are distinctive. When perched in the open, birds display to each other in a curious wing-waving action. They also flick their wings when they are shuffling along the ground in search of insects.*

# SEDGE WARBLER *Acrocephalus schoenobaenus*

*You will know that there is a sedge warbler around when you hear a chattering song and then see a swaying reedstem as the bird makes its jerky progress to the top. Its streaked appearance and creamy supercilium distinguish it from the reed warbler. Sedge warblers are known almost to double their body weight by laying on fat prior to their long migration to Africa in the autumn.*

A SUMMER MIGRANT from Africa to Europe, in the breeding season, the sedge warbler is present throughout much of Europe, except for central Scandinavia, Spain, parts of southern France, and Italy, where it is seen only on migration. The upperparts are brown with blackish streaking; the reddish buff, unstreaked rump is especially noticeable in flight, and the underparts are creamy white with buffish flanks. The prominent, creamy supercilium contrasts with the dark, streaked crown, and the blackish line through the eyes is conspicuous; the cheeks are brownish. Juveniles are yellower and have some fine speckling on the breast.

The call is a sharp scolding *tuc* or *tuc, tuc, tuc* and a *churr*. The song is a fast series of musical and chattering notes, mixed with a considerable amount of mimicry, and uttered from a prominent perch on a bush or on top of a reed stem, or in a vertical song flight.

Although it shares with the reed warbler a liking for wet areas like reedbeds, in which to breed, it nevertheless is not restricted to these and can be found in much drier habitats well away from water. It has been known to take advantage of young forestry plantations, as well as crops—notably that of rape-seed. Ditches with reed fringes or lush vegetation by ponds are also used.

It is a skulking bird, creeping among the vegetation and climbing up plant stems, making short, darting flights from one piece of cover to another. Its food consists mainly of mosquitoes, flies, spiders, small beetles and other insects picked off vegetation or taken in flight. In autumn, it also takes some berries.

The nest, situated on the ground or low down in thick

## FACTS AND FEATURES

**Plumage** Upperparts pale brown streaked with black; unstreaked rump; underparts creamy white; flanks buff. Bold, creamy supercilium contrasting with dark streaks on crown.
**Habitat** Young coniferous plantations, reedbeds, ditches and crops.
**Food** Flies and other small insects, spiders and berries.
**Nest** Low down, or on ground, in thick cover.

13 cm/5 in

cover, occasionally bound to reed stems over water, is a rounded, deep cup on a bulky foundation of grass, plant stems and moss and lined with leaves, hair and down.

The sedge warbler is a species for which there is cause for concern, as numbers seem to be declining at an alarming rate. The main cause is the Sahel drought in West Africa, their principal wintering ground.

You are not likely to see a sedge warbler in your garden unless you have a ditch, pond or river nearby, or unless the garden is on the coast, where migrants stop to rest.

# ICTERINE WARBLER *Hippolais icterina*

A LARGE-BILLED, LONG-WINGED WARBLER, often confused with the reed warbler, breeding in much of western Europe and north to the Arctic Circle. It is regular on passage in central and southern France, Italy and the western Mediterranean, and is seen mainly in autumn in eastern England and Scotland. It winters in Africa.

The adult upperparts are greenish olive, with a pale yellow patch on the folded wing. This does vary,

however, and some adults are greyish with a whitish patch. The underparts are pale to bright yellow, and the supercilium is yellowish. The wings and tail are browner. It is distinguished from the similar melodious warbler by a steeper forehead, and wings which project beyond the base of the tail. The legs are bluish and the bill is long, deep and broad. Juveniles are paler, greyer above and below and have a pale whitish wing-patch. The loud song is repetitive and sustained, and is a varied mixture of both musical, harsh and discordant notes, interspersed with harsh chattering. Other calls include a willow warbler-like *hooeet*, a blackcap-like *tak* and a churring alarm note, when the crown feathers are also raised.

A skulking bird, difficult to see at times, but its movements through undergrowth seem clumsy and heavy. It can be very active and inquisitive, popping out of the undergrowth to scold an intruder.

Preferred habitats are orchards, parks, gardens and hedgerows, bushy riverine scrub, broad-leaved woodland edges, and any cultivated land with trees and bushes.

In summer, food consists mainly of insects picked off the leaves of the tree tops and bushes. In autumn, fruit and berries are also consumed.

The nest is usually high up in the fork of a tree or tall shrub, and is a deep cup of grasses, leaves and roots, bound together (and to the branches) with plant fibre and cobwebs. The lining is hair, grass and feathers.

The icterine warbler is often confused with other warbler species, notably reed and garden warblers, and the melodious warbler (see that species for detailed differences), but with care and good views it should not present a great problem, except perhaps in autumn, when adults can look extremely pale and show no yellow.

Gardens with tall hedges or dense shrubs or those lined with broad-leaved trees should attract them. They may visit in autumn if berry-bearing bushes are present.

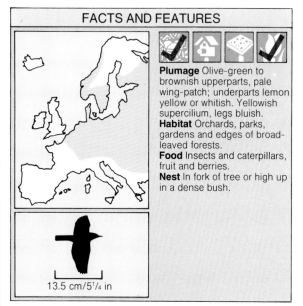

## FACTS AND FEATURES

**Plumage** Olive-green to brownish upperparts, pale wing-patch; underparts lemon yellow or whitish. Yellowish supercilium, legs bluish.
**Habitat** Orchards, parks, gardens and edges of broad-leaved forests.
**Food** Insects and caterpillars, fruit and berries.
**Nest** In fork of tree or high up in a dense bush.

13.5 cm/5¼ in

*In adult plumage, this species can be confused only with its close cousin, the melodious warbler. However, confusion is unlikely as their ranges barely overlap.*

# MELODIOUS WARBLER *Hippolais polyglotta*

THE MELODIOUS WARBLER IS the counterpart of the icterine warbler, breeding in areas south and west of this species, with little overlap. It is a regular passage migrant to Britain, mainly in the south, but it leaves Europe in autumn, to winter in Africa. It is thought that at one time the melodious warbler must have been simply a geographical race of the icterine, but that during the last Ice Age it became separated for such a time that, when the ice receded, the two forms were unable to interbreed.

Hence the two species. The wintering quarters are also well divided between the species. Although split geographically no major difference of habitat is recorded, except that the melodious does seem to select low bushes and ground vegetation more often than the icterine.

The adult's upperparts are brownish-olive (normally browner than in the icterine), and it possesses a rounded rather than a peaked crown, and shorter wings reaching only to the base of the tail, not beyond. In summer, adults may display a pale yellowish wing panel, but this is never as striking as its close relative. The underparts are rich yellow with the legs bluish, or brownish. Juvenile birds lack the yellow underparts, do not have a wing-patch and are generally browner above. In autumn, adults can be very bright or, more usually, a washed-out brown above and creamy-buff below. The long, broad, dagger-like bill is obvious, and is almost out of proportion to the head.

The habitat of the melodious warbler includes clumps of trees in parkland, oak woodland, forest edges; and trees and bushes near water. All habitats usually include low, dense ground cover with lush vegetation. Gardens are frequently used after the breeding season and while on passage. It shows a preference for waterside habitats.

Food consists of small insects and their larvae, and small fruits. The nest is similar in site and construction to that of the icterine—a cup formed of grass, plant fibres and cobwebs, lined with hair and plant down, and placed in a tree fork.

The melodious warbler's song is a long, fast, musical series of notes, quieter and softer than its cousin's, but harsh sounds may be introduced and it is known to mimic. The call is a sparrow-like twitter. A shy, secretive bird, showing itself mostly when in song. In autumn, beware of confusion with young, yellowish willow warblers. It will visit gardens with dense shrubbery and berry bushes, especially those with blackberries.

## FACTS AND FEATURES

**Plumage** Adult upperparts brownish, olive-green; underparts rich yellow. Juveniles: browner above; no yellow on the underparts. Legs bluish, or sometimes brown.
**Habitat** Woodland, parks, gardens and forest edges with dense ground vegetation, often near water.
**Food** Small fruits such as berries; insects and their larvae.
**Nest** High in bush or fork of tree.

13 cm/5 in

*This species has a more westerly range than the similar icterine warbler, from which it may be distinguished by slight differences. These include a less steep forehead, shorter wings, less blue legs and no yellow patch in the wings. The latter, however, can be lost by the icterine warbler in late summer.*

# GARDEN WARBLER *Sylvia borin*

NOT THE MOST APTLY NAMED BIRD, since it seldom visits gardens unless they are large and have dense cover. It is common in northern Europe as a breeding bird, except in Scotland and Ireland, where it is scarce, and Iberia and Italy, where it occurs only as a passage migrant. It is a relatively drab looking warbler, with uniform plumage lacking any distinctive features, a rounded head and a short stubby bill. The upperparts are brownish-olive, and the wings are a darker, greyish brown. The underparts are whitish with buff on the breast. Juveniles are similar. Seldom seen clearly, keeping well hidden in foliage, its presence is detected only by its call, a hard *tac tac* and a grating *churr*, or by its beautiful warbling song, similar to the blackcap's, but longer and lacking the top notes. It can, however, be very difficult to identify at times. When in flight, dashing from one tree or bush to another, and diving into cover, its plump build and uniformity of plumage can help you identify it, but, in autumn especially, it can be confused with the barred warbler.

The garden warbler inhabits mixed woodland and coniferous forest (especially young plantations with dense undergrowth of brambles or bushes), parks and gardens. It chooses sites similar to the blackcap, but it prefers denser undergrowth and can be found in bushy areas lacking in any trees.

The garden warbler's diet consists of caterpillars, small beetles, flies and spiders. In autumn, on passage, when putting on fat for the journey south to its winter quarters in Africa, it feeds a great deal on berries, elder being a favourite.

A cup-shaped nest is built low down in deep cover, and constructed of twigs and grass, and lined with hair.

It is not often seen in gardens, preferring quieter, less open areas, and unless an area of bramble or high, dense hedging is provided, you are unlikely to entice it. However, it may visit gardens for berries in the autumn and, occasionally, in winter, when a few remain in Britain and western Europe.

## FACTS AND FEATURES

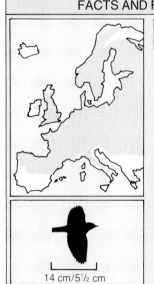

**Plumage** Uniform, no distinguishing features. Upperparts olive, browny grey; underparts whitish buff. Juveniles similar.
**Habitat** Mixed and coniferous woodland with dense undergrowth, bushes and scrub.
**Food** Insects such as flies, caterpillars, small beetles and spiders; berries in autumn.
**Nest** Low, in deep, dense vegetation, or low down in tree.

14 cm/5½ cm

*Although the plumage is nondescript, the song of this species is considered to be the most musical of all the European warblers, and is delivered from a perch in dense cover. During display, the male flutters his wings and spreads his tail while facing the female.*

# BLACKCAP *Sylvia atricapilla*

*The blackcap has a beautiful song which in many respects is similar to the garden warbler's, but it is more varied and has a blackbird's quality about it. Females and birds of the year all have brown caps. Young males obtain their black cap gradually during the autumn.*

♀  ♂

COMMON AND WIDESPREAD throughout Europe, but thinly distributed in Scotland, Ireland and northern Scandinavia, the blackcap is a very distinctive warbler. The body plumage is very similar to the garden warbler: brownish grey above, greyish or buffish white below. The distinguishing characteristic is the crown: glossy black on the male, reddish brown for the female. The upperparts of the male are greyish olive-brown, the wings and tail are darker, and the underparts are greyish white. The female is browner above and more buffy underneath. Juveniles in summer have brown caps, which, in the young males, slowly turn to black during the autumn. The blackcap is not to be confused with the Sardinian warbler, which has more black on the head, and white outer tail feathers.

The call is a harsh *tac* sometimes followed by a *churr*. The short song is very rich and musical, more varied than the similar song of the garden warbler and like a blackbird's, but thinner, consisting of clear, warbling notes, and uttered from dense cover. The flight is fast though jerky. The blackcap seldom travels far and is most often seen flitting from bush to bush.

Favoured habitats of the blackcap are mixed, broad-leaved woodlands, parks and gardens with dense bushes, hedges and shrubs, bramble thickets, clumps of elder, riverine woodland and coniferous forests. The cup-shaped nest, usually low down in a bush or tree, is made of dry grass, roots and moss and lined with hair.

The diet of the blackcap consists of insects and larvae, in the summer, changing in autumn and winter to mainly fruit and berries, such as blackberries, apples, pears, the berries of holly, ivy, the elder and the snowberry.

## FACTS AND FEATURES

**Plumage** Upperparts greyish olive-brown with darker wings; underparts greyish white. Male has black cap; female reddish brown cap.
**Habitat** Mixed broad-leaved woodland, hedges, and bramble in parks and gardens.
**Food** Insects, fruit and berries, especially elderberries and snowberries.
**Nest** Low down in bushes and trees.

14 cm/5½ in

Although mainly regarded as a summer visitor in northern Europe, the blackcap now regularly winters in Britain and Ireland in small numbers; the usual wintering grounds are Italy, southern France, Spain and North Africa, though it has been recorded, even further south.

In the breeding season, the blackcap is attracted to gardens if dense shrubs, bushes and hedges are grown—plant evergreens and snowberry. In autumn and winter, it will visit the garden for berries and the bird table for crumbs, oats and scraps.

# WHITETHROAT *Sylvia communis*

COMMON, AS A BREEDING BIRD, throughout the whole of Europe, the whitethroat, a summer visitor, is declining in numbers due to the drought in the Sahel, its principal wintering quarters. Once the commonest sylvia warbler in Britain, the population crashed in 1969, when only a quarter of the population returned—it has never recovered its former status. However, numbers have marginally improved.

The male upperparts are brownish grey, the wings are chestnut-brown, the head and nape are grey, and the throat is white. The underparts are white, and the breast is suffused with pink in the spring. The outer feathers of the dark tail are white. The female upperparts are similar to the male's but the head is browner and less grey. The breast and flanks are buffer and less pink. Juveniles are browner above than adults, and the white throat is less defined. The underparts are buffish, and the outer tail feathers are dirty white. Adults have a bright, clear, pale brown eye with a clear-cut iris, and a whitish eye ring. In juveniles the eye is a muddy brown. The call is a sharp, hard *tak-tak* with a scolding *churr*. The song, often emitted in a fluttering, dancing flight, is a short, scratchy warble consisting of rapid notes ending in a shrill chatter. It will also sing from a prominent perch on top of a bush or from deep cover.

A skulking, restless bird, constantly on the move, it dives in and out of cover, looping up in display flight, and appearing out of bushes and hedges with its crown feathers raised, its tail fanned and with a scolding voice.

The whitethroat is a bird of varied habitat ranging from low, thorny bushes, brambles, open areas of scrub, hedgerows and commons, to willow beds, banks of ditches and young conifer plantations. It is always found near any form of cultivation.

The diet consists of small insects caught among the foliage and, in the autumn especially, in common with most other sylvia warblers, it eats berries and soft fruit.

The nest, usually sited low down, consists of a loosely built cup of grass and roots made by the male. This is then lined by the female with fine roots, wool and hair.

It is not often seen in gardens in the breeding season. However, on autumn passage, it may be a frequent visitor searching for berries.

## FACTS AND FEATURES

**Plumage** Greyish brown upperparts, chestnut wings. Male: grey head and nape; female: browner grey. Both sexes have white throat and underparts, breast suffused with pink. Outer tail feathers white.
**Habitat** Scrub, thorn bushes and bramble, hedgerows and young coniferous plantations.
**Food** Insects and berries.
**Nest** Low down in vegetation; in thickets, hedges, scrub and tall plants.

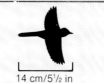

14 cm/5½ in

The whitethroat is a summer visitor which is more likely to be seen between late April and September. It is a skulking species and likes brambles in which to breed (above).

# LESSER WHITETHROAT *Sylvia curruca*

IN EUROPE, less common than the whitethroat, this handsome sylvia warbler, with its dark grey head and cheeks, shows by contrast an even whiter throat; it is also shorter-tailed, more compact and slimmer. It is a summer visitor, occurring mainly in eastern Europe from central France, north to Scandinavia. It is absent from Italy, western and southern France, except on passage, and rare at all times in Iberia. In Britain it is absent from Scotland and much of the north and west of England and Wales. In the breeding season, it is also absent from Ireland. The lesser whitethroat winters in north-east Africa and is one of the few birds, from Britain at least, that has a different migration route in spring and in autumn; it comes up through the Middle-East, Turkey and Greece for the summer, and returns to winter mainly via Italy.

Adults are grey brown above; their wings are darker and they lack the chestnut coloration of the whitethroat. The head has a grey crown, and the cheeks and ear coverts are dark grey, forming a mask across the face, and contrasting vividly with the white throat. The underparts are white, faintly suffused with pink, but less so than in the whitethroat. The tail is dark with white outer feathers. In summer, juveniles are browner above and buffer below, but by autumn they are difficult to separate, the only major difference being the buffish, not white, outer tail feathers. The call is a hard *tacc tacc* and a *charr-rrr*. The song is a soft, low warble followed by a loud, rattling, single note, repeated several times, *chicca-chicca-chicca;* this is usually delivered from cover. Unlike the whitethroat it has no song flight.

The preferred habitat is varied—it haunts parks, gardens, thick hedges, young conifer plantations, open broad-leaved woodland and areas of scrub, scattered bushes and dense foliage.

The nest, usually low down, is made of fine twigs, grass, leaves and cobwebs, and is lined with hair and plant down. It is smaller than that of the whitethroat, but, in common with that species, the nest is started by the male and then lined by the female.

Food largely consists of small insects; berries forming a large part of the diet in autumn. It is more commonly seen in gardens than the whitethroat, providing suitable cover and berry-bearing bushes are present.

## FACTS AND FEATURES

**Plumage** Grey brown above, head grey with dark mask across cheeks and ear coverts. White throat and underparts. Outer tail feathers white. Juveniles: browner above, buffer below.
**Habitat** Parkland, gardens, thick hedges and open broad-leaved woodland.
**Food** Small insects and berries.
**Nest** In thick, dark cover. Sited low down in undergrowth, tall shrubs or conifers.

13.5 cm/5¼ in

*Although less brightly coloured than its cousin, the whitethroat, the lesser whitethroat looks more streamlined and shorter tailed. Its most outstanding plumage feature is the blackish grey ear coverts.*

# SARDINIAN WARBLER *Sylvia melanocephala*

RESIDENT AND COMMON around the Mediterranean countries and central Iberia, the Sardinian warbler is rare elsewhere. In Britain, it has been only rarely recorded, mainly on the south coast. Similar in appearance to the blackcap, this warbler may be distinguished by its larger, dark cap and red eye ring. In the male, the upperparts are dark grey, with dark brown wings and tail, the latter having the outer tips white. The underparts are whitish, with a pure white chin and throat, and the flanks are grey. The hood or cap, which extends below the eye, is glossy black and there is a red eye ring. The female is similar to the male, but is brown above with buff flanks. The hood is dark greyish brown, and the eye ring is less red and more brownish. Juveniles are browner above and the tips to the outer tail feathers are brownish white. Beware of confusion with the orphean warbler which is similar, but much larger, and with whitish eyes, but also with white outer tail feathers and a hood.

The call is a *tack-tack,* and the song resembles a whitethroat, but is longer, more musical and includes a rattling alarm note. The flight is direct and undulating.

The Sardinian warbler can be extremely skulking, creeping about in dense undergrowth, showing only its head for brief periods, or flitting from bush to bush when its long, white-tipped tail becomes obvious. Equally, it can be seen singing from an exposed perch on top of a bush, fanning and cocking its tail in the process, at which time the crown feathers may be raised.

Favoured habitats are oaks, pines, orange and olive groves, parks, gardens, thorny scrub, oak woods, vineyards and urban areas. The diet consists mainly of small insects and larvae, also fruit and berries.

The untidy, saucer-shaped nest is fairly large and is constructed of grass and cobwebs—a cup is then built of down, and lined with fine grass or hair.

The Sardinian warbler is noticeably affected by hard weather: some areas, especially the south of France, have lost almost their entire populations in severe winters.

It is found in gardens, even in the most urban areas, providing dense foliage is present and disturbance is at a minimum. Plenty of evergreen shrubs, brambles and dense hedging will encourage it to visit and to breed; berry-bearing plants may entice it in winter.

## FACTS AND FEATURES

**Plumage** Dark grey or brownish grey upperparts; underparts whitish; chin and throat pure white. Tips to outer tail feathers white. Male has glossy black hood; female has greyish brown.
**Habitat** Olive groves, parks, gardens, oakwoods and scrub.
**Food** Small insects, fruit, seed and berries.
**Nest** In shrubs or brambles, often low down.

13.5 cm/5¼ in

*The Sardinian warbler is a typical bird of the warmer regions of Europe where it is almost entirely resident. Its black cap and red eye ring help to separate it from the larger orphean warbler. It is commonly found in gardens with a reasonable amount of low scrub.*

# WILLOW WARBLER *Phylloscopus trochilus*

*Although there are slight plumage differences between this species and the chiffchaff, the only reliable way to separate them is by their song. Nests are usually placed on the ground at the end of a grass tunnel.*

THE WILLOW WARBLER is the commonest *phylloscopus* warbler of the region. It is a summer migrant, inhabiting all of central and northern Europe and a small area of Spain. It is otherwise absent from Iberia, the extreme south of France and other Mediterranean countries, except on passage. A small percentage of the population winters in Portugal and the extreme southern areas of Europe; the main wintering grounds are in Africa.

Very similar in appearance to the chiff chaff, it is usually a slimmer, brighter looking bird with longer wings and a flatter head. However, the distinctive song is the only reliable characteristic in the field. Adult upperparts are olive-green to brownish green, including the crown. The supercilium is pale yellowish. The underparts are whitish with variable amounts of yellowish streaking, and the undertail coverts are yellowish. The legs are usually pale brown, but can be dark and are not a reliable field characteristic to separate it from the chiff chaff, which usually has dark blackish legs. Juveniles are initially browner than adults, but, in autumn, they are very similar, though usually much brighter and yellower below, with little white. The northern and eastern races of the willow warbler are greyer above and much whiter below.

The call is a *tso-eet* and the song is a beautiful cascade, beginning quietly, becoming clearer and stronger, descending into a flourishing, *tsooet-tsooew*.

Favoured haunts of the willow warbler are broad-leaved woodland featuring tall ground vegetation, riverine forests, birch woods, copses, scrub and parkland, in which it is extremely active, constantly foraging for food among the leaves and branches, and pausing only to sing. It frequently hovers in front of leaves searching for insects and it flycatches proficiently, flying out from a suitable perch and catching passing flies with an audible snap of the bill. On migration it also frequents reedbeds, hedgerows and orchards.

Flies, aphids, small caterpillars, small spiders and beetles are the main diet, but small berries and worms are also taken.

The nest, built by the female, almost always on the ground, in thick grass or beneath shrubs, is a domed structure with a side entrance, built of grass, moss and fine roots, and lined with feathers.

Outside the breeding season, it is commonly seen in gardens, searching for insects, especially among willow and fruit trees.

## FACTS AND FEATURES

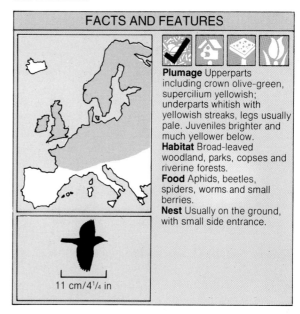

**Plumage** Upperparts including crown olive-green, supercilium yellowish; underparts whitish with yellowish streaks, legs usually pale. Juveniles brighter and much yellower below.
**Habitat** Broad-leaved woodland, parks, copses and riverine forests.
**Food** Aphids, beetles, spiders, worms and small berries.
**Nest** Usually on the ground, with small side entrance.

11 cm/4¼ in

113

# CHIFFCHAFF *Phylloscopus collybita*

THE FIRST OF THE SUMMER MIGRANTS to reach northern Europe, the chiffchaff arrives in Britain in mid-March. It has a similar but wider distribution in Europe than the willow warbler, except in Scandinavia and Scotland, where there are large, unexplained gaps. The chiffchaff breeds throughout the whole of Europe and, although most of the population winters in North Africa, some overwinter in southern Britain and Spain. Two main races occur and the northern races *albietinus* or *tristis* can be seen in Britain, mainly in autumn, on passage. The gaps in distribution in Scandinavia are thought to have been caused by the last Ice Age, when the population was split; since then the eastern form has moved westwards, and the southern race northwards.

Dumpier in appearance than the willow warbler, with a more rounded crown, and usually shorter wings, the chiffchaff is at once identified by its two note song *psilp psap* or *chiff chaff.* The upperparts are olive-brown to brown, seldom as green looking as the willow warbler, with a creamy supercilium. The underparts are buffish brown to buff, giving an overall drab appearance. The legs are usually dark brown, but pale legs have been known, though these are much rarer than willow warblers with dark legs. Juveniles are browner overall than adults, but appear similar in autumn. The northern race is greyer above, sometimes with a pale wing-bar, and whiter below. The call is a *hweet*, more pronounced than the similar *tsooeet* of the willow warbler. The song can be variable, including churring notes and phrases of *psilp-psilp-psilp-psap;* all notes are deliberate and well spaced.

When moving through the tree canopy, flitting from twig to twig, the chiffchaff flicks its wings and tail while searching for small insects and their larvae, spiders and small caterpillars. It makes frequent darting sorties to catch passing aerial insects and also hovers, picking prey from the underside of leaves.

It chooses broad-leaved or coniferous forest, parks, gardens and open areas of woodland and shrubs in which to build its nest. This, like the willow warbler's is domed, but generally above the ground. Made of plant stems and moss on a base of dead leaves, it is lined with feathers.

It frequently occurs in large gardens, but on passage may be seen in many different habitats.

## FACTS AND FEATURES

**Plumage** Upperparts olive-brown to brown, creamy white supercilium. Underparts buff. Legs usually dark. Juveniles similar.
**Habitat** Mixed broad-leaved woodland or coniferous forest and plantations, parks and gardens.
**Food** Flies, small caterpillars, aphids and small beetles.
**Nest** Often in hedges or bushes, ivy or tall vegetation, low down.

11 cm/4¼ in

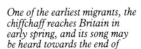

*One of the earliest migrants, the chiffchaff reaches Britain in early spring, and its song may be heard towards the end of* *March. Although a bird of the upper canopy, its nest is always placed close to the ground in dense vegetation (left).*

# GOLDCREST *Regulus regulus*

TOGETHER WITH THE FIRECREST, the goldcrest is the smallest bird found in Europe. It is a partial migrant, strangely absent in the breeding season from almost the whole of Spain and much of Italy, but present in all areas in winter, except perhaps northern Scandinavia.

The upperparts are a dull olive-green, the wings have a black patch and two whitish wing-bars, while the underparts are a dull, whitish buff. The most distinguishing feature is the head, with its black-bordered, bright crown—yellow in the female, yellow and orange in the male. The cheeks and throat are whitish, with a small, dark moustachial stripe. This stripe tends to give the bird a mournful, sad appearance. The short tail is dark green; the bill is small and fine. Juvenile birds lack the crown colours and moustachial stripe and are a more browny green above.

The call is a high-pitched *zee-zee-zee*, the song is a high, thin series of repeated notes, ending with a soft, twittering flourish. Goldcrests are extremely active, flitting about the tops of trees, constantly calling, often in association with tits whose flight is similar to theirs. They can be seen hovering under leaves and branches looking for food.

Coniferous woodland is the goldcrest's favoured habitat, especially in the breeding season, but it can be found in mixed woodland, hedges, bushes and gardens and, when migrating, is fond of gorse on the coast. In all habitats it is seen flicking among the twigs and branches, searching for spiders, tiny insects and their larvae in a warbler-like fashion.

The nest is a deep cup suspended under the tip of a conifer branch or, less often, in ivy or gorse in a finely woven mixture of moss and lichens. It is bound together and attached by cobwebs, and lined with feathers. When courting the female, the male raises and fans his crest, suddenly flashing the central, orange feathers.

It is increasing in numbers mainly because of re-afforestation (notably in Britain), but this species is hard hit in severe winters and numbers can drop dramatically.

It is a regular visitor to the garden and will come to bird tables or to any bits of fat you hang out for it. If possible, and if space permits, you can plant pine or larch trees to attract these birds; if open space permits you could plant yew hedges which are also a favourite.

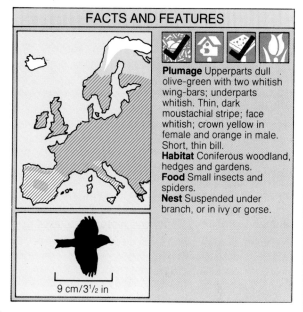

## FACTS AND FEATURES

**Plumage** Upperparts dull olive-green with two whitish wing-bars; underparts whitish. Thin, dark moustachial stripe; face whitish; crown yellow in female and orange in male. Short, thin bill.
**Habitat** Coniferous woodland, hedges and gardens.
**Food** Small insects and spiders.
**Nest** Suspended under branch, or in ivy or gorse.

9 cm/3½ in

*The goldcrest is the smallest European bird, and it may be seen throughout the year. It can be distinguished from the firecrest by its greenish, not bronzed, back and the lack of a white stripe above the eye.*

# FIRECREST *Regulus ignicapillus*

SIMILAR IN SIZE AND APPEARANCE to the goldcrest, the firecrest, a partial migrant, is found over much of central and southern Europe, but is absent in the breeding season from Scandinavia, parts of Spain, Denmark and northern France. In Britain it breeds only in the south-east of England and, although uncommon here, seems to be increasing, in common with a noticeable range expansion on the Continent. Eastern populations move south and west for the winter, and in the autumn especially, it is regular on the coasts of southern England, southern Ireland and northern France.

The plumage is much brighter overall than the goldcrest's: the upperparts are greener with a noticeable yellowy bronze wash over the shoulders; the wings have a dark patch and double wing-bar, and the underparts are cleaner and whiter. The most striking difference is the broad, white supercilium and black stripe through the eye, which is very distinctive. The male has a brilliant, orange crown with a thin, yellow border, while the female has a yellow crown—but she may have some orange feathers in the centre of this. Juveniles are very similar to juvenile goldcrests, but differ by having a dark line through the eye, and a faint supercilium. The firecrest is beautiful, and a favourite among ornithologists.

The call is hard and strong, *zit-zit-zit* notes sounding more separated than the rather run-together notes of the goldcrest. The song is also stronger, ending in a flourish.

The firecrest is seen more in low cover than the goldcrest and is less restricted to conifers, favouring mixed woodland of broad-leaved trees, as well as spruce, pine, scrub and dead bracken.

In terms of site and construction, the nest is similar to that of the goldcrest, but it is slightly smaller and more compact and there is a greater tendency to build in yew trees.

The firecrest's diet consists of spiders, small insects and their larvae. It may associate with feeding flocks of tits in winter, but less frequently than the goldcrest. It is usually seen singly or in small groups.

It is a frequent visitor to gardens, notably on passage, or in winter, in suitable areas, especially if large dense hedges or scattered bushes and trees are present. It has wintered in Britain.

## FACTS AND FEATURES

**Plumage** Upperparts green; double, white wing-bars; bronze shoulders; underparts white. Crown orange or yellow and orange, bordered with black; white supercilium and black stripe through eye; thin, dark moustachial streak.
**Habitat** Mixed woodland, bracken, spruce and pine.
**Food** Small insects and spiders.
**Nest** Suspended under branch, or in ivy or gorse.

9 cm/3½ in

*The firecrest's yellowy bronze wash over the shoulders shows clearly in flight (above), and the broad, white supercilium distinguishes it from the goldcrest. In display, the crest is raised and spread, showing a vivid flash of orange.*

# PIED FLYCATCHER *Ficedula hypoleuca*

THE PIED FLYCATCHER is a migrant species which winters in the scrubland areas of Africa. During the breeding season, however, this species can be considered a typical inhabitant of hilly, broad-leaved woodlands, although it may be encountered in sparsely wooded, mountainous regions. On migration, especially during the autumn passage, it may be observed flitting among bushes in town centres, gardens, parks and in low bushes close to the sea.

The male is black above and white below, with the black of the back being broken only by the white forehead, wing-bar and outer tail feathers. Females and birds of the year are similarly patterned, but are all brown above, and lack the white forehead.

It is a retiring species, and the call may be the only indication of its presence. This is made up of a sharp *whit*, or *tic* or a combination of the two. The song is a rather deliberate, repeated *zee-chi*, followed by a liquid phrase, which may be written as *tree-tree-tree, once more I come to thee*.

When feeding this flycatcher tends to keep to the tree canopy where it catches its insectivorous prey in aerial pursuit. After such a sortie the bird returns to another perch, where it will flick its wings and tail in an agitated fashion, while watching for another victim. Although most of its prey is taken on the wing, this species will sometimes drop to the ground, and occasionally cling to trees in search of food.

The fortunes of the pied flycatcher have fluctuated considerably since the beginning of the last century. For instance, there have been marked decreases to the west of their range, which has been due in part to competition for suitable nesting sites with more aggressive birds such as the common redstart and tits. This problem has been compounded by the felling of large tracts of old broad-leaved forests with their array of holes in which this species places its nest. In other areas, however, their numbers have increased, and there has been some recolonization where the replacement pine plantations have been supplied with nestboxes. This is particularly so in Britain, where the supply of artificial sites has enabled them to spread from Wales to many other areas during the past 40 years.

## FACTS AND FEATURES

**Plumage** Male: black above with a white forehead, wing-patches and outer tail feathers; underparts white. Female and young birds: similarly patterned, but lack white forehead, while the back is brown.
**Habitat** Broad-leaved woodlands, in hilly areas, and in parkland.
**Food** Insects of all kinds, usually taken in the air.
**Nest** Holes in mature, broad-leaved trees.

13 cm/5 in

*Pied flycatchers take readily to nestboxes, especially in pine and birch forests where natural holes are scarce. This female* *(above) is just about to enter to feed the young; the male plumage is blacker.*

# SPOTTED FLYCATCHER *Muscicapa striata*

THE SPOTTED FLYCATCHER is a bird of open woodland, but is commonly encountered in orchards, parks and gardens, especially if there is water close by. It is an unobtrusive species which is easily overlooked, for the plumage is nondescript. The adults are a dull mouse-brown above, and indistinctly streaked dark brown about the forehead and on the white breast. The juveniles, however, are more clearly marked and have distinctly scaly backs and spotted breasts.

Probably the first indication of this bird's presence will be its song. It is not melodious, but it is very characteristic, and recalls the squeaky wheel of a barrow. Other notes may also be uttered and include a *whee-tuc-tuc* and a robin-like *tzee*. If the bird is not in song, the posture is a good identification feature, for it always sits bolt upright when perched, from which position it makes frequent flights after insect prey.

While hunting prey, the flight is often extremely erratic, twisting and turning on many occasions as it compensates for the evasive actions taken by the insect. Rarely does this species miss the intended victim, and on contact the bill closes with an audible snap. After making its capture the bird, more often than not, returns to the same perch.

This species, like its relative the pied flycatcher, is a migrant, which does not return from its African wintering quarters until May, thus making it one of the latest breeding migrants.

Spotted flycatchers usually select a well-shaded spot in which to build their nests. These are often situated next to a building with creepers or trellis, a rock ledge, or open holes in trees. The nest is made up of plant material, roots and grasses, and is lined with feathers, hair and dead leaves. An open-fronted nestbox, placed on a tree, or wall, in a well-shaded position will attract this species. Once a bird has discovered and used the nestbox it will return to the same spot year after year.

*The spotted flycatcher is usually seen perched on the edge of a bush or on a fence waiting to catch passing insects. It is often seen in gardens where it will build its untidy nest, if an open-fronted nestbox or cavities in the walls (left) are provided.*

## FACTS AND FEATURES

**Plumage** Drab, mouse-brown above with indistinct streaking on the forehead and breast; white below. Juveniles: more clearly marked with a scalloped back and spotted breast.
**Habitat** Woodlands of many types, orchards, parks and gardens, especially close to streams.
**Food** Insects of many kinds, usually taken in aerial pursuit.
**Nest** Among creepers close to walls, trellises and trees.

14 cm/5½ in

# BLACK REDSTART *Phoenicurus ochruros*

*Adult males are dark sooty black with a rusty red tail and white wing patches; these patches are brighter and more obvious on older birds. Females are duller and lack the wing-patches. Juveniles are like the female, but are slightly speckled.*

THE BLACK REDSTART HAS SPREAD from its typical habitat of rocky slopes, to the towns and villages in most countries of continental Europe, where old buildings now provide a good substitute for their natural homes. They are absent, however, from much of Scandinavia, Britain and Ireland, as breeding birds. In Britain, this species was seen only on migration, until 1923, when a solitary pair bred, but it was not until after the Second World War, when bombed buildings provided suitable nest-sites, that they really became established. Unfortunately, now that many of these derelict buildings have been redeveloped, this redstart is on the decline.

The adult male is mainly black, with striking, white wing-patches and undertail coverts. When seen from the back and in flight, the rusty rump and tail, the latter with its darker centre, is conspicuous. In winter, the plumage becomes browner, and as a result is less striking. At all times, the female, and birds of the year, are dusky-brown above, and only slightly paler below, and lack the white wing flashes. Juveniles are browner than the female and are speckled above and below. The song consists of a fast warble with a scratchy hiss, and is normally delivered from a building, often at a considerable height.

The choice of nest-sites can be quite varied, for they may include holes in walls, rocky ledges, under bridges, or in a cavity on the ground. A particularly favourite site in Britain at present, is the cavities and ledges afforded by power station complexes. The nest is a loosely assembled cup of dry grass and plant stems; it is lined with wool, hair

and feathers, and is the work of the female.

Being a mainly insectivorous species, the black redstart will come to a bird table only in exceptional circumstances. If bees are kept, however, they may come for they have a liking for these insects. So much so, that in certain regions of the Continent they are regarded as pests for they can decimate a bee colony very quickly.

## FACTS AND FEATURES

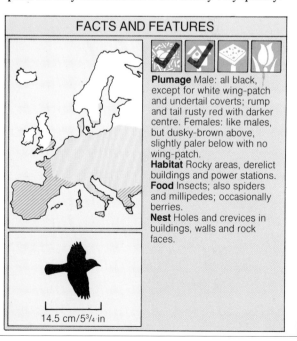

**Plumage** Male: all black, except for white wing-patch and undertail coverts; rump and tail rusty red with darker centre. Females: like males, but dusky-brown above, slightly paler below with no wing-patch.
**Habitat** Rocky areas, derelict buildings and power stations.
**Food** Insects; also spiders and millipedes; occasionally berries.
**Nest** Holes and crevices in buildings, walls and rock faces.

14.5 cm/5¾ in

# REDSTART *Phoenicurus phoenicurus*

THE MOST IMPORTANT REQUIREMENT of the redstart is the availability of suitable nest-holes. For this reason, therefore, it may select a wide range of dissimilar habitats from broad-leaved woodlands, parks, large gardens, tree-lined river banks and treeless, rocky areas with their vast array of rock crevices. It breeds throughout Europe, but only sporadically in Ireland, and is absent from the extreme north. Being a migrant, however, redstarts can turn up virtually anywhere. They are particularly common during the autumn passage in coastal situations, where they stop to feed in gardens and rock-strewn beaches, before continuing their journey to the African wintering quarters.

Probably the first glimpse of a redstart will be from the rear when its orange-red rump and tail may be seen clearly as it darts away into cover. The male is very handsome for it displays a white forehead, dove-grey back, black face and orange breast, rump and tail; the latter with a dark centre. In autumn, the demarcation between the body colours becomes obscured by the brown and whitish tips of the new feathers. The latter eventually abrade in winter to produce the full breeding dress. The female and birds of the year have brown backs and brownish white breasts. Juveniles are heavily spotted above and below, but possess the characteristic red rump and tail. The song is brief and somewhat variable, for they are known to mimic other species. It consists of a robin-like warble at the beginning petering out into a feeble jangle. The call is a plaintive *hweet* or *hweet tuc-tuc.*

The redstart's diet is mainly comprised of flying insects which it catches by chasing them through the branches of trees and bushes. Sometimes, however, they may hover to pick off a sitting insect on a wall or tree trunk and they will descend to the ground in search of prey. The nest is generally situated in a hole in a tree, wall, or nestbox, and lined with grass and hair. It is the responsibility of the female. As this species will utilize nestboxes it is possible to attract them to the garden, but this is most likely to occur in the west and north in the British Isles.

*Redstarts nest in holes in walls, ledges or sometimes in split trees (left). The female alone incubates the clutch of 6 to 7 eggs. During courtship, the bright orange red tail is flicked and fanned constantly by the male.*

♂

♀

## FACTS AND FEATURES

**Plumage** Male: white forehead, black face, grey back, rusty red rump and tail with a dark centre; underparts mainly orange. Female: brown above, buffish to off-white below; juveniles spotted darker above and below.
**Habitat** Broad-leaved woodland, parks and large gardens; also tree-lined river banks; upland areas with sparse trees.
**Food** Insects and berries.
**Nest** Hole in tree or wall.

14 cm/5½ in

# NIGHTINGALE *Luscinia megarhynchus*

THE NIGHTINGALE IS CONSIDERED BY MANY to be one of the best songsters in the European bird community. It is a migrant species which breeds through much of continental Europe and southern Britain, before returning to winter in Africa. Its favourite habitats include open broad-leaved woodlands where there is a dense undergrowth of thickets and low bushes, coupled with a protective ground cover of sweet briars, wild roses, brambles and nettles. In other instances, undisturbed or overgrown areas in parks and large gardens may also provide suitable breeding spots.

This bird is rarely seen, for it is very secretive and seldom ventures to the outer branches of the thickets it inhabits. The plumage also helps to make it inconspicuous: it is drab brown above, with rump and tail tinged chestnut, and with off-white underparts. The presence of a nightingale, therefore, is usually indicated by its song, which may be delivered from a concealed perch by day or by night.

The best time to listen to the male's song is just after it has returned from its wintering quarters, when it is setting up its territory prior to the arrival of the females. The song is unforgettable, not only for its variety of notes, but also for its volume. It consists of a mixture of hard and liquid notes ending with a series of *pioo* calls which build up slowly into a crescendo. Other calls that may be heard include a chiff chaff-like *hweet*, a grating *kurr* and a *tak-tak*.

After pairing, the female constructs a nest close to, or on the ground, deep within a suitable thicket. The nest is made up of a bulky cup of leaves and grasses, and is lined with hair and fine grass.

It will not be possible to attract the nightingale to a bird table, for its diet is almost entirely insectivorous, much of which is obtained from underneath ground litter. If you want to attract them as breeding species you will have to have a large garden and allow a selection of unkempt areas rich in brambles and nettles to develop.

*The nightingale's bulky nest of grass and dead leaves, usually near the ground, is often more concealed than this (left). The young are fed by both adults. When fledged, the young birds are heavily speckled, resembling young robins, but the reddish chestnut tail distinguishes them.*

## FACTS AND FEATURES

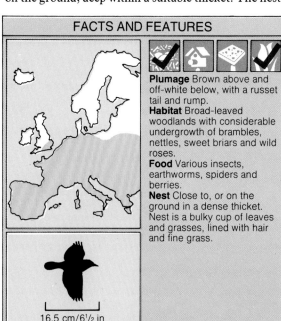

**Plumage** Brown above and off-white below, with a russet tail and rump.
**Habitat** Broad-leaved woodlands with considerable undergrowth of brambles, nettles, sweet briars and wild roses.
**Food** Various insects, earthworms, spiders and berries.
**Nest** Close to, or on the ground in a dense thicket. Nest is a bulky cup of leaves and grasses, lined with hair and fine grass.

16.5 cm/6½ in

# ROBIN *Erithacus rubecula*

*Although the robin appears to be a friendly little character (left), it is in fact a very pugnacious species which, for most of the year, will not tolerate other robins within its territory. In continental Europe it is a retiring species which can be particularly difficult to see, unless on migration.*

*Garden sheds, garages or disused buildings are often selected as nesting places (right).*

IN BRITAIN AT LEAST, the robin is so well-known that a description is hardly necessary: it is one of the best-known of all garden birds and certainly one of the best-loved. In much of Europe, however, it is not generally a garden bird at all, nor particularly tame. Adult robins are plain olive-brown above, with a bright orange face and breast, often vaguely, but visibly, edged with pale grey-blue, and otherwise whitish underparts. Males and females are indistinguishable. Juvenile robins lack the orange breast

and are strongly spotted and mottled with buff and brown. The commonest calls are a short *tsip*, a more drawn-out *seet* and a sharp, insistent *tic-tic-tic. . .;* the song is a pleasing, melancholic warbling and is one of the few songs to be heard in the garden in winter.

Conspicuous, tame and assertive in winter, robins become more retiring when nesting, giving rise to the frequent, but erroneous assertion that they only come into gardens in winter. Natural nest-sites are usually low down in good cover, perhaps in a recess somewhere or under vegetation on a low bank. A wide range of manmade sites is also used—in sheds and outhouses, in old kettles and flowerpots, in an old jacket left hanging behind a door, and so on. The list of recorded artificial sites is almost endless! Robins may take readily to open-fronted nestboxes placed in sheltered positions in ivy or on walls, or anywhere out of reach of cats, or to any discarded human artefact of the right shape and size.

Robins are primarily insectivorous birds and, except in hard weather, generally find enough to eat in the average garden. The often laborious task of digging in autumn and winter may be brightened by the close attendance of a robin, waiting for the spade to turn up various soil insects, pupae and small earthworms. With patience, the birds can sometimes be persuaded to take food from the hand, in these situations. Many robins will become tame very quickly, especially if offered mealworms, and will come readily to windowsills and even into houses, if encouraged by a steady supply of food. Otherwise, they are usually among the first customers at a bird table.

## FACTS AND FEATURES

**Plumage** Adult: olive-brown upperparts, bright reddish orange face and breast edged with grey; rest of underparts white. Juveniles: buffish brown with dark spots and scales.
**Habitat** Woodland, hedgerows, gardens, broad-leaved and coniferous forest.
**Food** Insects, spiders, worms and berries.
**Nest** In hole or hollow in banks, trees, walls.

14.5 cm/5³/₄ in

The natural nesting site is often at ground level, with the nest placed in dense vegetation (above) or under rocks — they are very difficult to locate.

Old tin cans and kettles (left) are readily accepted by robins as suitable places in which to nest. They will also commonly use open-fronted nestboxes.

# FIELDFARE *Turdus pilaris*

THE FIELDFARE FAVOURS woodland edges, or clearings, orchards, gardens and cultivated areas with trees, especially those close to water. During the nesting season it is restricted to northern Scandinavia and central and eastern Europe, although the occasional pair does breed in Scotland.

With the onset of winter, however, the more northerly breeding birds move southwards, and range over much of Europe as far west as Portugal and southwards to the Mediterranean coast, especially in severe winters. In these conditions, large flocks may be encountered virtually anywhere, feeding upon fallen fruits in orchards, berry-laden hedgerows, or on open fields, where they search out insects and grubs, often in association with other thrushes. During times of hard frosts, or after heavy snow falls, they may be seen flying over urban areas in loose flocks, sometimes hundreds strong. At this time, they are very vocal, and may be identified by their loud chattering call of *chack-chack*.

With the loss of their normal feeding sites these birds overcome their general shyness and venture into urban areas in search of food. They may be attracted to even the smallest of gardens where there are berry-bearing trees, or those with rotten fruits on the ground.

This species is the second largest of the European thrushes, and is without doubt the most colourful. The sexes are similarly marked having a delicate blue-grey head, which is spotted black-brown on the crown, a bright chestnut back, brownish wings and grey rump. The underparts are heavily spotted black on the breast and flanks, with the under colour being tinged buff, fading gradually to white on the belly. When in flight, the bird shows white underwing linings and a grey rump.

Females build a bulky nest of grass, moss, twigs and roots, with the cup being formed by mud which in turn is lined with fine grass. The nest is usually placed in a fairly open situation which may be in the fork of a tree, on a broken stump, or even on the ground. Unlike some related species the birds nest in loose colonies, where their combined aggression helps to ward off predatory animals.

## FACTS AND FEATURES

**Plumage** Head grey and spotted about the forehead; back chestnut; rump grey; underparts tinged buff, fading to white on the belly; the breast and flanks well marked with spots.
**Habitat** Woodland edges and clearing, orchards, gardens, especially close to water.
**Food** Insects, worms and grubs, fruits and berries.
**Nest** In the open, in the fork of a tree, or on the ground.

25.5 cm/10 in

*The almost entirely grey head, chestnut back and grey rump will immediately distinguish this species. It is normally a bird of the fields and hedgerows in winter but, during severe weather, it will often venture into urban gardens.*

# REDWING *Turdus iliacus*

*Like the fieldfare, this species is normally a winter visitor from Scandinavia. It may be separated from the song thrush by the presence of a creamy white stripe above the eye, and red, not yellow, underwings.*

IN RECENT TIMES the redwing has established itself as a breeding bird in Scotland, where a few pairs nest every year. Its main breeding area, however, is in Scandinavia and north-eastern Europe, where it inhabits young conifer forests, birch and alder woodlands as well as scrub and tundra areas. Like the fieldfare, this species leaves its breeding grounds during the autumn to winter over much of Europe, as far south as North Africa. During this period they may be seen in association with other thrushes, especially in open fields while they search for food. In particularly long periods of bad weather many perish, for once the ground has become frosted they are unable to obtain food. This is when they will come into gardens and parks in urban areas, sometimes in substantial numbers, in an effort to find food.

Redwings are similar in appearance to song thrushes, but they are smaller and generally darker brown above. You can distinguish them from song thrushes by the creamy stripe above the eye, which contrasts with the dark brown cap and ear coverts. The underparts are mainly white; they are heavily spotted dark brown about the throat and breast, and they have reddish flanks. In flight, the underwing can be seen to be a brick-red colour, rather than the yellow-gold of the song thrush.

The song is rarely heard away from the breeding area, but when you do hear it, it is a monotonous series of fluty notes ending with a warble. You are likely to hear, however, the characteristic soft *tseep* as it flies overhead.

Nests may be placed in a tree or shrub, on a dead

## FACTS AND FEATURES

**Plumage** Brown above with a distinct, creamy eye stripe; underparts white, sometimes washed with buffish-red, and heavily spotted on the throat and breast; underwing brick-red.

**Habitat** Young conifer forests, birches and alder woodlands and scrub.

**Food** Earthworms, snails, insects and their larvae; also fruits.

**Nest** Mainly in bushes and trees, but occasionally on the ground.

21 cm/8¼ in

stump, or in a bank cavity. It is built by the female, which may select a spot anywhere from ground level to 3 m/ 10 ft high. It consists of a cup of grass, moss and lichens with an inner cup of mud, lined in turn with fine grass.

Like the fieldfare, this species can be attracted to gardens during the winter by providing rotten fruit for them to eat. When food is particularly scarce they will also take berries, but less so than other thrushes at this period.

# BLACKBIRD *Turdus merula*

THE BLACKBIRD is one of the best-known inhabitants of urban gardens. It was originally, however, a bird of woodland areas, but its ability to adapt to manmade environments has enabled it to spread into almost every conceivable niche in the past 100 years. In Britain it can now be considered the most common of breeding birds.

The plumage of the adult male is unmistakable—jet black with a bright yellow bill. Females are drab brown above, slightly paler below, with a few indistinct streaks around a pale throat. Young birds are similar to the female in colour, but are more russet, with buff tips to the back feathers, and mottled below, giving an overall spotted appearance.

Its song is, without doubt, one of the most beautiful that can be heard in Europe, and is probably rivalled only by that of the nightingale. The dawn chorus appears to be dominated by the blackbird in many areas, as the males proclaim ownership of their territories. The song comprises a languid, clear fluty warble which carries for some distance, and is audible even above the noise of passing vehicles. Other calls include a scolding *chik-chik-chik*, a three-part *chook*, an hysterical *chewee* which is repeated many times when the birds is alarmed, and a plaintive *tsee* which is often uttered in flight.

A variety of nesting sites may be chosen, including trees, bushes, creepers attached to walls, trellises, garden sheds and in among disregarded bric-a-brac. The nest is built by the female and is a large, substantial cup, constructed of plant material mixed with mud, which is lined with dry grasses and dead leaves. Blackbirds may produce as many as four clutches a year, but the predation rate is high. Nests are often raided by magpies and squirrels, and young fledglings are easy prey for domestic cats.

There is no difficulty in attracting the blackbird to the garden, for they will eat almost any scraps of food. If you plant fruit-bearing trees, however, you will be sure of a larger population, especially if the crop is left on the ground.

## FACTS AND FEATURES

**Plumage** Male: all black with a yellow bill. Females: brown and slightly streaked about the throat. Juveniles: brown and spotted.
**Habitat** Woodlands, gardens, parks and urban areas.
**Food** Insects, worms, kitchen scraps, fruits and berries.
**Nest** Virtually any place that affords some cover—trees, bushes and buildings.

25.5 cm/10 in

*Ivy growing in the garden can attract many species of birds. This blackbird (left) is gorging himself on the berries. The species will also nest in ivy, as will many others and, although regarded as an unsuitable garden plant, it rarely does any damage. Blackbirds are also fond of the berries of cotoneaster, barbary, honeysuckle and hawthorn.*

The adult male is resplendent in his all-black plumage, yellow bill and eye ring (above). Young males are browner, lack the eye ring and have dark bills.

The clutch is usually 4 to 5, but larger numbers of eggs have been recorded. The inner layer of mud has been covered by a lining of dry grass (right). These eggs are typically marked, but coloration is variable.

Sheds are a favourite place for blackbirds to build their nests in (above) but, if they take up residence, you must be sure that you do not accidentally block up their entry point or leave the door open to let predators like cats in.

# SONG THRUSH *Turdus philomelos*

THE SONG THRUSH is a familiar garden visitor, though less so than its relative the blackbird. Outside the urban habitats, such as gardens and parks, this species prefers forest edges and clearings, but avoids the Taiga areas of northern Europe. It is widespread throughout the region, but does not breed in Spain and Portugal, visiting those countries only during particularly cold weather movements.

The plumage of both sexes is alike: warm brown above, well spotted below, and the upper breast and flanks washed with yellow on otherwise white underparts. It may be confused with both the redwing and mistle thrush, but it lacks the creamy eye stripe and red underwing of the former, and does not possess the white tips to the outermost tail feathers of the larger and deeper-chested mistle thrush. Juveniles are much like the adults, but have buff tips to the wing coverts. In flight, all show the characteristic yellow underwing coverts.

You can hear the song of this species almost every month of the year. It begins to declare its territory in early January and continues to do so up to July, when there is a break until September. The song is loud, clear and varied, and consists of phrases which may be uttered up to four times. The song thrush is a mimic, and the phrases often incorporate calls of many types of birds.

This species may be attracted to gardens by fruit-bearing bushes and trees as well as by kitchen scraps. One of its favourite natural food items is snails, which it breaks open by smashing the shell against a hard object in order to obtain the soft body. When looking for other live prey,

this species has a characteristic habit of cocking its head to one side so as to obtain a better view of its intended meal.

The nest is a well-shaped cup which is constructed by the female, and is made up of grasses, twigs, roots, dead leaves and lichens, with the inside lined with plain mud or decaying wood. It usually selects a well-shaded site, which may be in the fork of a tree, in a bush, or in creepers close to a building.

## FACTS AND FEATURES

**Plumage** Brown above and mainly white below, with the throat and breast washed with yellow and spotted dark brown. Underwing coverts yellow.
**Habitat** Edges of woodland, clearings, parks and gardens.
**Food** Snails, earthworms, insects and their larvae; fruits and seeds.
**Nest** Placed in the form of tree, or bush, in creepers and sometimes in buildings.

23 cm/9 in

*Snails form an important part of the song thrush's diet. The bird extracts the soft part of the snail by smashing the shell against a hard surface, which is often a rock or large stone (above), and is referred to as the 'thrush's anvil'.*

# MISTLE THRUSH *Turdus viscivorus*

THIS SPECIES is the largest of the thrushes commonly encountered in Europe, and takes its name from its habit of eating the berries from clumps of mistletoe. In some areas, however, it is known as the storm cock, for it will sing during the windiest of days.

The song is similar in some respects to that of the blackbird, but does not possess its mellowness, and it is faster, louder and with less time between the phrases. Further individual calls may also be heard and include a chatter resembling a wooden rattle, a *tuc-tuc-tuc* and a plaintive *tseep*.

The mistle thrush occurs throughout the whole region, except for the most northerly parts of Scandinavia. Its favoured habitats include gardens, parks, wooded avenues and orchards, but during the winter months it may be seen in open fields while searching for food. Its diet comprises berries, fruits, slugs, worms and insects, but it will take kitchen scraps during hard weather.

Although similar in many respects the mistle thrush may be distinguished from the song thrush by its larger size and deeper chest. In colour the upperparts are grey-brown, slightly paler about the head and on the rump, and boldly spotted white underparts. In flight the diagnostic white underwing coverts and white tips to the outermost tail feathers are obvious. The way in which this species flies is also a very good identification feature, for it closes its wings between flaps, thus giving it a 'shooting' appearance. Juvenile birds resemble the adults, but are spotted about the head and back.

This thrush is an early nester and will often have eggs before the end of February, long in advance of any leaf cover. The nest is usually located in more open areas with tall isolated trees. It is generally placed in a fork of a branch and is a bulky structure. The cup is built of plant material, mixed with earth and lined with fine grasses, and is the responsibility of the female. During the nesting period this species is at its most aggressive, for it has been known to attack even a man if he ventures too close to the nest site.

## FACTS AND FEATURES

**Plumage** Upperparts grey brown; grey about the head; underparts white, well-marked with spots on the throat and breast. Underwing and tips of outermost tail feathers white.
**Habitat** Gardens, parks, wooded avenues, and orchards.
**Food** Fruits, especially of mistletoe; slugs, worms and insects.
**Nest** Often in tall trees situated in open spaces or in orchards.

27 cm/10½ in

*The mistle thrush is larger, greyer and more boldly spotted than the song thrush. During the winter months, this thrush will often defend a berry crop against all comers. It is an early breeder and may have eggs in the nest before the end of February.*

# LONG-TAILED TIT *Aegithalos caudatus*

THE LONG-TAILED TIT is aptly named, for the tail is over half its total length. It is widespread throughout Europe, and is excluded only from the northernmost parts of Scandinavia. This species favours woods, hedgerows and other bushy places, where it may be seen in association with the more typical tits, as they forage for food in winter months. In some instances, it has been known for them to gather in family parties, forming flocks of 20 or more individuals.

Overall, the plumage is black and white, except for a pink flush on the wing coverts and lower abdomen. The only marking on the head is a band of black, which runs from avove the eye, backwards to the black back. Much of the wing is blackish-brown, but there are obvious white patches. The tail is very long and black, except for the white outertail feathers. The underparts are mainly white. In north-eastern Europe the head, in the adult, is all white, and the eye ring is yellow rather than red. Juvenile birds differ from the adults in having blackish-brown faces, and lack the pink flush on the wings and abdomen.

The nest is a beautiful, domed construction, which takes several weeks to complete. Both adults participate in the building, and, in some instances, may be helped by other individuals. Work is often begun during late winter, in order to be ready to receive the first egg, which can be laid as early as late March. The nest is usually sited in a bush, or tree anything from 1.25–21.5 m/4–70 ft from the ground. The material used consists of lichens, moss, cobwebs and animal hair, often woven around twigs to give it a firm anchorage. The entrance to the nest is through a hole in the upper half of the structure. So snug is the fit, the brooding adult has to fold its tail over its back.

Unlike the common tit, it is not an habitual frequenter of gardens, although sometimes it may be seen passing through them during one of its feeding sorties. Nor will you be able to attract it to a bird feeder since it is a mainly insectivorous species.

## FACTS AND FEATURES

**Plumage** Upperparts blackish, head white with blackish bands. Whitish patches on wing and pink band along scapulars. Underparts white, with pink belly and undertail. Long black tail, with white outer feathers.
**Habitat** Broad-leaved woodland, parks and gardens. Willows along rivers and streams.
**Food** Small insects, spiders, seeds and buds.
**Nest** Usually in dense bush or fork of tree.

14 cm/5½ in

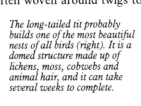

*The long-tailed tit probably builds one of the most beautiful nests of all birds (right). It is a domed structure made up of lichens, moss, cobwebs and animal hair, and it can take several weeks to complete.*

# MARSH TIT *Parus palustris*

THE DIFFERENCE BETWEEN THIS SPECIES and the willow tit is extremely slight. So small is the difference, that the latter was only separated from the marsh tit as late as 1897, and in consequence was the last British bird to be catalogued. In appearance, the marsh tit is a rather plain, brown bird with a glossy black cap, whitish cheeks and light buffish underparts. Juveniles are similar to the adults, but they have less glossy caps and are, therefore, indistinguishable from those of their close relatives unless a call is heard. The voice, in fact, is by far the most certain way of separating both the adults and juveniles of these species. The call consists of a scolding *chickabee-bee-bee-bee*, a soft *pitchu* or *pi*, which is sometimes followed by a scolding *tchay*. The song, made up of a high-pitched *schip-schip-schip*, or *schuppi-schuppi-schuppi*, may also identify it.

The marsh tit's name does not indicate its preferred habitat, in fact, it has a liking for broad-leaved woods, with both beech and oak, and usually with dense ground cover of tall bushes. Orchards, parks and large gardens are also commonly used, and, probably, the nearest this tit will come to a marsh habitat will be the riverine forests, and damp woodland areas which it sometimes inhabits. The breeding distribution covers much of Europe, but it is absent from Scotland, most of Norway and Sweden, the Iberian peninsula and Greece.

Like all tits of this family, this species nests in natural holes within trees and walls. The nest is built by the female alone, and consists of a cup formed from moss, and lined with hair and feathers to form a pad.

The diet of the marsh tit is made up almost entirely of insects, which it seeks out as it acrobatically hangs from the branches of trees and bushes; some seeds and wild fruit are also taken. Marsh tits are not particularly common in gardens, and, unless your property is adjacent to a suitable site as described above, the chances of attracting them to your garden are slim indeed. They are known, however, to visit tit feeders, especially during cold weather.

*The marsh tit is not easily distinguished from the willow tit, except by its song. However, the marsh tit's black cap is glossy and not sooty black, and it lacks the pale wing-patch of the closely allied species. Despite its name, it rarely frequents marshes, except when foraging for food during the winter.*

## FACTS AND FEATURES

**Plumage** Light brown above with glossy black cap and neat, black bib. Buffish below; pale flanks. No wing panel.
**Habitat** Broad-leaved mixed woodland, orchards, parks, riverine forests, but not marshes.
**Food** Insects, seeds and berries.
**Nest** In natural holes in trees, walls or in the ground. Unlike the willow tit, it does not excavate its own hole.

11.5 cm/4½ in

# WILLOW TIT *Parus montanus*

THE WILLOW TIT has a distribution in Europe similar to that of the marsh tit. However, it reaches further north in Scandinavia, but is absent from much of the Mediterranean region.

Its preferred habitats are damp, coniferous forests, especially where spruce predominates, mountainous, coniferous woods and subarctic, birch scrub. They will also take up residence in broad-leaved woodlands, where conifers are close by, as well as in swampy forests and thickets along river banks. In the mountainous regions of Europe it is sometimes called the alpine tit.

It is very difficult to separate, by sight alone, this species from its close cousin, the marsh tit. To identify by plumage requires close scrutiny, which will, under good conditions, reveal that the willow tit's black cap is sooty-brown and not glossy, and that there is an indistinct, pale wing-patch. Juvenile birds, however, are quite impossible to separate.

By far the most reliable method to identify this species is to listen to its song and call notes as they are quite unlike the marsh tit's. The song consists of a sad *piu-piu-piu*, and the calls are *zi-zi-zi* and *erz-erz-erz*.

Unlike the marsh tit, this species excavates its own nest hole in rotten trees. Sometimes, however, it will use a natural cavity, or even an old woodpecker hole. The female takes the responsibility for making the cavity and constructing the nest. The latter consists of wood chippings, occasionally moss, with an inner lining of hair and feathers. Although it is possible to encourage a pair to use a nestbox, the method is far from foolproof. The box should be placed on an old stump, and filled with small wood fragments or wood shavings for the bird to make an excavation.

The diet is not well established, but it generally obtains its food from low down on the trees. Insects appear to form the major part of the food taken, but a few seeds may also be eaten. As this tit has a particular liking for peanuts it will come readily to a bird feeder where they are supplied.

## FACTS AND FEATURES

**Plumage** Upperparts brown, cap dull, sooty-black. Closed wing shows a pale panel. Cheeks white, bib black; underparts white with buffish flanks.
**Habitat** Coniferous forest, mixed broad-leaved woodland, willows, alder and birch woods, especially trees along river banks.
**Food** Small insects, berries and seeds.
**Nest** In a hole in soft or decaying wood.

11.5 cm/4½ in

*Although you may be able to spot the willow tit by its sooty black cap and pale wing patches, the more reliable distinction between the willow and marsh tits lies in their songs.*

# CRESTED TIT *Parus cristatus*

THE CRESTED TIT IS WIDESPREAD IN EUROPE as a sedentary breeding species, but it is absent from the Netherlands, south-western Portugal, northern Scandinavia, Ireland and the Italian peninsula and its associated islands. In Britain, it has always been restricted to Scotland, but through the felling in the 17th and 18th centuries it was driven into a small area in the Highlands. Recently, however, there has been some recolonization of its former breeding range, thanks to the plantation of new forests. The Scottish population prefers to live in coniferous woods, but in other countries it may be found in mixed woodlands and thickets which are growing in both lowland and mountainous zones.

This species is the second smallest of the European tits, being only half a centimetre ($^1/_4$ in) larger than the diminutive coal tit. It is easily identified by the prominent white crest which is speckled black, the black, semicircular marking behind the eye, and the small black bib, which contrasts with the whitish face. The remainder of the body is warm, greyish-brown above, and off-white below, with buffish flanks. Its vocabulary consists of a deep, purring trill *chirr-chirr-chirr-r*, which is repeated several times to form the song; there is also a high-pitched, thin *tzee-tzee-tzee*.

The diet consists of a mixture of insects, aphids and caterpillars, but, on occasion, it will take conifer seeds and juniper berries. It is very acrobatic while searching for food—it will hang upside down on the thinnest of twigs, as it probes its bill into cones and small crevices.

While courting, the male produces a special, fluttering flight as it chases the female through the branches of a tree. The male may also display to his intended mate by raising his crest and flapping his wings. After pairing, the female seeks out a suitable nesting site, which may be a natural cavity in a tree or fence post, but she will also excavate a hole in a rotten stump. The nest consists of hair, feathers, moss and lichens usually collected by the female. Being a hole-nester, this species will utilize a nestbox placed on a tree or post.

## FACTS AND FEATURES

**Plumage** Upperparts warm greyish brown, prominent black and white crest on head, white face with black surround joining small black bib. Underparts whitish, flanks buff.
**Habitat** Mixed woodland and thickets, but predominantly coniferous forests.
**Food** Insects, caterpillars, conifer seeds and juniper berries.
**Nest** Excavates own hole in rotten wood.

11.5 cm/4$^1/_2$ in

*Although widespread in continental Europe, in Britain this tit is restricted to a small area of the Scottish Highlands. It is the only European tit with a distinct crest, which is speckled black and white. The remainder of the plumage is brownish above, off-white below with dark facial streaks.*

# COAL TIT *Parus ater*

THE SMALLEST OF THE EUROPEAN TITS, the coal tit can be found virtually anywhere, except for the more northerly parts of Scandinavia. Although quite common, it is often overlooked, for it is less bold than most other true tits, and it is less brightly coloured. In some views it can resemble the marsh tit, but the white stripe running down the back of the head will distinguish it from all other species. The face is whitish and is bordered by the black of the cap and bib. The remainder of the upperparts are a drab olive-buff, while the underparts are white, washed with a variable amount of buff, especially on the flanks and breast.

The song, which is remarkable, consists of a clear, high-pitched, repeated *seetoo* or *seetoooee*, while the calls may include a thin *tsui* followed by a short twitter, a *sissi-sissi-sissi* and a scolding *chi-chi-chi*.

Coal tits like woods of almost any type, but they do have a particular preference for conifers situated in large, mixed forests, parks and gardens. They can become quite tame in urban locations, and will visit bird tables, especially if peanuts and fat are provided. In some instances, they will lose their natural shyness completely and will take food from the hand.

Their natural food source is made up of insects such as beetles, flies and their grubs, caterpillars, spiders, seeds and wild nuts. During the adverse conditions of the winter period, they often associate with other species of tits, as well as treecreepers and goldcrests, while they are foraging for food.

The nesting site may be any suitable hole in a tree, bank, wall, and, occasionally, in the ground. They will readily use nestboxes. The nest construction is the responsibility of the female and consists of a cup of moss and spiders' webs, lined with hair, plant down and feathers, which is compacted to form a 'felty' mat. While incubating, the female, like other members of this family, is fed by the male. During the brooding period the female is often fearless, and reluctant to leave her young, even when a potential enemy approaches.

## FACTS AND FEATURES

**Plumage** Upperparts buff olive-grey; face white, topped with large black cap; large black bib below. Black on nape separated by broad white stripe. Underparts white; flanks buff. Juveniles: yellower on face and underparts.
**Habitat** Mixed woodland, parks, gardens, with coniferous trees.
**Food** Beetles, flies, spiders, seeds and nuts.
**Nest** In any suitable hole in a tree, bank, wall or in the ground.

11 cm/4¼ in

*The coal tit is a common visitor to gardens (above), especially in winter, when it will come for nuts and fat. Nuts are frequently taken and buried in the ground for future supplies.*

# BLUE TIT *Parus caeruleus*

WITHOUT DOUBT the blue tit is one of the best known birds in the garden, where it never ceases to amuse the observer with its bold, sometimes aggressive, and very agile behaviour. In some areas, however, it has become a problem, for it is a rather intelligent species, which has learned to open the foil tops of milk bottles to get at the creamy contents.

Although blue tits will now be found in almost any form of habitat, from town centres, gardens, parks and orchards, they were originally birds of the broad-leaved, woodland areas, especially those with good stands of oak. Their range extends throughout much of Europe, being absent only from central and northern Scandinavia.

They are attractively coloured, possessing an azure blue crown, wings and tail, with a white face marked with black, a greenish back and bright yellow underparts. Juveniles are similar to the adults, but have yellow instead of white on the face. The song consists of a strident, high-pitched *tsee-tsee*, which is followed by a long trill. Other calls are variable, but include the familiar *tsee-tsee-tsee-tsit*, and the scolding *chu-r-r*.

The natural diet of the blue tit is comprised of a large variety of insects, including aphids and caterpillars, as well as spiders, fruit, grain and seeds. During the winter period, they commonly associate with other tits while they forage for food in the tree canopy. Blue tits obtain insects by digging their bill into the bark of trees, which may be torn off in order to find the hibernating prey. They are easily attracted to the garden table in winter, if you provide fat or peanuts, or suspend coconuts by a piece of string, or wire from a tree. It is not good practice, however, to supply coconuts during the breeding season, for the flesh cannot be digested by the nestlings.

This species nests in holes in trees, or in a crevice in a wall, but it will readily use a nestbox. The nest itself is made of moss and grass, which is then lined with hair and feathers. The hatching of the eggs is timed to coincide with the emergence of the looping caterpillars in the early spring.

## FACTS AND FEATURES

**Plumage** Upperparts bluish green; crown, wings and tail azure blue. Head has white face edged with black and a dark line running through eye. Underparts bright yellow. Juveniles: overall paler, face yellowish.
**Habitat** Parks, gardens, orchards and broad-leaved woodland.
**Food** Aphids, spiders, caterpillars, fruit, grain and seeds.
**Nest** Holes in trees and crevices in walls.

11.5 cm/4½ in

*Together with the great tit, the blue tit is renowned for its habit of pecking through milk bottle tops and then drinking the cream (above).*

# GREAT TIT *Parus major*

THE GREAT TIT is the largest common tit, and is second only to the blue tit as a visitor to gardens where there are bird feeders. They are remarkably aggressive at feeders and will drive off even larger greenfinches from peanut holders. Like its commoner cousin, the blue tit, this tit also likes the cream of the milk, and so it, too, has developed the habit of removing, or puncturing the caps on milk bottles. Although infuriating, this habit is more than offset by the amount of harmful insects which it removes from fruit trees, rose bushes and other garden plants.

The plumage is quite striking—it has a glossy blue-black cap, white cheek patches, greenish back, and bluish-black tail, with white outer tail feathers. Beneath, it is citrous yellow with a black stripe running from the throat to the lower abdomen. Females are almost identical to males, but the black belly stripe is less pronounced, and does not widen towards the vent. Juveniles are more like the female, but differ in possessing yellow rather than white faces, and the black markings of the head are less glossy.

The vocabulary of the great tit is, perhaps, the most extensive of any British bird, for each population appears to have its own dialect. The song is striking and sounds like *teacher*, repeated many times. Calls include a *pink*, and a note resembling a saw being sharpened.

This species occurs throughout Europe being absent only from a central and northern wedge in Scandinavia. It is capable of inhabiting a large variety of woodland, including oak woods, olive groves, parks, and gardens in urban areas. Rarely, however, does it inhabit purely coniferous forests.

The natural food of the great tit consists of a great array of insects, including caterpillars, aphids and bugs, as well as seeds, fruit and buds. On occasions it has been known to eat nestlings of other species.

The nest is always placed in a hole, either in a tree, pipe or between rocks, and it will freely use nestboxes. The compartment is filled with roots, moss, lichens and grass and lined with hair, plant down and feathers.

## FACTS AND FEATURES

**Plumage** Glossy blue black cap, white cheek patch, greenish back, and bluish black tail; yellow below with black central stripe. Female: as male, but belly stripe less broad. Juveniles: yellowish faces and less glossy caps.
**Habitat** Woodlands, parks and urban gardens.
**Food** Mainly insects; also seeds, fruit and buds.
**Nest** Hole in tree, wall or pipe.

14 cm/5½ in

*Males have a dark stripe down the centre of the belly, widening towards the vent; in the female this is less obvious. Great tits are highly acrobatic when searching for small insects among the foliage. They readily use nestboxes and garden feeders containing nuts (far right).*

# NUTHATCH  *Sitta europea*

*The nuthatch is probably the only bird that is just as happy walking down a tree trunk as it is going up. In winter, it can be seen foraging with flocks of tits in woodland. A regular visitor to nut feeders in gardens, or where fat has been smeared on tree trunks.*

ALTHOUGH COMMON throughout much of Europe, the nuthatch spends much of its time clambering high up in the tree canopy, and often its presence is detected only by its call, a distinctive, ringing *chwit-chwit*. A resident species, it is absent only from the north of England, Scotland, Ireland, and northern Scandinavia.

Often described as a plump bird, when it is moving about with woodpecker-like actions, the long, chisel-like bill and tapering body can give the bird a very sleek appearance. Adult upperparts are a bluish grey, including the crown; the cheeks and throat are white. There is a long black line through the eye; the underparts are buff, the flanks are bright reddish buff in the male, and pale reddish buff in the female. The short tail has central feathers which are bluish grey, and outer feathers which are blackish with white tips. Juveniles are browner above, with a browner, less distinct eye stripe, and dull flanks. The song is a rapid trill, *chi-chi-chi-chi*. Other calls are a loud *tchui* and a quiet *tic*.

The nuthatch flies from tree to tree with an undulating flight, moving on tree trunks and branches with a short, jerky motion. It does not use its tail as a brace as woodpeckers do, and it is equally capable of going up or down a tree, or walking along the underside of branches, gripping with its sharp claws. Occasionally it feeds on the ground.

This species will be found in mixed, broad-leaved woods, parks and gardens, where there are plenty of trees, particularly oak trees. The nuthatch probes crevices in the bark for large insects and larvae, spiders, earwigs, seeds and nuts, including hazel, acorns and beechmast. When nuts are found, the nuthatch wedges them in a crevice in the bark or branch of a tree and hammers them

open with its bill; at these times it sounds very much like a woodpecker tapping.

The nest is in a hole or hollow in a tree, sometimes in an old woodpecker nest. The hole is usually plastered with mud to narrow the entrance. Nestboxes are also frequently used, and the lids of these are also plastered up with mud to seal the box. The lining of the chamber consists of dead leaves and chips of bark, which is used to cover the eggs when the female is away feeding.

The nuthatch will freely visit your garden for hanging fat, nuts and seeds.

## FACTS AND FEATURES

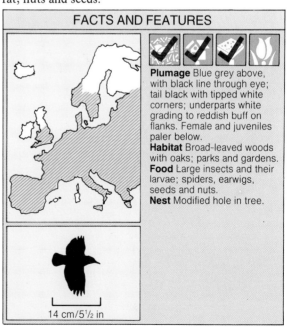

**Plumage** Blue grey above, with black line through eye; tail black with tipped white corners; underparts white grading to reddish buff on flanks. Female and juveniles paler below.
**Habitat** Broad-leaved woods with oaks; parks and gardens.
**Food** Large insects and their larvae; spiders, earwigs, seeds and nuts.
**Nest** Modified hole in tree.

14 cm/5½ in

# TREECREEPER *Certhia familiaris*

THE HABITAT OF THE TREECREEPER normally consists of dark, forested areas of spruces and firs in both lowland and mountainous regions. In Britain, however, this species, possibly through the lack of competition with the short-toed treecreeper, has been able to move into broad-leaved forests, and thus into parks and gardens in urban areas where it is not infrequent. It may be encountered through Britain and Ireland, the Pyrennees, central and northern Europe, including the central spine of Italy and Scandinavia.

The plumage above is a mixture of shades of brown and buffish streaks, while the underparts are silvery white. In flight, the wings display a distinct buffish wing-bar on an otherwise drab, brown bird. The tail feathers, which have been modified to function as braces for this species' climbing activities, are relatively long and stiff. While searching for food, it ascends tree trunks in an upward progression which is slow and mouse-like, and often takes the form of a spiral around the trunk. When it has reached the top it usually drops down to the base of the next tree, and then repeats the process.

The treecreeper's characteristic song consists of a *tee-tee-tee-titit-dooee*, while the normal call is a repeated high-pitched *tseee*.

The diet of the treecreeper includes numerous invertebrates, such as spiders, and many forms of insects and their larvae. The treecreeper probes its long decurved bill into small cavities and crevices where its prey may be skulking. In winter, it is possible to attract treecreepers to the garden—not by the conventional method of using feeders—but by preparing a mixture of crushed nuts and porridge, and spreading it over a tree or placing it in crevices.

In the breeding season, the pair seeks out a site—often behind loose bark, among ivy roots, in holes in trees and in rock crevices. They will also occupy a wedged-shaped nestbox with a side entrance placed against a tree. The nest is made of dried grass and roots, and lined with wool, feathers and bark fragments.

*Using its stiff tail as a prop, the treecreeper hops up tree trunks in search of insects and grubs under the bark. It then uses its long decurved bill to extract them. In winter, it can often be seen in association with roving tit flocks in woodland.*

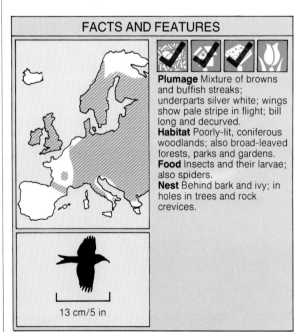

## FACTS AND FEATURES

**Plumage** Mixture of browns and buffish streaks; underparts silver white; wings show pale stripe in flight; bill long and decurved.
**Habitat** Poorly-lit, coniferous woodlands; also broad-leaved forests, parks and gardens.
**Food** Insects and their larvae; also spiders.
**Nest** Behind bark and ivy; in holes in trees and rock crevices.

13 cm/5 in

# SHORT-TOED TREECREEPER *Certhia brachydactyla*

THE SHORT—TOED TREECREEPER is virtually indistinguishable from its near relative the treecreeper, from which it may be separated with certainty only by its voice, and, in some areas, by distribution, or habitat. This species occurs in Britain only as a rare vagrant from the European mainland. In principle it can be said that the short-toed treecreeper replaces its counterpart over much of the Continent, but there is considerable overlap in central and eastern Europe, while it is absent from all of Scandinavia. In countries where both species are found, the short-toed treecreeper has a marked preference for broad-leaved forests in both lowland and mountainous regions, but, when there is no overlap in the distribution, this species will occupy open pine woods. The reason for two extremely similar species occurring in this way is not fully understood, but it is thought to have been one of the consequences of the last glaciation.

As already stated, the plumage of the two species is almost identical. The short-toed treecreeper may be separated, however, by a less rusty rump, brownish flanks, slightly longer bill and shorter claws. By far the most reliable identification features are the song and the call. The song of this creeper is somewhat richer, similar to that of the coal tit, and possessing a series of high-pitched rythmic notes *teet-teet, teeteroititt*, while the call is characterized by a shrill *srrich*.

This species is mainly insectivorous, and its food source consists of a variety of invertebrates, such as woodlice, weevels, beetles, earwigs, small caterpillars and spiders. On occasion it has been known to eat seeds.

The male courtship display includes chasing the female through the branches, a bat-like flight, and wing-quivering. Once paired, both sexes look for a suitable site in which to place their nest. This is usually a crevice, situated behind loose bark, or where ivy has climbed against a wall or tree. The nest is made up of a cup of twigs, roots, moss, grass and lined with feathers, wool and fine pieces of bark. Both sexes help to construct the nest. Nestboxes may be utilized.

## FACTS AND FEATURES

**Plumage** Mixture of browns and buffish streaks; underparts silvery white, flanks dusky; in flight, shows pale wing-bar; bill long and decurved.
**Habitat** Mainly broad-leaved woodlands; also coniferous forests.
**Food** Invertebrates, woodlice, weevels, beatles, earwigs; also seeds.
**Nest** Behind bark and ivy; holes in trees and rock crevices.

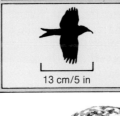

13 cm/5 in

*In the field, the short-toed treecreeper is almost impossible to separate from the treecreeper (above) except by its distribution and song. Generally it has a rufous tinge on the flanks, is greyer above and has a less rusty rump and less distinct supercilia. Its song may be uttered from an exposed perch.*

139

# HOUSE SPARROW *Passer domesticus*

*The house sparrow is probably the commonest species of bird to be found close to human habitation.*

DUE TO ITS OWN SPREAD IN DISTRIBUTION, following the expansion of both man and cultivated land, and helped with widespread introductions, the house sparrow now has a world-wide distribution and is common throughout Europe. There are many different races, and separation of these is difficult. Confusion is likely only with the tree sparrow, which has a similar range.

The male upperparts are brown and buff with heavy, black streaking; the rump is grey. The crown is grey, the nape and sides of the neck chestnut brown; the chin, throat and centre of the breast black and the rest of the underparts are greyish white. In flight, the short, white wing-bar is obvious. In summer, the bill is black, becoming yellowish in winter. Females are duller; they are greyer brown on the back, they lack the grey on the crown and rump, and show no black on the throat or breast. The wing-bar is indistinct. Juveniles are similar to females. Town and city birds are often duller and drabber than their country cousins.

The house sparrow is found anywhere in the vicinity of man, from city streets to the smallest cottage in remote areas. Often gathering in large, noisy flocks, busily chirping and twittering, they are the most familiar of birds. Feeding largely on seeds and grain in agricultural land, in towns and villages, they depend on scraps thrown out by man. They can be seen inspecting waste bins, and are forever attendant on picnickers in parks. In summer, the house sparrow's diet consists of small insects and spiders, plant shoots and buds of flowers and fruit trees. Freshly harvested fields attract large flocks, especially in autumn and winter.

The domed nest is built in a hole or crevice in buildings, trees, cliffs, or deep among ivy; it also builds in the base of rooks' nests. The nest is constructed of grass, root stems and frequently includes bits of string, waste paper and fabric, making an altogether untidy structure. It is lined with fine hair, wool and feathers. The house sparrow will use nestboxes if the holes are large enough to allow entry; they may be a pest in this way, preventing other, more welcome birds from breeding.

They will eat almost any scraps, particularly seeds, put out on the bird table, or in the garden, and if encouraged can oust other, smaller birds and prevent them feeding.

**Plumage** Male upperparts brown streaked with black, crown and rump grey, nape and sides of neck chestnut-brown; underparts greyish-white, but throat and breast black. Females like juveniles: greyish brown above, paler below, with white wing-bar.
**Habitat** Urban areas, farmyards; close to man.
**Food** Virtually anything, but especially seeds.
**Nest** Domed; in buildings, trees, cliffs, ivy and old nests of large birds.

14.5 cm/5³⁄₄ in

*They often take over house martins' nests (left) before they have been completed.*

*A typical example of a nest (below) placed in the roof of a building.*

*Partial to nuts, the house sparrow will habitually come to feeders (above). To prevent over use by this species, the holder should be suspended from a piece of wire.*

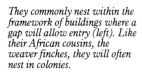

*They commonly nest within the framework of buildings where a gap will allow entry (left). Like their African cousins, the weaver finches, they will often nest in colonies.*

# TREE SPARROW *Passer montanus*

UNLIKE THE RESIDENT HOUSE SPARROW, the tree sparrow is a partial migrant. It is common throughout Europe, except in the north and west of Britain, where it is very localized, and in Ireland, where it is mainly confined to the coast. It is seen in all areas on passage, especially in the autumn. Less reliant on human habitation for its existence and rarely seen in large towns, this bird is also shyer than the house sparrow, with which it sometimes associates in the country at grain stores, farmyards and fields, to feed. Adults are rich brown on the back with dark blackish streaking; the rump is pale brown. The head has a bright, chocolate crown and nape; the white on the cheeks, with a crescent-shaped, black mark, almost joins up at the back of the neck, forming an incomplete white collar. There is a neat, black bib, and the underparts are cleaner and whiter than the house sparrow. It has thin, white, double wing-bars. The sexes are similar. Juveniles have a duller crown, buffish wing-bars, and the bib and cheek markings are dark grey. The flight call is distinctive—a hard *tecc-tecc*, the chirping notes are higher pitched, a more musical *chip, chip, chip.*

Tree sparrows inhabit open parkland, orchards, farmyards, scrub and bushes bordering cultivated land, open fields, cliffs, ruins and lines of pollarded willows. Lightly wooded areas are also favoured.

Gregarious and sociable, the tree sparrow often nests in small colonies, choosing holes in trees, walls, cliffs and thatch, as well as in rocks, dense creepers and haystacks. The nest, built of grass, straw, plant stems and twigs, is domed in the open, but may be just an untidy cup in a hole or a nestbox. It is lined with down and feathers.

The diet consists of plant and grass seeds, as well as small insects such as caterpillars, and flocks can be seen in autumn and winter feeding in stubble fields.

It will visit gardens for scraps and seeds and can be encouraged by the provision of nestboxes.

The numbers of the tree sparrow are very erratic, building up over a number of years and then declining rapidly; happily they are on the increase at the moment.

## FACTS AND FEATURES

**Plumage** Head bright chocolate; back brown, streaked darker; face white with black chin and crescent mark behind eye; underparts white. Juveniles have less chocolate brown on cap and the face is greyish.
**Habitat** Open parkland, orchards, farmyards, scrub, cliffs, ruins.
**Food** Mainly seeds; also insects.
**Nest** Holes in trees, buildings, cliffs, and haystacks.

14 cm/5½ in

*Tree sparrows readily use nestboxes (above) where they are provided. Note the chestnut brown crown and black mark on the cheek. Young birds leave the nest after about two weeks and have duller crowns, with cheek mark and a greyish bib.*

# CHAFFINCH *Fringilla coelebs*

UNTIL FAIRLY RECENTLY, the chaffinch was considered to be the commonest bird in Britain. Over the past decade, however, their numbers have declined dramatically through the systematic grubbing-out of one of its major nesting sites, the hedgerow. Even so, it is still common throughout its range, which includes the whole of Europe, where it may be encountered in numerous habitats.

It is quite catholic in its choice of environments, and it is regularly found in gardens, parks, woodlands of all types, hedgerows and in cultivated areas. During the winter, the chaffinch enlarges its options and will inhabit completely open areas, such as fields, marshes and even the tideline in particularly bad weather.

The plumage of the male is quite striking, consisting of a blue grey cap and neck, chestnut back, greenish rump and mainly brick-red underparts. The wings are predominately blackish, with a white forewing patch and a narrow wing-bar. The slightly forked tail is also blackish, but has white outertail feathers. The female differs in being yellowish brown above and paler below. In flight, the white forewing patch is obvious and is one of the characteristics. Chaffinches begin to proclaim their territories during February, the song consisting of a vigorous series of about a dozen notes, which are terminated in a flourishing *choo-ee-o*. Other vocalizations may include the well-known repeated *pink-pink* call, but a *wheet* and *chwit* may also be heard.

The food of this species varies according to the time of the year. In summer, for instance, they are mainly insectivorous, collecting their prey from bushes and trees. During the winter months, however, they search for seeds on the ground, often in association with sparrows and other finches. At this time, large flocks may form which may be sexually discrete. They regularly visit gardens, especially if grain is sprinkled either on the ground or on the bird table.

The nest is constructed by both sexes, and may be placed in a variety of sites. It is often situated in a dense hedgerow, tree or tall shrub and is made up of a neat, deep cup which is securely fitted to a tree fork. The material used consists of moss, mixed with lichens, grass, roots and feathers, bound together with spiders' webs and decorated with bark and more lichens. It is then lined with feathers, roots, hair, wool and plant down.

*The chaffinch is the southern counterpart of the brambling and one of the commonest birds in Europe. Northern and Eastern populations move south in winter. The bright plumage of the male becomes duller in winter, and the bill becomes whitish brown.*

## FACTS AND FEATURES

**Plumage** Male: grey crown and neck, back chestnut, rump greenish, tail black with white outertail feathers. Underparts brick-red; paler in winter. Female: yellowish brown above, paler below. In flight, both show white forewing patch and white wing-bar.
**Habitat** Woodlands, parks, gardens, open fields.
**Food** Seeds, fruit and insects.
**Nest** Hedgerows, tree or shrub.

15 cm/6 in

143

# Brambling *Fringilla montifringilla*

THIS CLOSE RELATIVE of the familiar chaffinch breeds only in the north of Europe, from central Scandinavia northwards, although in recent years it has begun to colonize in Scotland. A summer migrant to this area, the brambling moves south in the winter and is then found over much of Europe, including Britain and Ireland, but not quite reaching the southern most parts of Spain and Italy. The male, in summer, is a striking bird, with black head and mantle, and buff orange throat, breast and shoulder patch. It has less white in the black wings than the chaffinch, but, in flight, the white rump, not to be confused with the similar rump pattern of the bullfinch, is distinctive. The belly and undertail coverts are white. The male's winter plumage, most often seen outside the breeding habitat, is similar, but the buffy orange is retained only on the breast and shoulders; the mantle becomes mottled, like the head and crown, in shades of brown, buff and grey. The bill is black in summer, and yellow in winter. Females and juveniles are similar in appearance, having a browny black mottled head, duller shoulder patches and breast than males, and a mantle suffused with buff feather edgings. The call is very distinctive, a hoarse *tsweek* and a long *dszweee*. The song is a grating, monotonous note constantly repeated, *dshweea-dshweea-dshweea*.

Replacing the chaffinch in the northern birch and pine woods, as well as in areas of willow beside rivers and streams, other winter habitats are stubble fields and farmyards, but more especially beechwoods, where they feed on beechmast, an important food item.

Other food in the brambling's diet consists of large numbers of insects, caterpillars, butterflies and moths, in the breeding season; berries in the autumn.

The nest is a deep, luxuriant cup of moss, grass and hair, bound with cobwebs, lichens and birch bark, and lined with hair, down and feathers. It is usually placed near the trunk of the tree in a convenient fork.

An infrequent visitor to the garden, the brambling will appear for seeds and nuts, especially in severe winters.

## FACTS AND FEATURES

**Plumage** Male, in summer: head and mantle black, throat, breast and shoulders buffish orange; white rump. Winter: head, crown and mantle greyish, mottled with grey and buff. Female: duller than male, head streaked and mottled browny-black.
**Habitat** Birch and pine woods, stubble fields, beech forests.
**Food** Insects, caterpillars; seeds in winter.
**Nest** In a fork in birch or conifer trees.

14.5 cm/5¾ in

♂

♀

*During the winter this species migrates to much of Europe from its mainly Scandinavian breeding quarters. Nests are often placed near the trunk of a tree (above) and are constructed from moss, grass, cobwebs, lined with hair, down and feathers.*

# SERIN *Serinus serinus*

THE SMALLEST OF THE EUROPEAN FINCHES, the serin is a relative of the canary. It ranges throughout much of continental Europe, being absent only from Scandinavia, Britain and Ireland. The species, however, has been extending its range for many years, and several pairs are known to have nested successfully in some southern counties of England—it has even managed to reach the southern tip of Sweden. In these newly colonized regions it is a summer visitor only, withdrawing southwards in the autumn. The spread appears to be continuing as more individuals are consistently appearing along the southern shores of Britain in the spring.

The plumage of the male is mainly bright yellow, streaked brownish on the crown, back and flanks, with the wings and notched tail being dull blackish-brown. In flight, which is rapid and undulating, it displays a bright yellow rump and two indistinct, pale wing stripes. The female lacks much of the male's yellow, and is more heavily streaked, especially about the breast. Young birds are brown-buff, streaked darker brown above and below, the latter washed yellow-buff.

The song can be delivered from a perch, or in flight and consists of a rapid jingle which in may respects is similar to a canary-like trill. Call notes include a twittering trill, a weak *chip-chip* and an anxious *tsooeet*.

In displaying to the female, the male rises vertically into the air before returning to a perch in a circular descent. After pairing, a nest-site is selected. This is normally located in a bush, or tree, anything from 1.5–6.0 m (5–20 ft) above the ground, and is placed towards the extremity of a branch. It is built by the female and is comprised of a neat, compact cup made of plant stems, roots, moss and lichens; it is lined with hair, feathers and plant down.

Favoured habitats are the woodlands surrounding the Mediterranean, but, during the spread through Europe, it is now frequenting cultivated land, orchards, vineyards and hedgerows in or around villages as well as parks and gardens.

The main items of food taken by the serin are the seeds of weeds, grasses  insects, and, noticeably, the buds of elm; seeds of birch, catkins and brassica are also important.

*The serin is the smallest European finch. It is far commoner in the countries bordering the Mediterranean but, during the past decade, it has been extending its range northwards and it now breeds in small numbers along the southern coast of Britain.*

## FACTS AND FEATURES

**Plumage** Male: bright yellow with brownish streaking on crown, mantle and flanks; rump yellow; wings brown, with two yellow wing-bars. Female: duller, also streaked on the breast.
**Habitat** Woodland, farmland, orchards, parks and gardens.
**Food** Seeds, insects and elm buds.
**Nest** Placed near the top of a branch or in a small fork of a tall bush or tree.

11.5 cm/4¹/₂ in

145

# GREENFINCH *Carduelis chloris*

FOUND THROUGHOUT EUROPE except for a broad wedge in central and northern Scandinavia; the greenfinch is mainly resident, with the more northerly populations migrating south in winter. It is a solid, chunky bird with a short, stubby bill and a well forked tail, and it is a common visitor to gardens. In summer the plumage of the male is predominantly green—as the name suggests. It is olive-green on the back and crown, yellow on the rump, and bright, yellow-green below; the flanks are slightly greyish yellow. The wings appear greyish with bright yellow outer edges to the primaries. The short tail has a yellow base and sides, and is blackish towards the tip. The bill is pale. In winter, the upperparts become greyish to brownish green, the cheeks and flanks are grey and the rest of the underparts are yellowish, washed with grey. Females are much duller overall: greyish brown on the upperparts and yellowish tinged with grey on the underparts. The yellow on the wings and tail is less vivid. Juvenile upperparts are streaked brownish, with a green tinge; the underparts are brownish, yellowy-grey. In autumn, the plumage of juveniles and both sexes of adult birds can be very similar and difficult to distinguish. The call is a rapid, twittering *chwitt, chwitt, chwitt,* and a drawn-out, nasal whistling *psweeu.* The song is a combination of the calls and is sung from a prominent perch on top of a tall tree, or in a slow, bat- or butterfly-like display flight.

Habitat preferences include woodland edges, orchards, vineyards, tree-lined avenues, parks, tall hedges; and tall trees for displaying, singing and breeding.

The nest, situated high in a tree or in dense, tall hedging, is usually in a fork and comprises a deep cup of grasses and moss, lined with roots and hair.

In the breeding season, the adults feed the young largely on insects, but the main diet consists of seeds, some insects and the buds of flowers and trees. Berries of yew, ivy and elder are also consumed.

The greenfinch is a regular visitor to most gardens, having a tendency towards sunflower seeds. It readily adapts to nut feeders, but tends to take these over, preventing tits from enjoying the nuts.

## FACTS AND FEATURES

14.5 cm/5³/₄ in

**Plumage** Male, in summer: olive-green upperparts, yellow green underparts; rump and tail yellow. In winter: tinged with grey. Females: greyish brown above, greyish yellow below; yellow in wings and tail less bright.
**Habitat** Edges of woodland, tree-lined avenues, parks, orchards.
**Food** Seeds, tree and flower buds, berries and insects.
**Nest** In a fork or near the trunk of a tree or bush, or hedge.

♀ ♂

*The male greenfinch has a much brighter plumage than the female; he is seen here (below) regurgitating food to one of the nestlings.*

# SISKIN *Carduelis spinus*

THE SISKIN is a partial migrant with a very scattered breeding population, occurring in small isolated pockets in some countries in Europe. The reasons for this are not known, and it is certainly not due to food or habitat. It breeds in Ireland, Scotland and a few scattered localities in England. It is present in Scandinavia, except for some central and northern areas. In Italy, it is found in a small band through the centre and also in the far south; another small area is in the eastern Pyrenees. Otherwise it is found in a band running from the south of France north-westwards. In winter it is found throughout the region.

The male upperparts are a yellow green with faint streaking. The rump is yellow and unstreaked. The wings are black with double, yellow wing-bars. The crown and bib are black, the cheeks greenish, and the eyestreak yellow. The underparts and breast are yellow; the belly is whitish, and the flanks are streaked with black. The short, well forked tail has yellow sides to the base. Females lack the black on the head, are greyer green and not so yellow below, with a streaked rump. Juveniles are similar to females, but browner and more heavily streaked. The call, in flight, is a *tsyzin* or *tsu*. The song is a long, sweet twittering, ending in a nasal wheeze.

The siskin is found in mixed deciduous or coniferous forest, favouring spruce in the breeding season. At other times it frequents parkland, birch clumps and more commonly, alders alongside streams and rivers.

Feeding almost exclusively on seeds of spruce, pine, fir, alder and larch, it prises the seeds out of cones with its fine bill, while hanging tit-like from slender twigs.

The nest is usually high up in a conifer, and consists of a small cup of twigs, moss and grass, lined with hair, down and feathers.

In some years 'irruptions' take place, the birds dispersing to new areas when food is scarce. At times like this, the birds might stay on to breed—this may explain the strange distribution of the species. It often associates with redpolls, especially on migration and when in feeding flocks.

Siskins frequently visit gardens—if you want to attract them, hang some peanuts out in a red bag or container.

The siskin is recognizable by its forked tail, yellow wing-bars and yellow patches on the tail base. The male has a black crown and bib and is much brighter than the female. The siskin is mainly a winter visitor to gardens.

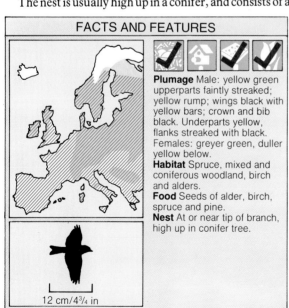

## FACTS AND FEATURES

**Plumage** Male: yellow green upperparts faintly streaked; yellow rump; wings black with yellow bars; crown and bib black. Underparts yellow, flanks streaked with black. Females: greyer green, duller yellow below.
**Habitat** Spruce, mixed and coniferous woodland, birch and alders.
**Food** Seeds of alder, birch, spruce and pine.
**Nest** At or near tip of branch, high up in conifer tree.

12 cm/4³⁄₄ in

# GOLDFINCH *Carduelis carduelis*

AT THE BEGINNING OF THIS CENTURY the numbers of goldfinches in Britain had reached a low ebb—this was the direct result of intensive trapping for the cage-bird market. Since that period, the species has built up its numbers again, and is now a regular sight in many areas of the British Isles. The recovery has been due to a concentrated conservation policy, initially introduced and maintained by the RSPB.

It is a widespread species which is to be found virtually everywhere in Europe, but is particularly common in Iberia. The only countries which have failed to attract this beautiful little finch are Norway, Finland and Iceland. Favoured habitats consist of gardens, parks, edges of woods, orchards and hedgerows. Their food consists of seeds of burdock, dandelion and other weeds, especially thistle heads, which they frequently sit on while pulling out the seeds. Other food sources include fruits of alder, birch and other trees, as well as insects on which they feed their young. While feeding, they often congregate into small parties, collectively referred to as a 'charm', but they may associate with other species during the winter.

The adult is brightly coloured and has a large, almost white bill. It has a red blaze on the face which is bordered above and below with black and white behind. The remainder of the upperparts are sandy-buff, with a white rump and a black tail, tipped with white. The wings are also black and, in good plumage, are tipped white on the primaries—these in turn have a broad, golden wing-bar. The underparts are mainly buff, but this gradually fades to whitish on the abdomen. Juveniles have smaller bills,

lack the red, black and white of the adult's head, and are generally a greyer buff below.

The female takes the responsibility for constructing the nest, which may be situated in the outer branches of trees in orchards and gardens. It is a neat cup of roots, grass, moss and lichens, lined with wool and plant down.

Although they cannot be readily attracted to bird tables it is possible to encourage them to the garden by planting thistles and other plants with large seed heads.

## FACTS AND FEATURES

**Plumage** Adult: pale, sandy buff upperparts, white rump and black tail; wings black with broad yellow bar and white tips; face with red blaze, and white cheeks; crown and nape black. Underparts buffish.
**Habitat** Parks, gardens, orchards and areas of bushy scrub.
**Food** Seeds of dandelion, thistles; insects and their larvae.
**Nest** Mainly in trees near the end of a branch.

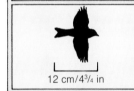

12 cm/4¾ in

*The nest, usually built by the female alone is of down, wool and plant materials. The young (far right) are stretching up to be fed by the attending parent. Goldfinches are one of the prettiest finches and their twittering, trilling song matches their appearance. In flight, the yellow wing-bars and white rump are conspicuous.*

# LINNET *Acanthis cannabina*

LIKE THE GOLDFINCH, the linnet was a popular cage bird during the Victorian and Edwardian eras in Britain, when the bright plumage of the male, and the twittering song, helped to add some colour to the dowdy lives of many urban inhabitants. In the wild this species has a liking for hedgerows and areas of scrub, especially those with a considerable amount of gorse, bramble thickets along river banks and woodland edges. Their range is extensive—they are absent only from northern Scotland,

and the majority of Scandinavia. The species is a partial migrant, with many British breeding birds moving south to winter in south-western France and Iberia.

The plumage of the male varies considerably through the year, and this can present considerable problems to the inexperienced observer. In full breeding dress the male has a greyish-brown head with a red forehead and breast, and a chestnut back. The flight feathers are edged white, as is the base of the forked tail. Moulting males lack the red, which is lost in late summer and does not return until spring. Females are duller brown above, and mainly white, streaked brown below. Juveniles are similar to the female. The song may be delivered from a perch, or during a bounding display flight, and consists of a musical twitter of fluty and nasal notes. Of its calls a *chichichichit* is the most characteristic.

The nest is usually placed close to the ground in a thicket or low bush. It is built by the female and consists of a cup of grass and moss, which is lined with hair, wool, and sometimes down and feathers. Linnets can be gregarious, and several nests may be placed in close proximity to one another.

Although the linnet is commonly found around gardens in rural areas, it very rarely ventures within their boundaries unless there are suitable thickets, or a bordering hedge in which they can breed. Food on bird tables will not attract them for they prefer fields and other open spaces where they can find an adequate supply of suitable seeds. In the breeding season they take considerable quantities of insects to feed their young.

♀

♂

*Resplendent in his breeding plumage the male, however, loses the red on the breast and forehead in late summer, and in winter is more like the female. Note the white in the wings and on the side of the well forked tail. Large flocks can occur in late autumn when some birds migrate south.*

## FACTS AND FEATURES

**Plumage** Male: chestnut upperparts; greyish brown head with red on fore-crown; primaries edged white. Underparts: reddish breast, pinkish flanks, whitish belly. Female: dull brown above, with streaked grey head; buffish underparts streaked brown.
**Habitat** Forest edges, heathland, orchards, open scrub.
**Food** Small insects, caterpillars and weed seeds.
**Nest** Low in bush, hedgerow, gorse or bramble.

11 cm/4¼ in

# REDPOLL *Acanthis flammea*

THIS PETITE FINCH has been expanding its range in Britain for the past few decades, thanks to the afforestation programme, which has included the planting of a large number of conifers—one of its favourite habitats. Its distribution, however, is still rather patchy and remains commoner to the north and west of these islands. Various habitats of this species include stands of birch, alder, willow and conifer, but it also has a liking for heathlands, parks and gardens. It may be encountered throughout the British Isles and much of Scandinavia, but it is restricted to the more mountainous regions of continental Europe. Being a partial migrant, however, the redpoll can be found virtually anywhere, but it rarely manages to reach Spain or southern France during its winter wanderings.

At first sight, the plumage appears rather drab, but on closer inspection the bright red forehead will become evident. In breeding dress, the male also sports a pinkish flush on both the breast and rump, but the amount and intensity of colour varies considerably. The remainder of the plumage is dull brown above, streaked buffish, with a blackish-brown tail edged white. It is mainly white below except for a black chin and a few brownish streaks on the flanks. Females are similar to winter males, and lack the pink flush on the breast and rump. Juveniles are more streaked and lack the red forehead. At all ages, and in both sexes, these birds possess a yellowish bill and two white-buffish wing-bars. The song, usually given during an aerial display, is not outstanding and consists of a ringing, rolling *rrrr, che-chee-chee*, which is also used as a contact call in flight and is very characteristic.

After pairing, the female builds the nest which takes the form of a flimsy, untidy cup constructed from grasses, moss, old flower-heads and roots; it is lined with plant down, hair and feathers. The site may be located anywhere from almost at ground level up to 4.25 m (14 ft), and is placed towards the extremities of branches of bushes or trees, especially in birch scrub and thickets of alder, sallow, hawthorn and gorse. They often nest gregariously in small loose colonies.

Their food consists mainly of birch, alder, conifer and willow seeds, but the young are given insects for some time. They will also come to feeders containing peanuts.

## FACTS AND FEATURES

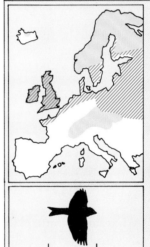

**Plumage** Brownish upperparts with dark streaking; two buffish wing-bars; pale rump streaked darker. Bright red forehead; black chin; bill yellow. Underparts buffish grey with darker streaking on the flanks. Male has pink flush on breast and rump.
**Habitat** Coniferous woodland, birch forest, woods, parks and gardens.
**Food** Insects and seeds.
**Nest** In bushes and trees; usually in loose colonies.

13 cm/5 in

*The untidy nest, often placed in a fork of a tree (above), is lined with down and feathers. The red forehead distinguishes the redpoll from all but the linnet, but note the shorter tail, black chin and the two buff wing-bars.*

♂  ♀

# CROSSBILL *Loxia curvirostra*

THIS LARGE, DUMPY, PARROT-LIKE FINCH has evolved to fit a special ecological niche—feeding almost exclusively on conifer seeds, it has developed a crossed bill. This adaptation enables it to open pine cones and extract the seeds with consummate ease. When food within its range is short, populations depart and seek food elsewhere, and, after overwintering, may be found breeding almost anywhere suitable. They seldom stay for more than one season, however, returning to their usual areas in late summer or autumn. In Britain, the main breeding areas are Scotland, where another species the Scottish crossbill, has also evolved, and East Anglia, though a few are scattered along the south coast. The European populations are widely separated, occurring in Spain, east and central Europe and central and southern Scandinavia.

Adult males are usually bright red, especially on head and rump; the wings and the short, forked tail are dark brown. Some males are more orange, and in certain rare instances, are the same colour as the female, which ranges from a highly variable yellowish green to greyish green. The juveniles are greyish overall and are heavily streaked. The crossed bill does not develop until some two weeks after the young bird leaves the nest.

The call, uttered usually in fast, undulating flight, is a distinctive *chip chip* or *jip-jip*. The song consists of a rapid trill and warbling notes including a *tjee, tjee*.

Found almost exclusively in spruce or fir and pine forests, but after 'invasions' or 'irruptions' the crossbill can be found in parks and gardens providing suitable cone-bearing trees.

The crossbill will eat berries and insects, but conifer seeds form the major part of its diet. It will pluck a cone from a branch with its bill, wedge it in a crack, or between the trunk and branch of a tree with its foot, and then open the seed cases, rotating the cone as it feeds. It does not always remove the cone, however, and crossbills can be seen hanging from branches, extracting seeds from hanging cones. It is only seen on the ground when drinking.

The nest, built of twigs, grass and lichen, is lined with hair and fine grass, and placed high up in conifers. The breeding season is extremely variable from January to July, but is usually February to March.

## FACTS AND FEATURES

**Plumage** Male: red overall, brighter red on head and rump; wings and tail brown. Female: yellowish green to greyish green. Juveniles: grey with heavy streaking.
**Habitat** Spruce and pine forests; parks and gardens with pine and fir trees.
**Food** Seeds of pine cones, insects and berries.
**Nest** In conifer trees, usually high up; built of pine twigs and grass, lined with hair and feathers.

16.5 cm/6½ in

*The heavy head, thick neck and crossed bill are distinctive features of the crossbill. The bill can be crossed either way.*

*Males are usually reddish, while females are greenish in colour. Juveniles are greyish and heavily streaked.*

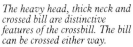

# BULLFINCH *Pyrrhula pyrrhula*

THERE CAN BE NO DOUBT that the male bullfinch is one of the most beautiful of European birds. The plumage consists of a glossy black cap, grey back and white rump. The tail and wings, except for a white wing-bar, which borders an almost entirely grey forewing, are gun metal blue. The underparts are a conspicuous blood-red which contrasts with a white abdomen. Females resemble males in pattern, but they are grey-brown above and only pinkish-brown below. Juveniles are similar in colour to the female, but lack the black cap—the head is completely brown. In flight, the white rump is very obvious as it passes through the branches of a bush or tree, or flies along a hedgerow. The song is not as spectacular as the plumage, for it consists of a broken, creaky warble, while the contact call of *deeu* is so plaintive that it is barely audible.

Unlike many other bird species, the bullfinch cannot be regarded as a gardener's friend, as it habitually feeds on the flowering buds of fruit trees. For this reason, farmers in fruit-producing areas consider them to be a major pest and consequently dispose of them in any way possible. It is very difficult to defend the bullfinch's position, as they certainly cause considerable damage, but it is possible that this habit became more frequent when farmers began clearing the ground of weeds within the orchard boundaries. The practice of removing unwanted weeds, in the autumn, takes away a considerable amount of natural food, thus forcing this finch to seek alternatives.

Its favourite habitats include woods, bushes, orchards, scrubland with dense bushes and scattered trees, parks, gardens and along hedgerows. They occur almost throughout Europe, but are excluded from much of Iberia, areas of central south-eastern Europe and northern Scandinavia. Some continental populations are partial migrants

The female builds the nest, which is made up of twigs, moss and lichens put together to form a cup. It is always well-concealed in a thick hedge or bramble, but on occasions the bullfinch will use a fruit tree.

*The males' brilliant plumage makes the female look quite drab. Northern birds are larger and more brightly coloured, and may migrate south in the winter.*

## FACTS AND FEATURES

**Plumage** Male: grey upperparts with white rump, black crown and chin; wings black with white patch; underparts bright reddish pink. Females: greyish brown above, pinkish brown below. Juveniles: resemble female, but lack black crown.
**Habitat** Parks, gardens, woods and orchards.
**Food** Insects, berries, seeds and buds of fruiting trees and flowers.
**Nest** In bush, hedge or tree, made of fine twigs and moss.

14.5 cm/5¾ in

# HAWFINCH *Coccothraustes coccothraustes*

*The Greek name* Coccothraustes *means kernel breaker and the hawfinch, with its immensely powerful bill, is quite capable of cracking cherry stones to get at the seed inside. The inner primaries are strangely shaped — they are notched and curled and are presumed to be for display. It often favours vegetable gardens where it shreds pea pods to get at the peas inside.*

♀

♂

THE HAWFINCH IS UNMISTAKABLE—a bull-necked, thickset bird with a short tail and an outsize pale-coloured bill. The plumage is beautifully subtle rather than colourful: there is a tawny head, a short, black bib, grey collar, brown back and pale brownish-pink underparts. The wings are black with broad and conspicuous white bands, and the brown tail has an obvious white tip. Females are somewhat duller than males and juveniles are drabber still, and barred with brown. In spring, the adult's bill is grey-blue, but is horn-coloured for the rest of the year. A short, sharp *ptik* is the commonest call, especially in flight, but also when groups are feeding together; the weak, rather uncertain song is usually delivered from a treetop, but is seldom heard.

Hawfinches build a fairly substantial nest, often quite high in a tree, but also in large bushes, usually in areas of woodland or continuous cover. They may nest in large, undisturbed gardens, but mainly appear as visitors in search of food or water.

In Britain, hawfinches have a somewhat patchy and rather local distribution, and to most people they are totally unknown or, at best, only irregular as garden visitors. In some favoured areas, however, they come regularly, either to fruit trees or hornbeams, or to drink at garden pools. They are normally shy and wary, but with patience and care can actually be watched fairly easily. Curiously, in many parts of Europe they are not only very much commoner, but also not nearly so shy.

They are unlikely to come to most artificial sources of food, but have a fondness for fruit, especially cherries, and berries, including yew; they are often most regular in large old gardens or orchards, generally in well-wooded districts. Their powerful bills (and the strong muscles which give their necks their characteristically thick appearance) enable them easily to crack open fruit stones to get at the kernels inside. Beech and, particularly, hornbeam are favoured trees, the birds often feeding in good numbers where beechmast is thick on the ground.

This is always an elusive and difficult bird in Britain: bird gardeners in known hawfinch areas may not be able to provide instant cherry trees or hornbeams, but a garden pool might be a worthwhile investment!

## FACTS AND FEATURES

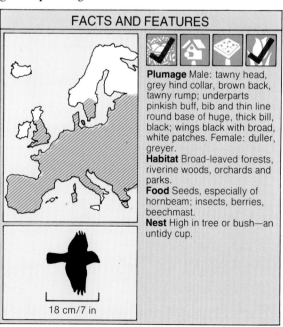

**Plumage** Male: tawny head, grey hind collar, brown back, tawny rump; underparts pinkish buff, bib and thin line round base of huge, thick bill, black; wings black with broad, white patches. Female: duller, greyer.
**Habitat** Broad-leaved forests, riverine woods, orchards and parks.
**Food** Seeds, especially of hornbeam; insects, berries, beechmast.
**Nest** High in tree or bush—an untidy cup.

18 cm/7 in

# YELLOWHAMMER *Emberiza citrinella*

THE YELLOWHAMMER'S FAMILIAR SONG, known in Britain as sounding like *little-bit-of-bread-and-no-cheese*, can be heard from late February. The bird sings from a favourite song perch high up in a tree or bush. It is not a shy bunting, but nevertheless is seldom seen in gardens, unless these are large, or near cultivated land. Present throughout northern Europe as a breeding bird, it is found in central southern Iberia and parts of southern Italy only in the winter, when some of the population moves south; most populations are resident.

The male is beautiful—bright yellow on the head and underparts, chestnut with heavy dark streaking on the upperparts. The rump is plain chestnut, and the head shows some olive markings on the cheeks and crown. The long, notched tail has white sides, which are conspicuous when the bird flicks its tail, and in flight. Females are duller, lacking much of the yellow; most females are yellow only on the upper breast and face. The head markings are more pronounced and browner. Both sexes have some streaking on the underparts, especially on the flanks, and this is more apparent in the female. Juveniles are a light brown with streaking all over, not showing any yellow until the late autumn. The call is a sharp *chip*, and the song is a series of rapid, high notes *chi, chi, chi, chi—chwie*.

With new agricultural practices involving the destruction of hedgerows, especially in England, the yellowhammer has shown a marked decline in population in its usual haunts, which comprise arable fields surrounded by dense hedging and scattered woodland. Other habitats include edges of broad-leaved forests, pine plantations, scrub and bracken on heathland, and in winter, stubble fields and farmyards.

Food consists of worms, insects, spiders and young plant shoots, while berries, grain and seeds are the main diet in winter.

The nest, a cup of grass stems and moss, lined with hair and fine grass, is built by the female, and is usually low down or on the ground in dense vegetation, rarely more than 91cm (3ft) up.

It is not a common garden visitor, but it may come if vegetables are grown, or if you can provide seeds for it during the winter.

*Males give the appearance of being almost entirely yellow, but they are variably streaked darker above. Females and young birds are less distinct, but the chestnut rump will separate it from similar buntings.*

## FACTS AND FEATURES

**Plumage** Male: upperparts chestnut with some streaking, except on rump which is plain; head and underparts bright yellow; white outer tail feathers. Females: duller, less yellow.
**Habitat** Arable fields, young pine plantations, heathland, farmyards.
**Food** Plant shoots, seeds, insects and worms.
**Nest** A cup of plant stems and moss, lined with hair. Sited low down, or on the ground.

16.5 cm/6½ in

# REED BUNTING *Emberiza schoeniclus*

*In breeding plumage, the male, with its black head, throat and breast, and white moustachial streak, is easy to identify. Out of breeding dress, the male, like the drabber female, may be confused with other species, especially when away from the normal, marshy habitat.*

♂

♀

NOT, PERHAPS, THE MOST OBVIOUS SPECIES to visit suburban gardens, but in winter the reed bunting is a comparatively regular visitor, searching for seeds and even coming to the bird table. Indeed, the reed bunting has been increasingly inhabiting, and breeding in, dry areas similar to that of the yellowhammer. This may be because of the reduction of suitable habitat and open water areas, due to the recent agricultural changes. It is common throughout Europe, where it is largely resident, but northern populations do move south in winter to Britain, central Europe and Iberia.

The male, in summer, is resplendent with a pure black head, chin and throat, contrasting with a white collar and moustachial stripe. The back is rufous buff, streaked black and the underparts are pure white with streaking on the flanks. It has a long tail with white outer feathers. The female is buffer above and below—more streaked on the underparts and with a brown head with a pale buffish eye stripe, moustache and collar. Males, in winter, resemble females, but the head is darker, with cleaner underparts. Juveniles are similar to females, but generally paler and the underparts are yellower.

The call is a high *chirk* or *see-ewe*. The song is squeaky, and is usually delivered from a prominent perch. It begins slowly, accelerating towards the end, and is rather monotonous—a *tseek, tseek, tseek, tsisisik*. The flight is low, undulating or bounding. When perched, the reed bunting often flicks open its tail, flashing the white outer tail feathers.

Originally, a bird of marshy regions, reedbeds or waterside margins, the reed bunting can now be found in young coniferous plantations, fields of cereals, hedges, hawthorn scrub and chalk downland.

Seeds of various plants form a large part of its diet, but in summer, during the breeding season, it resorts to insects, caterpillars beetles and snails.

The nest, often low down in vegetation, a bush, reedstems or on the ground, is a neat cup of grass, lined with hair and finer grass. It is built by the female.

A suitable, reed-fringed pond, or seed put out in winter, will entice this species to even the smallest of gardens.

## FACTS AND FEATURES

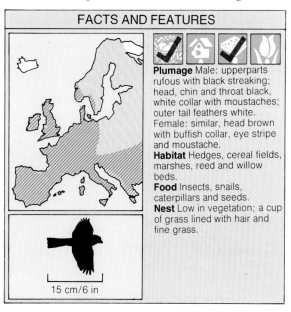

15 cm/6 in

**Plumage** Male: upperparts rufous with black streaking; head, chin and throat black, white collar with moustaches; outer tail feathers white. Female: similar, head brown with buffish collar, eye stripe and moustache.
**Habitat** Hedges, cereal fields, marshes, reed and willow beds.
**Food** Insects, snails, caterpillars and seeds.
**Nest** Low in vegetation; a cup of grass lined with hair and fine grass.

# USEFUL ADDRESSES

## ENGLAND
**British Trust For Ornithology**
Beech Grove
Tring
Hertfordshire HP23 5NR

**Royal Society For The Protection Of Birds**
The Lodge
Sandy
Bedfordshire SG19 2DL

**Fauna & Flora Preservation Society**
c/o Zoological Society of London
Regents Park
London NW1 4RY

**International Council For Bird Preservation**
219c Huntingdon Road
Cambridge CB3 0DL

## SCOTLAND
**Scottish Ornithologists Club**
21 Regent Terrace
Edinburgh EH7 5BT

## EIRE
**Irish Wildbird Conservancy**
Southview
Church Road
Greystones
Dublin

## BELGIUM
**Comité De Coord Pour La Protection Des Oiseaux**
8 Durentijdlei
2130 Brasschaat
Antwerp

## DENMARK
**Dansk Ornithologisk Forening**
Vesterbrogade 140
1620 Copenhagen

## FINLAND
**Ornitologiska Föreningen**
P. Rautatiekatu 13
SF — 00100
Helsinki 10

## FRANCE
**Ligue Française Pour La Protection Des Oiseaux**
La Corderie Royale
BP 263
F — 17315 Rochefort

**Société D'Etudes Ornithologiques**
Ecole Normale Supérieure
Laboratoire de Zoologie
46 Rue d'Ulm
F — 75230 Paris
(Cedex 05)

**Société Ornithologiques De France**
Muséum National d'Histoire
   Naturelle
55 Rue de Buffon
75005 Paris

## GERMANY
**Deutsche Ornithologen— Gesellschaft**
Hardenbergplatz 8
1000 Berlin 30

## GREECE
**Hellenic Ornithological Society**
Kyniskas 9
Athens 502

## ITALY
**Centro Italiano Studi Ornithologici**
c/o Instituto di Zoologica
Via Dell Universita 12
43100 Parma

## NETHERLANDS
**Nederlandse Ornithologische Unie**
Dr. G. C. Boere
Voorstraat 7
Beesd
Gld

## NORWAY
**Norsk Ornitologisk Forening**
Innherredsveien 67A
7000 Trondheim

## SPAIN
**Coda**
Aizgorri 5
Madrid 28

## SWEDEN
**Sveriges Ornitologiska Forening**
Runebergsgaten 8
11429 Stockholm

**Scandinavian Ornithologists Union**
Dept. of Animal Ecology
Ecology Building
S — 223 62 Lund

# FURTHER READING

**A Field Guide To The Birds Of Britain & Europe**
Peterson, Mountfort & Hollom
(Collins)

**The Birds Of Britain And Europe**
Heinzel, Fitter & Parslow
(Collins)

**The Hamlyn Guide To The Birds Of Britain And Europe**
Bruun & Singer
(Hamlyn)

**The Bird Table Book**
Soper & Gillmor
(David & Charles)

**Gulls, A Guide To Identification**
P.J. Grant
(T & AD Poyser)

**A Field Guide To The Nests, Eggs And Nestlings Of British & European Birds**
Colin Harrison
(Collins)

**Field Guide To The Birds Of Britain**
Readers Digest Nature Lovers
  Library
(Readers Digest)

**Nestboxes**
BTO Guide No. 3
(British Trust For Ornithology)

# INDEX

Numerals in bold type indicate the main entry for each species of bird. Numerals in italic type indicate illustrations.

## Picture Credits

*Key: t=top; b=bottom; r=right; l=left; i=inset.*

*6/7* Karen Bussolini. *7* Eric Crichton. *9* Eric Crichton. *10/11* Eric Hosking. *11* Frank Lane. *12(b)* Karen Bussolini. *12(t)* Eric Crichton. *12/13* Eric Crichton. *13* Frank Lane. *14(b)* Lennart Norström. *14(t)* Eric Crichton. *14/15* Karen Bussolini. *16(b)* Frank Lane. *16(t)* Eric Crichton. *17* David Hosking. *30* Nick Clark. *31* Trevor Wood. *31(i)* Trevor Wood. *32/33* Trevor Wood. *34* Eric & David Hosking. *40* Frank Lane. *43(b)* Eric & David Hosking. *43(tl)* Eric Hosking. *43(tr)* Frank Lane. *46(bl)* Frank Lane. *46(br)* Frank Lane. *47* Frank Lane. *55* Frank Lane. *61* Frank Lane. *63* Eric Hosking. *74* Frank Lane. *76* Frank Lane. *81* Eric Hosking. *86* Eric Hosking. *89(tl)* Frank Lane. *89(tr)* Eric & David Hosking. *89(b)* Eric & David Hosking. *96* Eric & David Hosking. *103* Eric & David Hosking. *110* Eric & David Hosking. *114* Eric & David Hosking. *116* Eric & David Hosking. *117* Eric & David Hosking. *118* Frank Lane. *120* David Hosking. *121* David Hosking. *122/123(c)* David Hosking. *(tr)* David Hosking. *(b)* David Hosking. *126* Frank Lane. *127(l)* Frank Lane. *127(r)* Eric Hosking. *128* Frank Lane. *130* David Hosking. *134* Frank Lane. *135* Frank Lane. *136* Frank Lane. *139* David Hosking. *140/141* Eric Hosking. *142* Eric Hosking. *144* Eric Hosking. *146* Frank Lane. *148* Eric Hosking. *150* David Hosking.